D1736795

CONSOLIDATION, TRANSLATION, AND THE EQUITY METHOD

THE WILEY/RONALD SERIES IN PROFESSIONAL ACCOUNTING AND BUSINESS

Lee J. Seidler, Series Editor

Consolidation, Translation, and the Equity Method

CONCEPTS AND PROCEDURES

PAUL ROSENFIELD
STEVEN RUBIN

A RONALD PRESS PUBLICATION

JOHN WILEY & SONS

New York · Chichester · Brisbane · Toronto · Singapore

Library of Congress Cataloging in Publication Data
Rosenfield, Paul.
  Consolidation, Translation, and the Equity Method

  "A Ronald Press publication."
  Includes index.
  1. Financial statements, Consolidated.   I. Rubin,
Steven.   II. Title.

HF5681.B2R647   1985   657'.3   85-614
ISBN 0-471-81357-5

Printed in the United States of America

10 9 8 7 6 5 4 3 2 1

Preface

This book is intended to fill a void in the essential library of financial accountants who prepare consolidated financial statements and independent accountants who audit or review them. Until now, the concepts and procedures needed to consolidate, translate, and apply the equity method have only been discussed in textbooks and handbooks, along with many other topics. This book is devoted solely to those subjects.

Such concentrated attention should also prove valuable to students and teachers of financial accounting, as a supplement to textbooks that deal with consolidation, translation, and the equity method.

This book is designed to take the mystery out of those topics by:

Explaining clearly the concepts underlying consolidation, translation, and the equity method

Presenting easy-to-follow, step-by-step descriptions of the procedures used to consolidate, translate, and apply the equity method

Illustrating the procedures fully and understandably

Providing examples from annual reports of consolidated financial statements and of disclosures

Identifying and discussing unsettled issues related to consolidation, translation, and the equity method

Acknowledgments

We gratefully acknowledge the comments we received on draft sections of this book from several members of the staff of the American Institute of Certified Public Accountants. The views expressed are, of course, solely our responsibility. Further, the views are not necessarily those of the AICPA, our employer. Official AICPA positions are determined through specific committee procedures, due process, and deliberations.

We appreciate the permission granted by the AICPA and the Financial Accounting Standards Board to quote from their pronouncements and by the AICPA to present excerpts from its *1983 Accounting Trends and Techniques*.

Grateful, too, are we to Margaret Rosenfield, for her deft transformation of raw drafts into this finished product.

Finally, we thank our editor, Richard Lynch, for proposing the book and for his support during its preparation.

PAUL ROSENFIELD
STEVEN RUBIN

New York, New York
April 1985

Contents

CHAPTER ONE

Concepts Underlying Consolidation, Translation, and the Equity Method

Consolidation, translation, and the equity method are related sets of accounting practices used mainly in preparing consolidated financial statements. Such statements report the financial position, results of operations, and changes in financial position of a consolidated group[1] of companies. A consolidated group consists of a parent company and its consolidated subsidiaries, companies controlled by the parent company. The purpose of consolidated financial statements is to provide information for the benefit of persons interested in the financial affairs of the parent company. Such information is believed to be helpful to those persons, either in addition to the information in the parent company's financial statements or as the only financial information those persons need.

Translation changes the currencies in which financial statements of foreign operations of members of a consolidated group are stated to the domestic currency, the currency of the parent company's country, so those statements can be consolidated with the financial statements of the parent company and domestic subsidiaries.

The equity method of accounting is used to account for unconsolidated subsidiaries and investments in which the investor has the ability to exercise significant influence over the operating and financial policies of the investee.

---

[1]Consolidated financial statements are called *group accounts* in the United Kingdom and elsewhere.

The major authoritative pronouncements on consolidation, translation, and the equity method are described at the end of this chapter.

A number of concepts underlie consolidation, translation, and the equity method, reflecting their unique features in financial reporting. Those concepts are discussed in this chapter. Issues concerning those concepts and concerning concepts and procedures discussed in subsequent chapters are considered in Appendix B.

CONSOLIDATION POLICY

A consolidated group of companies includes a parent company and some or all of its subsidiaries. Selection of the subsidiaries to include is called the *consolidation policy;* it establishes the reporting entity for the statements. Accounting Research Bulletin (ARB) No. 51, "Consolidated Financial Statements," the major authoritative pronouncement on consolidated financial statements at present, sets forth criteria to use in establishing consolidation policies.[2] The criteria concern (1) control and (2) similarity of activities.

Criteria Concerning Control

Because subsidiaries are controlled companies, the major determinant in consolidation policy concerns control. According to ARB No. 51, paragraph 2, "the usual condition for a controlling financial interest is ownership . . . by one company, directly or indirectly, of over fifty percent of the outstanding voting shares of another company. . . ."

Paragraph 2 of ARB No. 51 indicates that in unusual circumstances, a subsidiary is not consolidated, "for example, . . . where control is likely to be temporary, or where it does not rest with the majority owners (as, for instance, where the subsidiary is in legal reorganization or in bankruptcy)." Also,

> there may . . . be situations where the minority interest in the subsidiary is so large, in relation to the equity of the shareholders of the parent company in the consolidated net assets, that the presentation of separate financial statements for the two companies would be more meaningful and useful. [paragraph 2]

---

[2]The major authoritative pronouncements on consolidation, translation, and the equity method are described at the end of this chapter.

ARB No. 51 sets limits on exclusion of subsidiaries from consolidation: "the fact that the subsidiary has a relatively large indebtedness to bondholders or others is not in itself a valid argument for exclusion of the subsidiary from consolidation" (paragraph 2).

ARB No. 51 refers to Accounting Research Bulletin No. 43, "Restatement and Revision of Accounting Research Bulletins," Chapter 12, "Foreign Operations and Foreign Exchange," which provides criteria to determine whether to include foreign subsidiaries in the consolidated group, subsidiaries whose financial statements are stated in foreign units of currency.

Paragraph 8 of ARB No. 43 states that "careful consideration should be given to the fundamental question of whether it is proper to consolidate the statements of foreign subsidiaries" that are "subject to controls and exchange restrictions and the consequent unrealistic statements of income that may result from the translation of many foreign currencies into dollars." So, ARB No. 43 provides a broad choice:

> (a) To exclude foreign subsidiaries from consolidation . . . (b) To consolidate domestic and foreign subsidiaries . . . (c) To furnish (1) complete consolidated statements and also (2) consolidated statements for domestic companies only. . . . (d) To consolidate domestic and foreign subsidiaries and to furnish in addition parent company statements. . . . [paragraph 9]

Criteria Concerning Dissimilarity of Activities

ARB No. 51 gives latitude to exclusion of subsidiaries from consolidation based on the "heterogeneous . . . character" of the parent company and the subsidiary or subsidiaries. It says:

> . . . separate statements or combined statements would be preferable for a subsidiary or group of subsidiaries if the presentation of financial information concerning the particular activities of such subsidiaries would be more informative to shareholders and creditors of the parent company than would the inclusion of such subsidiaries in the consolidation. For example, separate statements may be required for a subsidiary which is a bank or an insurance company and may be preferable for a finance company where the parent and the other subsidiaries are engaged in manufacturing operations. [paragraph 3]

ARB No. 51 does, however, caution that "it may be better to make a full consolidation than to present a large number of separate statements" (paragraph 3).

SPECIAL FEATURES OF CONSOLIDATED
FINANCIAL STATEMENTS

Because the reporting entity for consolidated financial statements, the consolidated group of companies, transcends the legal boundaries of single companies, consolidated financial statements have special features, which require consideration in preparing and interpreting them.

Intercompany Amounts

Only legal entities can own assets, owe liabilities, issue capital stock, earn revenues, enjoy gains, and incur expenses and losses. A group of companies as such cannot do those things. So the elements of consolidated financial statements are the elements of the financial statements of the members of the consolidated group of companies—the parent company and its consolidated subsidiaries. They are the assets owned by the member companies, the liabilities owed by the member companies, the equity of the member companies, and the revenues, expenses, gains, and losses of the member companies.

Some elements of the financial statements of member companies are not elements of the consolidated financial statements, however. The elements of the financial statements of a reporting entity are relationships and changes in relationships between the reporting entity and outside entities. But some elements of the financial statements of members of a consolidated group are relationships and changes in relationships between member companies, called *intercompany amounts*. (They would more accurately be described as *intragroup amounts*.) Intercompany amounts are excluded from consolidated financial statements.

As discussed and illustrated in Chapters 4, 5, and 7, it is convenient to prepare consolidated financial statements by starting with the financial statements of the member companies, which include intercompany amounts. The intercompany amounts are removed by adjustments and eliminations in consolidation. The items are:

Intercompany Stockholdings.   Ownership by the parent company of capital stock of the subsidiaries and ownership, if any, by subsidiaries of capital stock of other subsidiaries or of the parent company

Intercompany Receivables and Payables.   Debts of member companies to other member companies

Intercompany Sales, Purchases, Fees, Rents, Interest, and the Like.   Sales of goods or provision of services from member companies to other member companies

Intercompany Profits.   Profits recorded by member companies in transactions with other member companies reflected in recorded amounts of assets of member companies at the reporting date

Intercompany Dividends.   Dividends from members of the consolidated group to other members of the consolidated group

After the intercompany amounts are eliminated, the consolidated financial statements present solely relationships and changes in relationships with entities outside the consolidated reporting entity. They present:

Amounts receivable from and amounts payable to outside entities

Investments in outside entities

Other assets helpful in carrying out activities with outside entities

Consolidated equity equal to the excess of those assets over those liabilities

Changes in those assets, liabilities, and equity, including profits realized or losses incurred by dealings with outside entities

Consolidated financial statements present the financial affairs of a consolidated group of companies united for economic activity by common control.

Controlling Interest

The parent company of a consolidated group controls the subsidiaries, and the stockholders of the parent company control the parent company. The stockholders of the parent company therefore have the controlling interest in the consolidated group of companies. The capital stock of the parent company (other than any owned by subsidiaries eliminated in consolidation, discussed in Chapter 7) and the other paid-in capital of the parent company are treated as the capital stock and other paid-in capital of the consolidated reporting entity.

Minority Interest

A wholly owned subsidiary in a consolidated group is a subsidiary whose capital stock is all owned by the parent company or other members of the consolidated group. All the capital stock and other paid-in capital of a wholly owned subsidiary are eliminated in consolidation. But only a majority of the capital stock of a company needs to be owned by the parent company or other member companies of a consolidated group for the company to qualify as a subsidiary eligible for consolidation. A minority of the capital stock of a member company may be owned by outside entities.

The capital stock of such a member company owned by other member companies and the related portions of its other paid-in capital are eliminated in consolidation. But its capital stock held by outside entities and the remainder of its other paid-in capital are carried over to the consolidated financial statements as minority interest.

Minority interest in consolidated financial statements has no counterpart in the financial statements of single companies. It does not fit neatly into any usual balance sheet category. The authoritative literature is silent on its classification, and authors and the preparers of consolidated financial statements disagree on it. Minority interest is treated or advocated for treatment as (1) liabilities of the consolidated group, (2) part of the equity of the consolidated group, or (3) a separate category in the consolidated balance sheet between liabilities and equity.

In consolidated income statements, net income is allocated between consolidated net income and net income attributable to minority interest.

BUSINESS COMBINATIONS

A company can start a subsidiary by having it incorporated and investing resources in it. Including such a subsidiary in consolidated financial statements presents no special problem. The amount of the investment recorded by the parent company equals the initial equity of the subsidiary, each of which is eliminated in consolidation.

Types of Business Combinations

Most parent and subsidiary relationships, however, are formed by *business combinations,* events in which separate, active companies become related as parent company and subsidiary. Accounting for business combinations is discussed and illustrated in Chapters 2, 4, and 7. Business combinations occur in several ways, for example:

Purchase of Stock for Cash.   The parent company buys for cash a majority of the capital stock of another company from the other company's stockholders, and the other company becomes a subsidiary.

Purchase of Assets for Cash and the Assumption of Liabilities.   The parent company buys for cash the assets of another company, assumes its liabilities, and forms a new company to assume the business of the other company as a subsidiary.

Stock for Stock.   The parent company issues some of its capital stock to stockholders of another company and receives from a them a majority of the capital stock of the other company, which becomes a subsidiary.

Some business combinations occur in one event; others occur in a series of events, as discussed and illustrated in Chapter 7, complicating accounting for the combinations.

Methods to Account for Business Combinations

Alternative views on the nature of the events that occur in business combinations and how best to account for them have led to two different methods of accounting for the combinations, the *purchase method* and the *pooling of interests method*. Differences between the financial statement results of applying the method applicable to a business combination and the results that would have been obtained had the other method been applicable are ordinarily substantial for current statements and those of many years following the combination.

Business combinations accounted for by the purchase method usually produce balance sheet amounts referred to as *goodwill on consolidation*. Such purchased goodwill is measured by the excess of the amount paid or the fair market value of the stock issued by the parent company to acquire the subsidiary over the fair values of the identifiable assets and liabilities of the subsidiary at the date of combination.

TRANSLATION

Financial statements of a parent company are stated in the domestic unit of currency, such as the U.S. dollar for U.S. parent companies. Financial statements of a foreign subsidiary are stated in a foreign unit of currency, a unit of currency other than the domestic unit of currency, such as the U.K. pound for U.K. subsidiaries. Such foreign currency financial statements cannot be consolidated with domestic currency financial statements; the result would be a set of financial statements stated in more than one unit of currency, which would make them unintelligible.

Before the financial statements of a foreign subsidiary can be consolidated with the financial statements of its parent company, therefore, the amounts in its foreign currency financial statements are changed to amounts stated in the domestic unit of currency. Changing the amounts from those stated in the foreign unit of currency to those stated in the domestic unit of currency is called *translation,* analogous to translation from one language to another. Translation is discussed and illustrated in Chapter 3.

Translation uses foreign exchange rates. Such rates are ratios of exchange, prices of units of one kind of currency in terms of units of another kind of currency, such as $(U.S.) 1.50 for £(U.K.) 1. Foreign exchange rates change, as all other prices do. That causes two problems in translation: (1) how to select the foreign exchange rates to use for translation; and (2) how to treat translation differences, items unique to translated financial statements caused by translating amounts in a single set of financial statements at two or more foreign exchange rates.

UNCONSOLIDATED SUBSIDIARIES AND THE EQUITY METHOD OF ACCOUNTING

Some companies controlled by a parent company are excluded from consolidation by the consolidation policy adopted and accounted for by the equity method. Generally accepted accounting principles require reported consolidated net income generally to be the same regardless of whether a particular subsidiary is consolidated or accounted for by the equity method, though it permits the balance sheet to be affected by the choice. The equity method of accounting, discussed and illustrated in Chapter 6, is used to achieve those results.

Generally, under the equity method of accounting for an unconsolidated subsidiary:

1. The difference between (a) consolidated net income as it would be computed by excluding the subsidiary entirely from the consolidated financial

statements and (b) consolidated net income as it would be computed with the unconsolidated subsidiary consolidated is presented in one line in the consolidated income statement.

2. The parent company's investment in the unconsolidated subsidiary is presented as an asset on one line in the consolidated balance sheet, at the amount required to achieve the result in number 1.

The equity method is sometimes called *one-line consolidation*,[3] but that is not strictly correct. The equity method does not have the single characteristic that distinguishes consolidation from other types of presentations—it does not include the unconsolidated subsidiary in the reporting entity of the consolidated financial statements.

Present authoritative literature gives considerable freedom to consolidate or not consolidate a subsidiary. Because net income is the item of primary focus in the consolidated income statement, and because consolidated net income is generally the same regardless of whether a subsidiary is consolidated or accounted for by the equity method, the effects on the consolidated income statement of the choice of consolidating or not consolidating a subsidiary are of relatively little concern.

But several balance sheet amounts are also of considerable interest, especially total current assets, total current liabilities, and total liabilities. Those amounts in a consolidated balance sheet with a subsidiary included in the consolidated group differ from those amounts in a consolidated balance sheet with the subsidiary excluded from the consolidation group and accounted for by the equity method. The effects on the consolidated balance sheet of the choice of consolidating or not consolidating a subsidiary are therefore of more concern.

LIMITATIONS OF CONSOLIDATED FINANCIAL STATEMENTS

The control of a parent company over its subsidiaries is not absolute. The parent company may do nothing to prevent other entities that have interests in the subsidiaries from the full enjoyment of their rights. Major categories of such other interests are creditors and minority stockholders of the subsidiaries. Re-

---

[3]For example, in AICPA Accounting Interpretation 1 of APB Opinion 18, paragraph 2.

sources may not be transferred from subsidiaries to the parent company under the direction of the parent company to harm those other interests, as intercompany transfers, intercompany dividends, or otherwise.

Restrictions on the transfer of resources between members of the consolidated group affect interpretation of consolidated financial statements. For example, the assets of one member may not be available to pay the liabilities of another member. Showing both the assets and the liabilities in a single consolidated balance sheet can erroneously imply that all reported assets are available to pay all reported liabilities. Full disclosure requires such erroneous implications to be avoided, by indicating significant barriers to the free flow of resources within the consolidated group of companies.

COMBINED FINANCIAL STATEMENTS

Paragraph 22 of ARB No. 51 states that circumstances exist in which combined financial statements of commonly controlled corporations are likely to be more meaningful than their separate financial statements. Such circumstances include, for example, ownership by one person of a controlling interest in several corporations related in their operations.

If combined financial statements are prepared, they present only relationships and changes in relationships with entities outside the combined group. That means that intercompany sales and purchases, profit, and receivables and payables are eliminated. Intercompany stockholdings, if any, are eliminated.

The separate components of equity of each corporation are aggregated with the corresponding separate components of the other corporations. Presentation of a table showing each corporation's portion of each component of combined equity in either the balance sheet or the notes, though not required by ARB No. 51, would likely enhance the usefulness of the combined statements.

CONSOLIDATING STATEMENTS

If all else fails to present information on a group of related companies in a helpful way, ARB No. 51 recommends in paragraph 24 the use of consolidating statements, as "an effective means of presenting the pertinent information." Such statements are essentially presentations as in worksheets used to derive consolidated financial statements, illustrated in succeeding chapters, together with notes and other kinds of necessary disclosures.

SEC RULES AND REGULATIONS ON CONSOLIDATED FINANCIAL STATEMENTS

Beyond the concepts and procedures involving all consolidated financial statements, the Securities and Exchange Commission, in its Regulation S-X, has published regulations for registrants that file their consolidated financial statements with the commission.

Selection of Reporting Entity

The rules require that the application of principles for inclusion of subsidiaries in consolidated financial statements "clearly exhibit the financial position and results of operations of the registrant and its subsidiaries." A company not majority owned may not be consolidated. A subsidiary whose financial statements are as of a date or for periods different from those of the registrant may not be consolidated unless all the following conditions apply:

The difference is not more than 93 days.

The closing date of the subsidiary's financial information is expressly indicated.

The necessity for using different closing dates is briefly explained.

Due consideration must be given to consolidating foreign subsidiaries operating under political, economic, or currency restrictions. If such foreign subsidiaries are consolidated, the effects, if determinable, of foreign exchange restrictions on the consolidated financial position and results of operations must be disclosed.

Intercompany Items and Transactions

Intercompany items and transactions between members of a consolidated group generally are eliminated in consolidated financial statements, and unrealized intercompany profits and losses on transactions with investees accounted for by the equity method are also eliminated. If such items are not eliminated, the registrant is required to state its reason for not doing so.

Other Disclosures

The SEC rules require brief descriptions in the notes to consolidated financial statements of the principles of consolidation followed and any changes in principles or in the composition of the companies constituting the consolidated group since the last set of consolidated financial statements was filed with the commission.

The rules require that consolidated financial statements also present:

An explanation and reconciliation of differences between (1) the amount at which investments in consolidated subsidiaries are carried on the registrant's books and (2) the equity of the registrant in the assets and liabilities of the subsidiaries

An explanation and reconciliation between (1) dividends received from unconsolidated subsidiaries and (2) earnings of unconsolidated subsidiaries

An analysis of minority interest in capital stock, in retained earnings, and in net income of consolidated subsidiaries

MAJOR AUTHORITATIVE PRONOUNCEMENTS

A number of authoritative pronouncements cover consolidation, translation, and the equity method. This section describes the major pronouncements in effect at the time of publication of this book.

Consolidations

ARB No. 43, Chapter 12, "Foreign Operations and Foreign Exchange," provides criteria for the treatment of foreign subsidiaries in consolidated financial statements.

ARB No. 51, "Consolidated Financial Statements," describes the purpose of consolidated financial statements and selection of a consolidation policy, and it discusses concepts underlying consolidation and procedures to prepare consolidated financial statements.

Business Combinations

APB Opinion 16, "Business Combinations," describes the conditions for each of the two methods of accounting for business combinations and the accounting principles that apply to each method.

AICPA interpretations of APB Opinion 16 were issued by the AICPA to elaborate on some points made in the Opinion.

FASB Statement No. 38, "Accounting for Preacquisition Contingencies of Purchased Enterprises," amends APB Opinion 16 to clarify how an acquiring enterprise should account for contingencies of an acquired enterprise that existed at the time of a business combination.

FASB Statement No. 79, "Elimination of Certain Disclosures for Business Combinations by Nonpublic Enterprises," amends APB Opinion 16 to eliminate the requirement for nonpublic companies to disclose:

> . . . the following information in financial statements of the period in which a business combination accounted for by the purchase method occurs:
>
> a. Results of operations for the current period as though the enterprises had combined at the beginning of the period, unless the acquisition was at or near the beginning of the period.
>
> b. Results of operations for the immediately preceding period as though the enterprises had combined at the beginning of that period if comparative financial statements are presented.

Foreign Currency Translation

ARB No. 43, Chapter 12, "Foreign Operations and Foreign Exchange," provides criteria for the treatment of foreign subsidiaries in consolidated financial statements.

FASB Statement No. 52, "Foreign Currency Translation," specifies the accounting for foreign operations reported in the financial statements of a domestic company. It supersedes FASB Statement No. 8, "Accounting for the Translation of Foreign Currency Transactions and Foreign Currency Financial Statements." FASB Interpretation No. 37, "Accounting for Translation Adjustments upon Sale of Part of an Investment in a Foreign Entity," prescribes that the accounting in Statement No. 52 that applies to a sale or complete or substantially complete liquidation of an investment in a foreign entity also applies to a partial disposal by an enterprise of its ownership interest.

Investments

APB Opinion 18, "The Equity Method of Accounting for Investments in Common Stock," specifies the circumstances in which an investment in common stock should be accounted for by the equity method of accounting and the principles that apply to the method.

FASB Statement No. 12, "Accounting for Certain Marketable Securities," describes the accounting principles for investments in capital stock if neither consolidation nor the equity method applies.

CHAPTER TWO

Accounting for Business Combinations

The two generally accepted methods of accounting for business combinations are the *pooling of interests method* and the *purchase method*. They are not alternatives. A business combination that meets all 12 conditions relating to (1) attributes of the combining companies before the combination, (2) the manner in which the companies are combined, and (3) the absence of certain types of planned transactions, as set forth in paragraphs 45 to 48 of APB Opinion 16, is accounted for by the pooling of interests method. A business combination that fails to meet even one of the 12 conditions is accounted for by the purchase method. Transfers of assets and liabilities or securities between companies owned by the same parties, including newly formed corporations, are not considered business combinations for purposes of APB Opinion 16. However, Interpretation 39 of APB Opinion 16 provides that in those circumstances the assets and liabilities so transferred are accounted for at their recorded amounts.

THE POOLING OF INTERESTS METHOD

The pooling of interests method accounts for a business combination as the uniting of the ownership interests of two or more companies resulting from a transfer of equity securities. Preexisting ownership interests continue (in modified form), preexisting bases of accounting are retained, and preexisting recorded amounts of assets and liabilities are carried forward to the consolidated financial statements.

Conditions for the Pooling of Interests Method

A business combination that meets all 12 conditions is accounted for by the pooling of interests method. The following discusses the 12 conditions. Though more than two companies may be combined at the same time, the conditions are discussed in terms of a business combination of two entities.

Attributes of the Combining Companies

Two of the 12 conditions pertain to attributes of the combining companies:

1. The combining companies are autonomous, meaning neither has been a subsidiary or division of another company within the two years immediately preceding the date the plan of combination is initiated.

    A plan of combination is considered to be initiated on (a) the date the major terms of a plan, including the ratio of transfer of stock, are announced publicly or are otherwise formally made known to the stockholders of either combining company or, if earlier, (b) the date stockholders of a combining company are notified in writing of a transfer offer.

    A combining company is considered autonomous though it was a subsidiary of another company (not one of the combining companies) within the two years immediately preceding the date the plan of combination is initiated if it was divested as a result of a governmental order.

2. The combining companies are independent of each other, meaning that, at the date the plan of combination is initiated and at the date the plan of combination is consummated neither, combining company owns more than 10% of the outstanding voting common stock of the other combining company acquired before the date the plan of combination is initiated.

    A plan of combination is considered to be consummated on the date ownership interests are transferred. The date the plan is consummated is often called the *date of combination*.

Manner in Which Companies Are Combined

Seven of the 12 conditions pertain to the manner in which the companies are combined:

3. The companies are combined in a single transaction or in accordance with a specific plan within one year after the plan of combination is initiated.

    Altering the terms of the transfer of stock after the plan of combination is initiated renders the original plan void and causes a new plan of combination to be initiated (unless earlier transfers of stock reflect the new ratio).

    A business combination may be consummated more than one year after the plan of combination is initiated and not violate this condition if proceedings of a governmental body or litigation beyond the control of the combining companies caused the delay.

4. One combining company offers and issues only common stock with rights identical to those of the majority of its outstanding voting common stock and receives substantially all, that is, 90% or more, of the voting common stock of the other company.

    The plan of combination may include provisions for the company issuing stock to distribute cash or other consideration for fractional shares and for shares held by stockholders not participating in the combination.

5. Neither combining company changes the equity interest of the voting common stock in contemplation of the combination within the two years immediately preceding the date the plan of combination is initiated until the date the plan is consummated.

    Changes in equity interests include distributions by a combining company to its stockholders, declarations of dividends, or additional issuances, transfers, or retirements of securities other than in the ordinary course of business.

6. If either combining company reacquires shares of voting common stock, it does so only for purposes other than the business combination, and it does not reacquire more than a normal number of shares between the date the plan of combination is initiated and the date it is consummated.

Stock reacquired for purposes other than the business combination includes shares reacquired for stock option and other compensation plans and other recurring distributions, if such plans have existed for at least two years preceding the date the plan of combination is initiated.

7. The ratio of an individual common stockholder's interest in a combining company to those of other common stockholders in a combining company remains the same after the transfer of stock that combines the companies.

Each common stockholder in a combining company who transfers stock retains the same relative interest as before the combination. For example: M owns 75% of S and J owns 25% of S. If they transfer all their shares to P for P's shares, M will receive three shares for each share J receives.

8. After the combination, the voting rights of the common stock ownership interests in the combining company that issues stock are not restricted in any way.

9. The combination is resolved at the date the plan of combination is consummated with no provisions of the plan pending that relate to the issue of securities or other consideration.

At the time of combination, the combining companies issue stock or have already issued stock and agree to issue no additional shares and to distribute no other consideration at a later date to the former stockholders of either combining enterprise, either directly or through an escrow account. Notwithstanding that, a plan may provide that the number of shares issued to combine the companies may be revised for the later settlement of contingencies that existed at the date the combination is consummated.

Absence of Planned Transactions

Three of the 12 conditions pertain to the absence of planned transactions:

10. The company issuing stock agrees not to retire or to reacquire, either directly or indirectly, any of the common stock issued to combine the companies.

11. Each combining company agrees not to enter into any other financial arrangements for the benefit of former stockholders of a combining company, for example, to guarantee loans secured by stock issued to combine the companies.

12. Neither combining company intends to dispose of a significant part of the assets of either combining company within the two years immediately after the combination other than in the ordinary course of business or to eliminate duplicate facilities or excess capacity.

Accounting for Combinations by the Pooling of Interests Method

Chapter 4 illustrates procedures to prepare consolidating worksheets at the date of a business combination accounted for by the pooling of interests method. Chapter 5 illustrates procedures to prepare consolidating worksheets after the date of such a business combination. Those procedures are affected by concepts discussed in this section.

Assets and Liabilities

Under the pooling of interests method, the assets and liabilities of the consolidated group generally are stated initially in the financial statements of the group at the amounts at which they were stated in the separate financial statements of the member companies, except for items of intercompany relationships—intercompany stockholdings, debt, and profit—eliminated because they do not represent relationships or transactions with outside entities.

The combining enterprises may have had accounting policies different from each other. For example, one may have determined the cost of its inventories on the first in, first out (FIFO) method and another may have determined the cost of its inventories on the last in, first out (LIFO) method. Though not required, the existing recorded amounts of the assets and liabilities of one combining company may be adjusted to conform its accounting principles to those of the other combining company.

Equity

The individual components of equity—common stock, preferred stock, additional paid-in capital, retained earnings, and so forth—of each member company are aggregated under the pooling of interests method with the corresponding individual components of equity of the other member company, except for items of intercompany relationships, which are eliminated. The aggregated common stock and additional paid-in capital may include amounts attributable to minority interests.

Reporting Combined Results of Operations in the Period of Combination

Results of operations for the entire period in which a business combination accounted for by the pooling of interests method is consummated are reported as though the companies had been combined at the beginning of that period, regardless of when during the period they were combined. Items of intercompany transactions—intercompany sales, purchases, and profit—are eliminated for the entire period. Indeed, retained earnings of all members of the consolidated group accounted for by the pooling of interests method are treated as the retained earnings of the consolidated group, as though the companies had always been combined.

Expenditures incurred for a business combination accounted for by the pooling of interests method, such as legal fees, accounting fees, registration fees, and so forth, are charged to expense in the consolidated income statements in the periods in which they are incurred.

A member of the consolidated group may dispose of assets after the combination. If such assets are part of duplicate facilities or excess capacity, a resulting gain or loss from disposition is included in income from operations. If such assets are not part of duplicate facilities or excess capacity, however, a resulting gain or loss from disposition is normally included in income from extraordinary items.

Though a consolidated group may be reasonably assured that a business combination initiated but not consummated will qualify for the pooling of interests method, it applies the purchase method in its consolidated financial statements prepared between the date a controlling interest is acquired and the date the plan of combination is consummated. Once the combination qualifies for the pooling of interests method, that method is applied retroactively in financial statements issued on or after that date, as discussed in Chapter 7.

Comparative consolidated financial statements of prior years presented with the consolidated financial statements of the year in which the combination accounted for by the pooling of interests method is consummated are restated as if the combination had been consummated in the prior year.

Disclosures Under the Pooling of Interests Method

A consolidated group that applies the pooling of interests method in accounting for a business combination discloses the following information in its financial statements or related notes for the period in which the combination is consummated:

The fact that a combination accounted for by the pooling of interests method was consummated

The basis of current presentation and restatements of prior periods

The names and brief descriptions of the companies combined, except those of a company whose name is carried forward to the consolidated group

A description of stock issued and the number of shares issued in the combination

Details included in current consolidated net income of the results of operations of the previously separate companies for the portion of the year before the combination is consummated. The details include revenues, extraordinary items, net income, and other changes in equity and the amounts of intercompany transactions and the manner of accounting for them.

Descriptions of adjustments to assets and liabilities of a combining company to conform its accounting principles to those of the consolidated group and descriptions of the effects of the changes on net income reported previously by the separate companies and presented in comparative financial statements

Details of an increase or decrease in retained earnings from changing the fiscal year of a combining company. The details include, at a minimum, revenues, expenses, extraordinary items, net income, and other changes in equity for the period excluded from the reported results of operations.

Reconciliations of amounts of revenues and earnings reported before the combination by the company that issues the stock to combine the companies with the consolidated amounts currently presented in financial statements and summaries. A new company formed to combine the companies may instead disclose the earnings of the separate companies for prior periods.

Appendix A presents examples of disclosures.

THE PURCHASE METHOD

A business combination not meeting all 12 conditions discussed above is accounted for by the purchase method. The purchase method, in effect, accounts for the combination as the acquisition of a controlling interest in a company by another company. The assets and liabilities of the acquired company are initially reported in consolidation at their fair values at the date of combination. A difference between the aggregate of those amounts and the cost incurred by the acquiring company to acquire the controlling interest is treated as goodwill, or, in some rare instances, negative goodwill.

Method of Acquisition

In a business combination accounted for by the purchase method, one enterprise, say, Corporation P, can acquire the voting stock of another enterprise, say, Corporation S, in several ways:

1. For cash
2. In exchange for noncash assets
3. By incurring debt
4. By issuing its own stock
5. In a combination of two or more of those ways

S makes no entry, because it has given up nothing and received nothing. It merely updates its list of stockholders. P records these entries based on various facts:

1. In the simplest type of acquisition, P acquires S's voting stock for cash. If P buys all 100,000 shares of S's voting stock for $10 a share, P makes this entry:

Investment in Corporation S	1,000,000	
Cash		1,000,000

2. P acquires for cash 90% of S's voting stock, 90,000 shares, for $9 a share plus a $1 a share commission:

Investment in Corporation S	900,000	
Cash		900,000

3. P acquires all the voting stock of S, 100,000 shares, by paying $5 a share now and agreeing to pay $5 a share to S's former stockholders two months from now:

Investment in Corporation S	1,000,000	
Cash		500,000
Payable		500,000

4. P acquires 80% of S's voting stock, 80,000 shares, in exchange for parcels of land it owns. The book value of the land is $700,000 and its fair value at the date of the exchange is $800,000. The market value of S's stock is not readily discernible, because S is a private, closely held corporation. According to APB Opinion 29, "Accounting for Nonmonetary Transactions," paragraph 18, the fair values of the assets received or of the assets given, whichever is more clearly evident, are used to record such a barter transaction. This entry records the exchange:

Investment in Corporation S	800,000	
Land		700,000
Gain on disposal		100,000

5. P acquires S by issuing 10,000 shares of its $100 par value voting common stock to S's stockholders who, in turn, transfer to P all their 100,000 $100 par value voting shares of S. Neither security has a readily discernible market value:

Investment in Corporation S	1,000,000	
Common stock		1,000,000

6. Same as number 5 except P's shares have a readily discernible market
    value of $110 a share:

Investment in Corporation S	1,100,000	
Common stock		1,000,000
Additional paid-in capital		100,000

Costs of Acquisition

Direct costs of a business combination accounted for by the purchase method,
such as legal fees, are capitalized and amortized, generally over the same period
that goodwill is amortized. Indirect and general expenses incidental to the combination are charged to income as incurred.

Allocation of Purchase Price

The parent company's cost to acquire the subsidiary (its investment) by the
purchase method comprises two pieces:

1. The total of the fair values of the subsidiary's assets and liabilities as
    determined under APB Opinion 16
2. Purchased goodwill

APB Opinion 16, "Business Combinations," provides the following guidance
on how the fair values of the subsidiary's assets and liabilities are determined:

Type of Asset or Liability	Amount at Which Subsidiary's Assets or Liabilities Are Initially Included in Consolidation
Marketable securities	Current net realizable value
Receivables	Discounted amount of expected future net cash inflows

Type of Asset or Liability	Amount at Which Subsidiary's Assets or Liabilities Are Initially Included in Consolidation
Inventories	
a. Finished goods	Current net realizable value
b. Work in process	Current net realizable value
c. Raw materials	Current replacement cost
Buildings and equipment	
a. Used in operations	Current replacement cost
b. To be sold or held for sale	Current net realizable value
c. Used only temporarily in operations	Current net realizable value, recognizing expected depreciation
Patents, trademarks, copyrights, customer lists, and the like	Appraisal value
Land, natural resources, and nonmarketable securities	Appraisal value
Accounts payable, notes payable, obligations under capital leases, accrued expenses, and the like	Discounted amount of expected future net cash outflows
Deferred income taxes	Zero
Operating loss carryforwards	Expected tax savings only if realization is assured beyond a reasonable doubt
Unused investment tax credits	Expected tax savings only if realization is assured beyond a reasonable doubt
Preacquisition contingencies (other than operating loss carry forwards)	Discounted amount of expected future net cash inflows or outflows, if determinable. The effects of preacquisition contingencies resolved after the combination at amounts different from

Type of Asset or Liability	Amount at Which Subsidiary's Assets or Liabilities Are Initially Included in Consolidation
	those at which they are recorded in the combination are charged or credited to income in the periods in which they are resolved.
Research and development costs	Zero. But assets resulting from research and development activities such as formulas, blueprints, and the like are recorded at appraisal value.

The following describe some of the terms used:

Current Net Realizable Value. The amount of cash (or its equivalent) expected to be derived from sale of an asset, net of costs required to be incurred as a result of the sale

Current Replacement Cost. The amount of cash (or its equivalent) that would have to be paid to acquire currently the best asset available to undertake the function of the asset owned (less depreciation or amortization, if appropriate)

Discounted Amount of Expected Future Net Cash Inflows or Outflows. The discounted amount of expected future cash inflows into which the asset is expected to be converted in due course of business less the discounted amount of expected future cash outflows necessary to obtain those inflows

Fair Value. The price at which an asset could be exchanged in a transaction, within a reasonably short time, between a buyer and a seller each of whom is well informed and willing to buy or sell and neither of whom is under a compulsion to buy or sell

Chapter 4 illustrates procedures to prepare a consolidating worksheet at the date of a business combination accounted for by the purchase method. Chapter 5 illustrates procedures to prepare consolidating worksheets after the date of such a business combination. Those procedures are affected by concepts discussed in this section.

Effects of Differences between Book and Tax Bases

The amounts initially assigned in consolidation to the subsidiary's assets and liabilities for financial reporting purposes may differ from the amounts allowable for income tax purposes. Those are permanent differences, not timing differences, under APB Opinion 11, "Accounting for Income Taxes," and, therefore, no deferred taxes are provided. However, the estimated future tax effects of such differences, if material, affect the amounts to assign to the subsidiary's assets and liabilities for financial reporting purposes. For example, the fair value initially assigned to an asset for financial reporting purposes is normally less than its market value or appraisal value if all or a portion of the market value or appraisal value is not deductible for income tax purposes.

Purchased Goodwill

Purchased goodwill is measured by the difference between (1) the cost of the parent company's investment accounted for by the purchase method and (2) the fair values of the subsidiary's assets and liabilities as determined under APB Opinion 16 at the date of the combination. Subsequent accounting for goodwill depends on whether (1) equals (2), in which case there is no goodwill; (1) exceeds (2), in which case there is goodwill; or (1) is less than (2), in which case there is negative goodwill resulting from a bargain purchase. Those three possibilities take the form shown in Exhibit 2.1.

EXHIBIT 2.1.   The Two Types of Goodwill Compared

	1	2	3
Fair values of subsidiary's assets	500,000	500,000	500,000
Fair values of subsidiary's liabilities	200,000	200,000	200,000
Net	300,000	300,000	300,000
Amount of investment	300,000	400,000	200,000
Amount of goodwill	-0-	100,000	
Amount of negative goodwill			100,000

Accounting for Purchased Goodwill

Goodwill is initially reported in the consolidated balance sheet as an intangible asset and is subsequently amortized to income over the periods expected to be benefited or 40 years, whichever is shorter. The straight line method is typically used.

APB Opinion 17, "Intangible Assets," paragraph 27, identifies the following factors to be considered in determining the estimated useful life of goodwill or other intangible assets:

a.   Legal, regulatory, or contractual provisions may limit the maximum useful life.

b.   Provisions for renewal or extension may alter a specified limit on useful life.

c.   Effects of obsolescence, demand, competition, and other economic factors may reduce a useful life.

d.   A useful life may parallel the service life expectancies of individuals or groups of employees.

e.   Expected actions of competitors and others may restrict present competitive advantages.

f.   An apparently unlimited useful life may in fact be indefinite and benefits cannot be reasonably projected.

g.   An intangible asset may be a composite of many individual factors with varying effective lives.

Negative Goodwill

Negative goodwill is allocated to reduce proportionately the fair values initially assigned to noncurrent assets (except for long-term investments in marketable securities). If the allocation reduces the affected noncurrent asset amounts to zero, the remainder is classified in the consolidated balance sheet as a deferred credit and, like goodwill, discussed above, is amortized to income over the periods expected to be benefited or 40 years, whichever is shorter. The straight line method is typically used. To illustrate: The fair values assigned S's noncurrent assets other than long-term investments total $300,000 and there is $100,000 in negative goodwill. The negative goodwill is allocated as shown in Exhibit 2.2.

If the unadjusted fair values of noncurrent assets totaled less than $100,000, they would be reduced to zero and the remaining negative goodwill would be accounted for as discussed above.

EXHIBIT 2.2.   Allocation of Negative Goodwill

	Fair Values of Noncurrent Assets (unadjusted)		Negative Goodwill Allocation		Adjusted Fair Values
Buildings and equipment	100,000		(33,333)		66,667
Land	200,000		(66,667)		133,333
	300,000		(100,000)		200,000

Comparative Financial Statements

Comparative financial statements of prior years presented with the financial statements of the year in which a combination accounted for by the purchase method occurs are not restated.

Disclosures under the Purchase Method

A consolidated group that applies the purchase method discloses the following information in its consolidated financial statements or related notes for the period in which the parent company acquired a controlling interest in a subsidiary:

That there was a business combination accounted for by the purchase method

The name and a brief description of the acquired company

The period for which results of operations of the acquired company are included in the consolidated income statement

The cost to acquire the subsidiary, including, if applicable, the number of shares of stock the parent company issued to acquire the subsidiary

A description of the plan for amortizing goodwill (method and period)

Contingent payments, options, or commitments specified in the acquisition agreement and the proposed accounting treatment

A consolidated group whose parent company's stock trades publicly also discloses as supplemental pro forma information:

Results of operations for the current period as though the member company had been combined at the beginning of the period (unless the members were combined near the beginning of the period)

Results of operations for the immediately preceding period as though the members had been combined from the beginning of that period

Appendix A presents examples of disclosures.

CHAPTER THREE

Foreign Currency Translation

A subsidiary or another unit within a consolidated group of companies (or within a company or an affiliated group of companies), such as a joint venture, a division, or a branch, may be a foreign operation, an operating unit that prepares foreign currency financial statements. Before such statements can be included in domestic currency consolidated financial statements, they ordinarily have to be translated into the domestic currency used in the consolidated financial statements, the currency of the parent company's country. FASB Statement of Financial Accounting Standards No. 52, "Foreign Currency Translation," sets forth current generally accepted accounting principles for translation.

OBJECTIVES OF TRANSLATION

Statement No. 52 states objectives to be achieved in translation in the face of changes in foreign exchange rates, ratios of exchange between two currencies. The principles in Statement No. 52 were adopted with the intention of achieving those objectives. The basic objective is:

Compatibility with Expected Effects. Information concerning foreign operations should be generally compatible with the expected effects of changes in foreign exchange rates on the parent company's cash flows and equity. If a change in an exchange rate is expected to have an overall beneficial effect, translation should reflect that. If a change is expected to have an overall adverse effect, translation should likewise reflect that. The expected effects of a change in a foreign exchange rate on the carrying amounts of all assets and liabilities of a foreign operation should therefore be recognized currently.

Other major objectives are:

Conformity with GAAP.   Translation should produce amounts that conform with generally accepted accounting principles. For example, inventories and land, buildings, and equipment should be stated at acquisition cost after translation.

Retaining Results and Relationships.   The financial results and relationships in the foreign currency financial statements of a foreign operation should be retained in its statements after translation. Profits should translate into profits and losses should translate into losses. Relationships before translation such as a current ratio of two to one or a ratio of gross profit to sales of 35% should be the same after translation.

ASSUMPTIONS CONCERNING TRANSLATION

FASB Statement No. 52 states these assumptions concerning translation on which the principles in the statement are based:

Two Types of Foreign Operations.   Foreign operations are of two types, which differ from each other so much that translation procedures for the two types have to differ. The two types are (1) self-contained and integrated foreign operations and (2) components or extensions of the parent company's domestic operations.

Self-Contained and Integrated Foreign Operations.   A foreign operation may be relatively self-contained and integrated in a foreign country. Such an operation should be treated in consolidated financial statements as a net investment of the parent company. The entire net investment, not merely certain assets and liabilities of the foreign operation, is exposed to the risk of changes in the exchange rate between the currency of the foreign country and the domestic currency. Though such changes affect the parent company's net investment, they do not affect its cash flows. The effects of such changes on a foreign operation should therefore be excluded from reported consolidated net income unless the parent company sells part or all of its investment in the foreign operation or completely or substantially liquidates its investment in the foreign operation.

Components or Extensions of Parent Company Domestic Operations.   A foreign operation may be a direct and integral component or an extension of the parent company's domestic operations, such as an import or export business. It should be treated as an integral part of the parent company's operations. Changes in the exchange rate between the currency of the country in which the foreign operation is conducted and the domestic currency directly affect certain individual assets and liabilities of the foreign operation, for example, its foreign currency receivables and payables, and thereby affect the parent company's cash flows. The effects should be recognized currently in reported consolidated net income.

Functional Currencies.   The most meaningful measuring unit for the assets, liabilities, and operations of a foreign operation is the currency of the primary economic environment in which the operation is conducted, its functional currency. Consolidated financial statements should therefore use one measuring unit for each functional currency of the operating units in the consolidated group of companies, including the domestic currency, which is the functional currency of the parent company. If only one measuring unit were used, the resulting information generally would be incompatible with the expected effects of changes in foreign exchange rates on the parent company's cash flows and equity. It would therefore be contrary to the basic objective of translation.

Highly Inflationary Economies.   Currencies of countries with highly inflationary economies are unsatisfactory as measuring units for financial reporting. A highly inflationary economy is one that has cumulative inflation of approximately 100% or more over three years. An operation in the environment of such a currency should be treated as if the domestic currency were its functional currency.

Effective Hedges.   Some contracts, transactions, and balances are, in effect, hedges of foreign exchange risks. They should be treated that way regardless of their form.

TASKS REQUIRED FOR TRANSLATION

Statement No. 52, "Foreign Currency Translation," paragraph 69, states that to achieve the objectives of translation and to conform with its assumptions, these major tasks are required for each foreign operation:

a. Identifying the functional currency of the [operation's] economic environment

b. Measuring all elements of the financial statements in the functional currency

c. Using the current exchange rate for translating from the functional currency to the reporting currency, if they are different

d. Distinguishing the economic impact of changes in exchange rates on a net investment from the impact of such changes on individual assets and liabilities that are receivable or payable in currencies other than the functional currency

Identifying the Functional Currency

Statement No. 52 indicates that identifying the functional currency of a foreign operation by determining the primary economic environment in which the operation is conducted is essentially a matter of management judgment. Management assesses the economic facts and circumstances pertaining to the foreign operation in relation to the objectives of translation, discussed above. Economic factors are considered both individually and collectively to determine the functional currency, so that the financial results and relationships are measured with the greatest degree of relevance and reliability.

Exercise of management's judgment is simplified if a foreign operation is either clearly self-contained and integrated in a particular foreign country, so that the currency of that country obviously is its functional currency, or clearly a direct and integral component or extension of the parent company's operations, so that the domestic currency obviously is its functional currency.

The functional currency of a foreign operation normally is the currency of the environment in which it primarily generates and expends cash. But sometimes observable facts are ambiguous in pointing to the functional currency. For example, if a foreign operation conducts significant amounts of business in two or more currencies, its functional currency might not be easily identifiable. For those operations, individual economic facts and circumstances need to be assessed.

Appendix A of Statement No. 52 provides guidance for making those assessments in particular circumstances. The guidance is grouped in sets of indicators: cash flow indicators, sales price indicators, sales market indicators, expense indicators, financing indicators, and intercompany transactions and arrangements indicators.

Measuring in the Functional Currency

Most foreign operations prepare their financial statements in their functional currencies. Some, however, prepare their financial statements in other foreign currencies.[1] Before the financial statements of a foreign operation are translated from its functional currency to the domestic currency, its foreign currency financial statements obviously have to be stated in its functional currency. If its financial statements are stated in another currency because its records are maintained in the other currency, they have to be remeasured into the functional currency before translation.

Statement No. 52, "Foreign Currency Translation," paragraph 10, distinguishes between remeasurement and translation. It states the goal of remeasurement to be "to produce the same results as if the . . . books of record had been maintained in the functional currency."

Remeasurement requires, as does translation, use of foreign exchange rates. For remeasurement, they are the rates between the foreign currency in which the financial statements of a foreign operation are stated and its foreign functional currency. Unlike translation, however, remeasurement requires the use of historical foreign exchange rates in addition to the current foreign exchange rate. Historical rates are rates at dates before the reporting date as of which certain financial statement items are recorded, such as items recorded at acquisition cost.

Remeasurement takes three steps. First, amounts to be remeasured at historical rates are distinguished from amounts to be remeasured at current rates. Second, the amounts are remeasured using the historical and current rates, as appropriate. Third, all exchange gains and losses identified by remeasurement are recognized currently in income. Such gains and losses are identified by remeasuring amounts at rates current at the reporting date, mainly monetary assets and liabilities not denominated in the functional currency, that differ from rates current at the preceding reporting date or an intervening date at which they were acquired.

---

[1]Even an operation that prepares its financial statements in the domestic currency uses translation procedures if application of the guidance in Statement No. 52 for identification of functional currencies clearly points to a foreign currency as its functional currency. That is necessary to prevent circumvention of the principles in FASB Statement No. 52.

Amounts remeasured at historical rates generally are amounts stated in historical terms, such as acquisition cost, and related revenue and expenses, such as depreciation. Appendix B of Statement No. 52 lists the following common items remeasured at historical rates:

Marketable securities carried at cost
  Equity securities
  Debt securities not intended to be held until maturity

Inventories carried at cost

Prepaid expenses such as insurance, advertising, and rent

Property, plant, and equipment

Accumulated depreciation on property, plant, and equipment

Patents, trademarks, licenses, and formulas

Goodwill

Other intangible assets

Deferred charges and credits, except deferred income taxes and policy acquisition
  costs for life insurance companies

Deferred income

Common stock

Preferred stock carried at issuance price

Examples of revenues and expenses related to nonmonetary items
  Cost of goods sold
  Depreciation of property, plant, and equipment
  Amortization of intangible items such as goodwill, patents, licenses, etc.
  Amortization of deferred charges or credits except deferred income taxes and
    policy acquisition costs for life insurance companies

Also, Statement No. 52 specifies that amounts resulting from interperiod income tax allocation and amounts related to unamortized policy acquisition costs of stock life insurance companies are to be remeasured using the current rate.

To remeasure an amount recorded in a currency other than the functional currency at the lower of cost and market, its cost in the foreign currency is first remeasured using the historical exchange rate. That amount is compared with market in the functional currency, and the remeasured amount is written down if market is lower than remeasured cost. If the item had been written down in the records because market was less than cost in the currency in which it was recorded, the writedown is reversed if market in the functional currency is more than remeasured cost.

If an item is written down to market in the functional currency, the resulting amount is treated as cost in subsequent periods in which it is held in applying the lower of cost and market rule.

The financial statements of a foreign operation in a highly inflationary economy are remeasured to the domestic currency the way they would be remeasured were the domestic currency its functional currency.

Illustration of Remeasurement

To illustrate remeasurement of French franc financial statements of a company whose functional currency is U.K. pounds: Corporation S was started on January 1, 19A. Exhibit 3.1 shows its franc financial statements for the year 19C, the third year of its life.

EXHIBIT 3.1.   Corporation S, Financial Statements (French francs) for the Year 19C

Income Statement		
Sales	FF	1,125,000
Cost of goods sold		(550,000)
Depreciation		(135,000)
Other expenses, including interest and taxes		(187,500)
Net income	FF	252,500
Statement of Changes in Retained Earnings		
Retained earnings, beginning of year	FF	135,000
Net income		252,500
Dividends		(75,000)
Retained earnings, end of year	FF	312,500
Balance Sheet		
Cash	FF	630,000
Accounts receivable (net)		245,000
Inventories		421,875
Equipment		540,000
Accumulated depreciation		(405,000)
	FF	1,431,875
Current liabilities	FF	105,000
Long-term debt		175,000
Deferred income taxes		35,000
Common stock		720,000
Additional paid-in capital		84,375
Retained earnings		312,500
	FF	1,431,875

S bought its equipment on January 1, 19A; the equipment has a four-year life. Sales, other expenses, dividends, and purchases of inventories on hand at December 31, 19C, occurred evenly throughout the year 19C. Inventories sold during the year were held an average of six months. The market value of the inventories in francs at December 31, 19C, exceeds its cost in francs. The pound equivalent of its franc cost exceeds its market value in pounds at December 31, 19C, by £6,250.

Exchange rates were FF9.00/£1 on January 1, 19A, FF8.00/£1 on December 31, 19B, FF7.50/£1 on June 30, 19C, and FF7.00/£1 on December 31, 19C.

EXHIBIT 3.2.   Corporation S, Remeasurement of Financial Statements (francs into pounds) for the Year 19C

	French Francs(i)	Exchange Rate	U.K. Pounds
Income Statement			
Sales	1,125,000	7.50	150,000
Cost of goods sold	(550,000)	(1)	(75,000)
Depreciation	(135,000)	9.00	(15,000)
Other expenses, including interest and taxes	(187,500)	7.50	(25,000)
Exchange gain		(2)	10,625
Net income	252,500		45,625
Statement of Changes in Retained Earnings			
Retained earnings, beginning of year	135,000	(3)	20,000
Net income	252,500	as above	45,625
Dividends	(75,000)	7.50	(10,000)
Retained earnings, end of year	312,500		55,625
Balance Sheet			
Cash	630,000	7.00	90,000
Receivables (net)	245,000	7.00	35,000
Inventories	421,875	(1)	50,000
Equipment	540,000	9.00	60,000
Accumulated depreciation	(405,000)	9.00	(45,000)
	1,431,875		190,000

EXHIBIT 3.2. *(Continued)*

	French Francs(i)	Exchange Rate	U.K. Pounds
Current liabilities	105,000	7.00	15,000
Long-term debt	175,000	7.00	25,000
Deferred income taxes	35,000	7.00	5,000
Common stock	720,000	9.00	80,000
Additional paid-in capital	84,375	9.00	9,375
Retained earnings	312,500	as above	55,625
	1,431,875		190,000

(i) From Exhibit 3.1.

(1) Inventories and cost of goods sold

	French Francs	Exchange Rate	U.K. Pounds	
Inventories				
Type A	300,000	7.50		40,000
Type B	121,875	7.50	16,250	
Writedown to market value in pounds			6,250	
Market value in pounds			10,000	10,000
Inventories, December 31, 19C	421,875			50,000

Cost of Goods Sold

	French Francs	U.K. Pounds
In francs income statement	550,000	
Exchange rate	÷ 8.00	68,750
Writedown of inventories to market value, as above, charged to cost of goods sold		6,250
Cost of goods sold, year 19C		75,000

(2) Exchange gain

Average monetary items during the year 19C: 595,000 francs

Change in pound equivalent during the year 19C:

	U.K. Pounds
December 31, 19C: 595,000 ÷ 7	85,000
January 1, 19C: 595,000 ÷ 8	74,375
Exchange gain	10,625

(3) Pound amount determined by difference. In practice, the amount is taken from the preceding year's financial statements.

Translation Using the Current Rate

Amounts remeasured into the domestic currency need not be translated, because the domestic currency is used as the reporting currency in the consolidated financial statements. Amounts measured in a foreign currency or remeasured into a foreign currency are all translated using the current foreign exchange rate between the foreign currency and the domestic currency.

For assets and liabilities, that is the rate at the reporting date. For income statement items, that is the rates as of the dates during the reporting period at which the items are recorded. An appropriately weighted average rate may be used to translate such items if they are numerous.

Translation Adjustments

Translation adjustments result from translating all amounts in foreign currency financial statements at rates current at the reporting date or during the reporting period different from rates current at the previous reporting date or during the previous reporting period. As discussed above, remeasurement of a foreign operation's foreign currency financial statements involves recognition in current income of exchange gains and losses. In contrast, translation adjustments are

EXHIBIT 3.3.   Corporation S, Translation of Financial Statements (pounds into dollars) for the Year 19C

	U.K. Pounds(i)	Exchange Rate	U.S. Dollars
Income Statement			
Sales	150,000	1.55	232,500
Cost of goods sold	(75,000)	1.55	(116,250)
Depreciation	(15,000)	1.55	(23,250)
Other expenses, including interest and taxes	(25,000)	1.55	(38,750)
Exchange gain	10,625	1.55	16,469
Net income	45,625		70,719
Statement of Changes in Retained Earnings			
Retained earnings, beginning of year	20,000	(1)	32,000
Net income	45,625	as above	70,719
Dividends	(10,000)	1.55	(15,500)
Retained earnings, end of year	55,625		87,219

EXHIBIT 3.3. *(Continued)*

	U.K. Pounds(i)	Exchange Rate	U.S. Dollars
Statement of Changes in Translation Adjustments			
Accumulated translation adjustments, beginning of year		(1)	4,718
Translation adjustments during year		(2)	(8,500)
Accumulated translation adjustments, end of year			(3,782)
Balance Sheet			
Cash	90,000	1.50	135,000
Accounts receivable (net)	35,000	1.50	52,500
Inventories	50,000	1.50	75,000
Equipment	60,000	1.50	90,000
Accumulated depreciation	(45,000)	1.50	(67,500)
	190,000		285,000
Current liabilities	15,000	1.50	22,500
Long-term debt	25,000	1.50	37,500
Deferred income taxes	5,000	1.50	7,500
Common stock	80,000	1.50	120,000
Additional paid-in capital	9,375	1.50	14,063
Retained earnings	55,625	as above	87,219
Accumulated translation adjustments		as above	(3,782)
	190,000		285,000

(i) From Exhibit 3.2

(1) Chosen for illustrative purposes. In practice, the amounts are taken from the preceding year's financial statements.

(2) Translation adjustment

	U.K. Pounds
Average monetary items during the year 19C:	85,000

	U.S. dollars
Change in dollar equivalent during the year:	
January 1, 19C: 85,000 × 1.60	136,000
December 31, 19C: 85,000 × 1.50	127,500
Translation adjustment	8,500

not recognized in current income but are accumulated in a separate component of equity.

The translation adjustments pertaining to a foreign operation are transferred from equity to gain or loss on disposition of the foreign operation when it is partly or completely sold or completely or substantially liquidated.

Illustration of Translation

Exhibit 3.3 illustrates translation of S's U.K. pound financial statements for the year 19C, derived in the illustration of remeasurement above, to U.S. dollar financial statements. Exchange rates were $1.60/£1 at December 31, 19B, $1.55/£1 at June 30, 19C, and $1.50/£1 at December 31, 19C.

TREATMENT OF FOREIGN COMPONENTS OR EXTENSIONS OF PARENT COMPANY OPERATIONS

The functional currency of a foreign operation that is a component or extension of the parent company's operations is the domestic currency. If it prepares its financial statements in a foreign currency, those financial statements are remeasured into the domestic currency by procedures discussed and illustrated above. No translation is required for such a foreign operation.

TREATMENT OF FOREIGN CURRENCY TRANSACTIONS

Some transactions of a unit in a consolidated group of companies may take place in a currency other than the functional currency of the unit. For example, a unit whose functional currency is the Mexican peso may buy a machine on credit for U.K. pounds or may sell securities on credit for French francs. Except in a forward exchange contract (discussed below), the amounts in such a foreign currency transaction are measured at the transaction date at the foreign exchange rate at that date—in the example, between the peso and the pound or between the peso and the franc.

At the next reporting date or at an intervening date at which the receivable or payable is settled, the receivable or payable is remeasured at the rate current at that date. Changes in its amount as measured in the functional currency since the previous reporting date or an intervening date at which it was acquired are

EXHIBIT 3.4.   Corporation S, Transaction Gain on Forward Exchange Contracts for the Year 19C

			U.S. Dollars
Liability			
January 1, 19C	£1,000,000 × $1.60/£1	=	1,600,000
December 31, 19C	£1,000,000 × $1.50/£1	=	1,500,000
Transaction gain			100,000

transaction gains or losses, to be included in current reported consolidated net income, except as discussed later.

To illustrate: Corporation P, whose functional currency is U.S. dollars, borrowed £(U.K.)1,000,000 on January 1, 19C, and agreed to repay £100,000 on December 31, 19C, and £1,100,000 on December 31, 19D. Exchange rates were $1.60/£1 at January 1, 19C, and $1.50/£1 at December 31, 19C.

The payment of £100,000 on December 31, 19C, is remeasured as interest expense of $150,000. The liability in dollars at December 31, 19C, is remeasured for the change in exchange rate and a transaction gain of $100,000 is determined, for presentation in P's income statement for the year 19C, as shown in Exhibit 3.4.

FORWARD EXCHANGE CONTRACTS

Forward exchange contracts are contracts that require currencies of two countries to be traded in specified amounts at specified future dates and specified rates, called *forward rates*. Such contracts are foreign currency transactions that require special treatment.

Discounts or Premiums on Forward Exchange Contracts

A forward exchange contract may involve a discount or premium, a difference between the foreign exchange rate specified in the contract and the rate at the date the contract is entered into, multiplied by the amount of foreign currency specified in the contract. Ordinarily, a discount or premium is allocated to income over the duration of the forward exchange contract. However, a discount or premium may be treated differently in these circumstances:

> If the contract is designated as and is effective as a hedge of a net investment in a foreign operation (discussed further on). If so, the discount or premium may be included with translation adjustments and thus not be reported in income.
>
> If the contract meets the tests of a hedge of an identifiable foreign currency commitment (also discussed further on). If so, the discount or premium may be included in the amount at which the foreign currency transaction related to the commitment is stated.

Gains or Losses on Forward Exchange Contracts

A gain or loss on a forward exchange contract to be reported in the current reporting period is computed by multiplying the amount of the foreign currency to be exchanged by the difference between (1) the foreign exchange rate at the reporting date and (2) the rate (a) on the date on which the contract was made or (b) the previous reporting date, whichever is later. A gain or loss on a forward exchange contract is recognized in income as a transaction gain or loss in the period of the gain or loss, unless it is in one of the categories of transaction gains and losses excluded from net income, discussed later.

To illustrate a forward exchange contract: On January 1, 19B, P and Q enter into a contract in which Q agrees to buy £(U.K.)1,000,000 from P for $(U.S.)1,550,000, incorporating a forward rate of $1.55/£1, on December 31, 19C. The exchange rate at January 1, 19B, is $1.60/£1. The contract therefore involves a premium to P and a discount to Q of £1,000,000 × ($1.60/£1 − $1.55/£1) = $50,000. Q makes this entry:

Foreign currency receivable	1,600,000	
Payable to P		1,550,000
Discount on foreign exchange contract		50,000

P makes this entry:

Receivable from Q	1,550,000	
Premium on foreign exchange contract	50,000	
Foreign currency payable		1,600,000

P and Q allocate the $50,000 to forward exchange gain or loss over the years 19B and 19C. P makes this entry in each of the two years:

Amortization of premium on forward exchange contract	25,000	
Premium on forward exchange contract		25,000

Q makes this opposite entry in each of the two years:

Discount on forward exchange contract	25,000	
Amortization of discount on forward exchange contract		25,000

The exchange rate changes to $1.50/£1 at December 31, 19B, and $1.45/£1 at December 31, 19C. P records these entries based on the changes in the exchange rate:

December 31, 19B

Foreign currency payable	100,000	
Forward exchange gain		100,000

$£1,000,000 \times (\$1.60/£1 - \$1.50/£1) = \$100,000$

December 31, 19C

Foreign currency payable	50,000	
Forward exchange gain		50,000

$£1,000,000 \times (\$1.50/£1 - \$1.45/£1) = \$50,000$

Q records these opposite entries based on the changes in the exchange rate:

December 31, 19B

Forward exchange loss	100,000	
Foreign currency receivable		100,000

December 31, 19C

Forward exchange loss	50,000	
Foreign currency receivable		50,000

On settlement of the contract on December 31, 19C, P makes this entry:

Foreign currency payable	1,450,000	
Cash	100,000	
Receivable from Q		1,550,000

*To record payment of $1,450,000 to buy
£1,000,000 to give to Q, receipt of $1,550,000
from Q, and cancellation of the forward exchange
receivable from Q.*

Q makes this opposite entry:

Payable to P	1,550,000	
Foreign currency receivable		1,450,000
Cash		100,000

*To record receipt of $1,450,000 on sale of
£1,000,000 received from P, payment of
$1,550,000 to P, and cancellation of the
forward exchange payable to P.*

The contract may be summarized as shown in Exhibit 3.5.

The net gain of P and loss of Q of $100,000 equal the difference between the forward rate and the rate on the settlement date times the amount of currency transferred:

$$(\$1.55/\pounds1 \ - \ \$1.45/\pounds1) \ \times \ \pounds1,000,000 \ = \ \$100,000$$

EXHIBIT 3.5. Corporation P or Corporation Q, Gain or Loss on Forward Exchange Contracts Beginning in the Year 19B

	Gain by P, Loss by Q, U.S. Dollars
Foreign exchange gain or loss on contract:	
The year 19B—£1,000,000 × ($1.60/£1 − $1.50/£1) =	100,000
The year 19C—£1,000,000 × ($1.50/£1 − $1.45/£1) =	50,000
	150,000
Premium or discount on contract	(50,000)
Net gain or loss over the life of the contract	100,000

EXCLUSION OF TRANSACTION GAINS AND LOSSES FROM INCOME

Gains and losses on some foreign currency transactions are not recognized in income when they occur.

Treatment as Translation Adjustments

FASB Statement No. 52, "Foreign Currency Translation," paragraph 20, requires amounts that otherwise fit the definition of gains and losses on foreign currency transactions to be treated as translation adjustments if

a. [They] are designated as, and are effective as, economic hedges of a net investment in a foreign entity, commencing as of the designation date [or]

b. [They are] intercompany foreign currency transactions that are of a long-term investment nature (that is, settlement is not planned or anticipated in the foreseeable future), when the [units that are parties] to the transaction[s] are consolidated, combined, or accounted for by the equity method in the reporting [entity's] financial statements.

Deferral of Transaction Gains and Losses

Recognition of transaction gains and losses in consolidated income is deferred for such gains and losses resulting from transactions intended to hedge identifiable foreign currency commitments; they are included in accounting for the transaction resulting from the commitment. However, recognition of losses is not deferred if deferral would lead to recognition of losses in subsequent periods.

Statement No. 52, "Foreign Currency Translation," paragraph 21, states two conditions that have to be met for a foreign currency transaction to be considered a hedge of an identifiable foreign currency commitment:

a. The foreign currency transaction is designated as, and is effective as, a hedge of a foreign currency commitment.

b. The foreign currency commitment is firm.

To illustrate: On December 15, 19A, Corporation F, a U.S. company, agrees to buy equipment from Corporation G in Austria. The equipment is to be delivered on January 15, 19B, and F is to be billed Sh(Aus.)1,000,000 at that time. To fix the cost of the equipment in U.S. dollars, F enters into a forward exchange contract on December 15, 19A, for the purchase of Sh1,000,000 to be delivered on January 15, 19B. Forward and spot rates on December 15, 19A, are both $.05/Sh1. The spot rate is $.055/Sh1 on December 31, 19A, and $.0525/Sh1 on January 15, 19B.

Because (1) the life of the forward exchange contract extends from the foreign currency commitment date to the anticipated transaction date, (2) the forward contract is denominated in the same currency as the foreign currency commitment (purchase price), and (3) the foreign currency commitment (purchase agreement) is uncancelable, the forward contract is accounted for as a hedge of an identifiable foreign currency commitment.

F makes the following entry on December 15, 19A:

Austrian shillings receivable	50,000	
Cash		50,000

Sh1,000,000 × $.05/Sh1 = $50,000

On December 31, 19A, the gain resulting from the forward contract is Sh1,000,000 × ($.055/Sh1 − $.05/Sh1) = $5,000. On December 31, 19A, F makes the following entry:

Austrian shillings receivable	5,000	
Deferred gain or loss on forward exchange contract		5,000

The equipment is delivered on January 15, 19B, and the forward exchange contract expires on the same day. The deferred gain is now only Sh1,000,000 × ($.0525/Sh1 − $.05/Sh1) = $2,500. F makes the following entries on January 15, 19B:

Deferred gain or loss on forward exchange contract	2,500	
Austrian shillings receivable		2,500
Austrian shillings	52,500	
Austrian shillings receivable		52,500

Equipment	50,000	
Deferred gain or loss on forward exchange contract	2,500	
Austrian shillings		52,500

Forward exchange transactions involving losses are accounted for in the same manner unless deferral of the loss would lead to recognizing losses in later periods. If so, the loss is recognized immediately.

To illustrate: If the spot rate on January 15, 19B, were $.04/Sh1 instead of $.0525/Sh1, there would be an unrealized loss on January 15 of Sh1,000,000 $\times$ ($.05/Sh1 $-$ $.04/Sh1) = $10,000. If the net realizable value of the equipment in the U.S. were only $45,000, F would make the following entries on January 15, 19B:

Deferred loss on forward exchange contract	10,000	
Exchange loss	5,000	
Austrian shillings receivable		15,000
Austrian shillings	40,000	
Austrian shillings receivable		40,000
Equipment	45,000	
Deferred loss on forward exchange contract		5,000
Austrian shillings		40,000

The amount to be deferred has these limitations:

1. The gain or loss has to be on the portion of the hedging transaction that is no greater than the amount of the commitment hedged after taxes. The part of the deferred gain or loss on the portion of the transaction that exceeds the amount of the commitment hedged, that is, the part related to taxes, offsets the related tax effect in the period in which the tax effect is recognized. A gain or loss so deferred is included as an offset to the related tax effects in the period in which such tax effects are recognized. The part of the deferred gain or loss that relates to the commitment

hedged is included in accounting for the transaction resulting from the commitment.

2. A gain or loss pertaining to a period after the transaction date of the related commitment is not deferred. However, if a foreign currency transaction previously considered a hedge of a foreign currency commitment is terminated before the transaction date of the related commitment, a deferred gain or loss on the transaction that remains continues to be deferred until the transaction date.

To illustrate limitation 1: Corporation N, the U.S. parent company of Corporation M, wishes to fix M's selling price of the equipment in U.S. dollars. Because a gain or loss on a forward exchange contract bought by N would be subject to U.S. taxes at a rate of 46%, N would have to buy a forward exchange contract for $Sh1,000,000/(1 - 46\%) = Sh1,851,852$ to make sure the effect of an exchange rate change on the selling price of the equipment would be offset by the after-tax gain or loss on the forward contract.

Because N wishes to hedge a specific exposed monetary item in addition to the sale of the equipment, N enters into a forward contract on December 15, 19A, to buy Sh3,000,000 to be delivered on January 15, 19B. The transaction is assumed to be not subject to Austrian taxes. The forward rate is $.05/Sh1, so the dollar amount of the contract is $150,000.

On December 15, 19A, N makes the following entry:

Austrian shillings receivable	150,000	
Payable to exchange broker		150,000

On December 31, 19A, N has a gain of $Sh3,000,000 \times (\$.055/Sh1 - \$.05/Sh1) = \$15,000$ resulting from the forward exchange contract. However, only the gain related to the portion of the forward contract that was intended to be an after-tax hedge of the selling price of the equipment may be deferred. On December 31, 19A, N makes this entry:

Austrian shillings receivable	15,000	
Deferred gain on forward exchange contract		9,259
Exchange gain		5,741

$9,259 = $5,000 [$15,000 × (Sh1,000,000/Sh3,000,000)] gain on foreign currency sales commitment + $4,259 [$15,000 × (Sh1,851,852 − Sh1,000,000)/Sh3,000,000] net related tax effects. $5,741 = [$15,000 × (Sh3,000,000 − Sh1,851,852)/Sh3,000,000] exchange gain

On January 15, 19B, the forward exchange contract expires and the gain is now only Sh3,000,000 × ($.0525/Sh1 − $.05/Sh1) = $7,500. N buys dollars for its shillings. It makes the following entries:

Deferred gain on forward exchange contract	4,630	
Exchange loss	2,870	
Austrian shillings receivable		7,500

$4,630 = $2,500 [$7,500 × Sh1,000,000/ Sh3,000,000] gain on forward currency sales commitment + $2,130 [$7,500 × (Sh1,851,852 − Sh1,000,000)/Sh3,000,000] related tax effects. $2,870 = $7,500 × (Sh3,000,000 − Sh1,851,852)/Sh3,000,000 exchange loss

Austrian shillings	157,000	
Austrian shillings receivable		157,000

Cash	157,000	
Austrian shillings		157,000

Income tax expense	1,320	
Deferred gain on forward exchange contract	2,130	
Income taxes payable		3,450
$3,450 = $7,500 × 46%		

To illustrate limitation 2: Corporation P sells its forward exchange contract on January 1, 19B, for Sh55,000, and makes this entry:

Austrian shillings	55,000	
Austrian shillings receivable		55,000

On January 15, 19B, when the equipment is delivered, P makes this entry:

Equipment	50,000	
Deferred gain on forward exchange contract	5,000	
Austrian shillings		52,500
Exchange gain		2,500

OTHER TOPICS IN FOREIGN CURRENCY TRANSLATION

Other topics concerning translation by the current rate method include income tax considerations, intercompany profit eliminations, selection of exchange rates, approximations, and required disclosures.

Income Tax Considerations

Treatment of foreign operations involves these special income tax accounting treatments:

Unremitted Earnings.   Deferred taxes are not recognized on translation adjustments that meet the tests in APB Opinion 23 concerning unremitted earnings.

Intraperiod Allocation.   Income taxes related to transaction gains and losses or translation adjustments reported in separate components of the income statement or the statement of changes in equity are allocated to the separate components.

Intercompany Profit Eliminations

An exception in the current rate method to the use of the current exchange rate for translation is the method to eliminate intercompany profits on transactions between combined or consolidated companies or between affiliates accounted for by the equity method. They are eliminated at the rates at the dates of the transactions, because those are the rates at which the profits are embedded in the recorded amounts. Such eliminations precede applying the current exchange rates to the foreign currency amounts.

To illustrate: Corporation P, a domestic parent company, sold a parcel of land last year to Corporation S, its foreign subsidiary, at a profit of $24,000, when the exchange rate was $1/Z8 (Polish zlotys). S recorded the land in zlotys.

The current exchange rate is Z6 = \$1. The profit is eliminated at Z8/\$1. The remaining amount at which S has the land recorded is translated at Z6/\$1.[2]

Selection of Exchange Rates

The current foreign exchange rate is used for most translation required by FASB Statement No. 52, "Foreign Currency Translation." Circumstances in which the rates at the dates of transactions are used instead are discussed above. These are other special considerations in selecting exchange rates:

If the two currencies involved could not be exchanged on the date of the transaction or the reporting date, the rate at which they could be exchanged at the first succeeding date is used.

If the inability to exchange the two currencies is not merely temporary, including the foreign operation in a consolidated group or accounting for it by the equity method is questioned.

Foreign currency transactions are translated at the rates at which they could have been settled at the dates of the transactions. Resulting receivables and payables are translated subsequently at the rates at which they could be settled at the reporting dates.

If there is more than one rate at a particular date, the rate at which foreign currency could be exchanged for domestic currency to remit dividends is used.

If the reporting date of the foreign currency financial statements being translated differs from the reporting date of the reporting entity in which the foreign operation is included, the current rate is the rate in effect on the reporting date of the foreign currency financial statements.

Approximations

Approximations of the results of applying the required translation principles are acceptable if the cost of applying them to every detail exceeds the benefits of such precision and the results do not materially differ from what they would be by applying them to every detail. Judgment is required to determine whether to

---

[2]Exchange restrictions between dollars and zlotys may be severe enough to call into question the soundness of including S in the consolidated reporting entity.

use approximation, because determining the extent of the differences precisely would require the very calculations to be avoided by approximations.

DISCLOSURES CONCERNING FOREIGN OPERATIONS

These disclosures are required concerning foreign operations:

The total transaction gains or losses, including, for this purpose, gains and losses on forward contracts other than those excluded from income

An analysis of the changes in the separate component of equity for translation adjustments, including at least:

The beginning and ending accumulated balances

The net change from translation adjustments and gains and losses from hedges and intercompany balances treated the way translation adjustments are treated

Income taxes allocated to translation adjustments

Transfers from the equity component into income because of the partial or complete sale of an investment in a foreign operation or the complete or substantial liquidation of a foreign operation

CHAPTER FOUR

Consolidated Balance Sheet at the Date of Business Combination

Amounts that would be presented in a consolidated balance sheet at the date of a business combination are determined for use in presenting a consolidated balance sheet as of that date or for use in consolidated financial statements for subsequent periods.

The separate balance sheets of the combining companies at the date of the combination include intercompany stockholdings and may include intercompany receivables and payables, all of which are eliminated in consolidation. The eliminating entries are recorded only on a consolidating worksheet, not in the books of any of the companies.

This chapter illustrates worksheet procedures to prepare consolidated balance sheets at the date of a business combination under five different sets of circumstances:

Pooling of interests method

    100% transfer of stock

    90% transfer of stock

Purchase method

    100% acquisition of stock for cash

    90% acquisition of stock for cash

    80% acquisition of stock by transfer of stock

POOLING OF INTERESTS METHOD: 100% TRANSFER OF STOCK

Corporation P acquires all Corporation S's voting stock on December 31, 19A, by issuing 1,100 shares of its $100 par value common stock to S's stockholders, who transfer to P all their voting stock in S. The combination qualifies for treatment by the pooling of interests method. Also, S owes P $3,000. Just before the combination, the December 31, 19A, balance sheets of P and S are as shown in Exhibit 4.1.

P makes this entry to record the issuance of its stock:

Investment in Corporation S	110,000	
Common stock		110,000

S has no entry to make; it merely updates its stockholder list. The December 31, 19A, balance sheets of P and S immediately after the combination are as shown in Exhibit 4.2.

As illustrated in Exhibit 4.3, those balances are transferred to the first two columns of a worksheet. The next two columns are for eliminations. The last column is for the consolidated balance sheet, which represents the aggregate of the members' balance sheets after the eliminations. The excess of the stated amount of P's stock issued to S's stockholders over the stated amount of S's

EXHIBIT 4.1. Corporation P and Corporation S, Balance Sheets, December 31, 19A (just before combination accounted for by the pooling of interests method: 100% transfer of stock)

	P	S
Cash	$500,000	$ 50,000
Accounts receivable (net)	50,000	20,000
Inventories	100,000	60,000
Buildings and equipment (net)	150,000	20,000
	$800,000	$150,000
Current liabilities	$ 20,000	$ 10,000
Long-term liabilities	140,000	20,000
Common stock	400,000	100,000
Retained earnings	240,000	20,000
	$800,000	$150,000

EXHIBIT 4.2. Corporation P and Corporation S, Balance Sheets, December 31, 19A (just after combination accounted for by the pooling of interests method: 100% transfer of stock)

	P	S
Cash	$500,000	$ 50,000
Accounts receivable (net)	50,000	20,000
Inventories	100,000	60,000
Buildings and equipment (net)	150,000	20,000
Investment in S	110,000	
	$910,000	$150,000
Current liabilities	$ 20,000	$ 10,000
Long-term liabilities	140,000	20,000
Common stock	510,000	100,000
Retained earnings	240,000	20,000
	$910,000	$150,000

EXHIBIT 4.3. Corporation P and Corporation S, Worksheet to Develop Consolidated Balance Sheet, December 31, 19A (just after combination accounted for by the pooling of interests method: 100% transfer of stock)

	P(i)	S(i)	Eliminations Dr.		Eliminations Cr.		Consolidated Balance Sheet
Cash	500,000	50,000					550,000
Accounts receivable (net)	50,000	20,000			(2)	3,000	67,000
Inventories	100,000	60,000					160,000
Buildings and equipment (net)	150,000	20,000					170,000
Investment in S	110,000				(1)	110,000	
	910,000	150,000					947,000
Current liabilities	20,000	10,000	(2)	3,000			27,000
Long-term liabilities	140,000	20,000					160,000
Common stock	510,000	100,000	(1)	100,000			510,000
Retained earnings	240,000	20,000	(1)	10,000			250,000
	910,000	150,000		113,000		113,000	947,000

(i) From Exhibit 4.2
(1) To eliminate intercompany stockholding: investment of $110,000 in S's stock charged first against common stock—$100,000—and the excess—$10,000—charged against retained earnings
(2) To eliminate intercompany debt

stock received from S's stockholders is charged to consolidated additional paid-in capital, with any further excess charged to consolidated retained earnings at the date of combination. (An excess of the stated amount of S's stock received over the stated amount of P's stock issued would be credited to consolidated additional paid-in capital.)

POOLING OF INTERESTS METHOD: 90% TRANSFER OF STOCK

P acquires 90% of S's voting stock (900 shares) on December 31, 19A, by issuing 1,000 shares of its $100 par value common stock to those of S's stockholders who transfer to P their voting stock in S. The combination qualifies for the pooling of interests method. Also, S owes P $3,000. Just before the combination, the December 31, 19A, balance sheets of P and S are as shown in Exhibit 4.4. P makes this entry to record the issuance of its stock:

Investment in Corporation S	100,000	
Common stock		100,000

The December 31, 19A, balance sheets of P and S immediately after the combination are as shown in Exhibit 4.5. The December 31, 19A, balance sheets are consolidated as shown in Exhibit 4.6.

PURCHASE METHOD: 100% ACQUISITION OF STOCK

P acquires all S's voting stock on December 31, 19A, for $170,000. The combination does not qualify for the pooling of interests method, so the purchase method is used. Also, S owes P $3,000. Just before the combination, the December 31, 19A, balance sheets of P and S are as shown in Exhibit 4.7.

P makes the following entry to record the purchase of S's stock:

Investment in Corporation S	170,000	
Cash		170,000

EXHIBIT 4.4.   Corporation P and Corporation S, Balance Sheets, December 31, 19A (just before combination accounted for by the pooling of interests method: 90% transfer of stock)

	P	S
Cash	$500,000	$ 50,000
Accounts receivable (net)	50,000	20,000
Inventories	100,000	60,000
Buildings and equipment (net)	150,000	20,000
	$800,000	$150,000
Current liabilities	$ 20,000	$ 10,000
Long-term liabilities	140,000	20,000
Common stock	400,000	100,000
Retained earnings	240,000	20,000
	$800,000	$150,000

The December 31, 19A, balance sheets of P and S immediately after the combination are as shown in Exhibit 4.8. For its $170,000, P acquired S's assets and liabilities, whose fair values are $144,000 and goodwill, whose acquisition cost is calculated to be $26,000, as shown in Exhibit 4.9. The December 31, 19A, balance sheets are consolidated as shown in Exhibit 4.10.

EXHIBIT 4.5.   Corporation P and Corporation S, Balance Sheets, December 31, 19A (just after combination accounted for by the pooling of interests method: 90% transfer of stock)

	P	S
Cash	$500,000	$ 50,000
Accounts receivable (net)	50,000	20,000
Inventories	100,000	60,000
Buildings and equipment (net)	150,000	20,000
Investment in S	100,000	
	$900,000	$150,000
Current liabilities	$ 20,000	$ 10,000
Long-term liabilities	140,000	20,000
Common stock	500,000	100,000
Retained earnings	240,000	20,000
	$900,000	$150,000

EXHIBIT 4.6. Corporation P and Corporation S, Worksheet to Develop Consolidated Balance Sheet, December 31, 19A (just after combination accounted for by the pooling of interests method: 90% transfer of stock)

	P(i)	S(i)		Eliminations Dr.		Eliminations Cr.	Consolidated Balance Sheet
Cash	500,000	50,000					550,000
Accounts receivable (net)	50,000	20,000			(2)	3,000	67,000
Inventories	100,000	60,000					160,000
Buildings and equipment (net)	150,000	20,000					170,000
Investment in S	100,000				(1)	100,000	
	900,000	150,000					947,000
Current liabilities	20,000	10,000	(2)	3,000			27,000
Long-term liabilities	140,000	20,000					160,000
Common stock	500,000	100,000	(1)	90,000			510,000*
Retained earnings	240,000	20,000	(1)	10,000			250,000**
	900,000	150,000		103,000		103,000	947,000

(i) From Exhibit 4.5
(1) To eliminate intercompany stockholding: investment of $100,000 in 90% of S's stock charged first against common stock—$90,000—and the excess—$10,000—charged against retained earnings
(2) To eliminate intercompany debt
 *Includes $100,000 × 10% = $10,000 of S's common stock owned by outsiders (minority interest)
 **Includes $20,000 × 10% = $2,000 of retained earnings attributable to minority interest

EXHIBIT 4.7. Corporation P and Corporation S, Balance Sheets, December 31, 19A (just before combination accounted for by the purchase method: 100% acquisition of stock)

	P	S
Cash	$500,000	$ 50,000
Accounts receivable (net)	50,000	20,000
Inventories	100,000	60,000
Buildings and equipment (net)	150,000	20,000
	$800,000	$150,000
Current liabilities	$ 20,000	$ 10,000
Long-term liabilities	140,000	20,000
Common stock	400,000	100,000
Retained earnings	240,000	20,000
	$800,000	$150,000

EXHIBIT 4.8. Corporation P and Corporation S, Balance Sheets, December 31, 19A (just after combination accounted for by the purchase method: 100% acquisition of stock)

	P	S
Cash	$330,000	$ 50,000
Accounts receivable (net)	50,000	20,000
Inventories	100,000	60,000
Buildings and equipment (net)	150,000	20,000
Investment in S	170,000	
	$800,000	$150,000
Current liabilities	$ 20,000	$ 10,000
Long-term liabilities	140,000	20,000
Common stock	400,000	100,000
Retained earnings	240,000	20,000
	$800,000	$150,000

EXHIBIT 4.9. Corporation P and Corporation S, Book Values, Fair Values, and Calculation of Goodwill, December 31, 19A (combination accounted for by the purchase method: 100% acquisition of stock)

	Fair Values	Book Values(i)	Excess of Fair Values over Book Values
Cash	50,000	50,000	-0-
Accounts receivable (net)	20,000	20,000	-0-
Inventories	80,000	60,000	20,000
Buildings and equipment (net)	30,000	20,000	10,000
Current liabilities	(10,000)	(10,000)	-0-
Long-term liabilities	(26,000)	(20,000)	(6,000)
	144,000	120,000	24,000
Amount of investment	170,000		
Goodwill	26,000		
Equity:			
Common stock		100,000	
Retained earnings		20,000	
Total, as above		120,000	

(i) From Exhibit 4.8

61

EXHIBIT 4.10. Corporation P and Corporation S, Worksheet to Develop Consolidated Balance Sheet, December 31, 19A (just after combination accounted for by the purchase method: 100% acquisition of stock)

	P(i)	S(i)		Eliminations Dr.		Cr.	Consolidated Balance Sheet
Cash	330,000	50,000					380,000
Receivable (net)	50,000	20,000			(2)	3,000	67,000
Inventories	100,000	60,000	(1)	20,000			180,000
Buildings and equipment (net)	150,000	20,000	(1)	10,000			180,000
Investment in S	170,000				(1)	170,000	
Goodwill			(1)	26,000			26,000
	800,000	150,000					833,000
Current liabilities	20,000	10,000	(2)	3,000			27,000
Long-term liabilities	140,000	20,000			(1)	6,000	166,000
Common stock	400,000	100,000	(1)	100,000			400,000
Retained earnings	240,000	20,000	(1)	20,000			240,000
	800,000	150,000		179,000		179,000	833,000

(i) From Exhibit 4.8
(1) To eliminate intercompany stockholdings, adjust S's assets to their fair values, and record the difference as goodwill, from Exhibit 4.9
(2) To eliminate intercompany debt

EXHIBIT 4.11. Corporation P and Corporation S, Balance Sheets, December 31, 19A (just before combination accounted for by the purchase method: 90% acquisition of stock)

	P	S
Cash	$500,000	$ 50,000
Accounts receivable (net)	50,000	20,000
Inventories	100,000	60,000
Buildings and equipment (net)	150,000	20,000
	$800,000	$150,000
Current liabilities	$ 20,000	$ 10,000
Long-term liabilities	140,000	20,000
Common stock	400,000	100,000
Retained earnings	240,000	20,000
	$800,000	$150,000

EXHIBIT 4.12. Corporation P and Corporation S, Balance Sheets, December 31, 19A (just after combination accounted for by the purchase method: 90% acquisition of stock)

	P	S
Cash	$350,000	$ 50,000
Accounts receivable (net)	50,000	20,000
Inventories	100,000	60,000
Buildings and equipment (net)	150,000	20,000
Investment in S	150,000	
	$800,000	$150,000
Current liabilities	$ 20,000	$ 10,000
Long-term liabilities	140,000	20,000
Common stock	400,000	100,000
Retained earnings	240,000	20,000
	$800,000	$150,000

EXHIBIT 4.13. Corporation P and Corporation S, Book Values, Fair Values, and Calculation of Goodwill, December 31, 19A (combination accounted for by the purchase method: 90% acquisition of stock)

	Fair Values	Book Values(i)	Excess of Fair Values over Book Values	90% of Excess of Fair Values over Book Values
Cash	50,000	50,000	0	-0-
Accounts receivable (net)	20,000	20,000	-0-	-0-
Inventories	80,000	60,000	20,000	18,000
Buildings and equipment (net)	30,000	20,000	10,000	9,000
Current liabilities	(10,000)	(10,000)	-0-	-0-
Long-term liabilities	(26,000)	(20,000)	(6,000)	(5,400)
	144,000	120,000	24,000	21,600
	× 90%	× 90%	× 90%	
	129,600	108,000	21,600	
Amount of investment	150,000			
Goodwill	20,400			

Equity:		Total	90% Acquired
Common stock		100,000	90,000
Retained earnings		20,000	18,000
Totals, as above		120,000	108,000

(i) From Exhibit 4.12

PURCHASE METHOD: 90% ACQUISITION OF STOCK

P acquires 90% of S's voting stock (900 shares) on December 31, 19A, for $150,000. The combination does not qualify for the pooling of interests method, so the purchase method is used. Also, S owes P $3,000. Just before the combination, the December 31, 19A, balance sheets of P and S are as shown in Exhibit 4.11.

P makes the following entry to record the purchase of S's stock:

Investment in Corporation S	150,000	
Cash		150,000

EXHIBIT 4.14.   Corporation P and Corporation S, Worksheet to Develop Consolidated Balance Sheet, December 31, 19A (just after combination accounted for by the purchase method: 90% acquisition of stock)

	P(i)	S(i)		Eliminations Dr.		Eliminations Cr.	Consolidated Balance Sheet
Cash	350,000	50,000					400,000
Accounts receivable (net)	50,000	20,000			(2)	3,000	67,000
Inventories	100,000	60,000	(1)	18,000			178,000
Buildings and equipment (net)	150,000	20,000	(1)	9,000			179,000
Investment in S	150,000				(1)	150,000	
Goodwill			(1)	20,400			20,400
	800,000	150,000					844,400
Current liabilities	20,000	10,000	(2)	3,000			27,000
Long-term liabilities	140,000	20,000			(1)	5,400	165,400
Common stock	400,000	100,000	(1)	90,000			410,000*
Retained earnings	240,000	20,000	(1)	18,000			242,000**
	800,000	150,000		158,400		158,400	844,400

(i) From Exhibit 4.12
(1) To eliminate intercompany stockholding, adjust S's assets and liabilities to their fair values, and record the difference as goodwill, from Exhibit 4.13
(2) To eliminate intercompany debt
*Includes $100,000 × 10% = $10,000 of S's common stock owned by outsiders (minority interest)
**Includes $20,000 × 10% = $2,000 of retained earnings attributable to minority interest

The December 31, 19A, balance sheets of P and S immediately after the combination are as shown in Exhibit 4.12. For its $150,000, P acquired 90% of the fair value of S's assets and liabilities for $129,600, and goodwill, whose acquisition cost is calculated to be $20,400, as shown in Exhibit 4.13. The December 31, 19A, balance sheets are consolidated as shown in Exhibit 4.14.

PURCHASE METHOD: 80% ACQUISITION OF STOCK (FOR STOCK)

P acquires 80% (800 shares) of S's outstanding voting stock on December 31, 19A, by issuing 600 shares of its own $100 par value common stock to S's stockholders, who, in turn, transfer S's voting shares to P. The combination does not qualify for the pooling of interests method, so the purchase method is used. The market value of P's stock is not readily discernible, but S's stock is selling for $140 a share. Also, S owes P $3,000. Just before the combination, the December 31, 19A, balance sheets of P and S are as shown in Exhibit 4.15.

The investment in S is recorded at $112,000, the fair value of S's shares (800 shares at $140 = $112,000). P issues 600 shares of its $100 par value stock, for a total of $60,000. The $52,000 difference is credited to additional paid-in capital.

EXHIBIT 4.15.   Corporation P and Corporation S, Balance Sheets, December 31, 19A (just before combination accounted for by the purchase method: 80% acquisition of stock)

	P	S
Cash	$500,000	$ 50,000
Accounts receivable (net)	50,000	20,000
Inventories	100,000	60,000
Buildings and equipment (net)	150,000	20,000
	$800,000	$150,000
Current liabilities	$ 20,000	$ 10,000
Long-term liabilities	140,000	20,000
Common stock	400,000	100,000
Retained earnings	240,000	20,000
	$800,000	$150,000

EXHIBIT 4.16. Corporation P and Corporation S, Balance Sheets, December 31, 19A (just after combination accounted for by the purchase method: 80% acquisition of stock)

	P	S
Cash	$500,000	$ 50,000
Accounts receivable (net)	50,000	20,000
Inventories	100,000	60,000
Buildings and equipment (net)	150,000	20,000
Investment in S	112,000	
	$912,000	$150,000
Current liabilities	$ 20,000	$ 10,000
Long-term liabilities	140,000	20,000
Common stock	460,000	100,000
Additional paid-in capital	52,000	
Retained earnings	240,000	20,000
	$912,000	$150,000

EXHIBIT 4.17. Corporation P and Corporation S, Book Values, Fair Values, and Calculation of Goodwill, December 31, 19A (combination accounted for by the purchase method: 80% transfer of stock)

	Fair Values	Book Values(i)	Excess of Fair Values over Book Values	80% of Excess of Fair Values over Book Values
Cash	50,000	50,000	-0-	-0-
Receivables (net)	20,000	20,000	-0-	-0-
Inventories	80,000	60,000	20,000	16,000
Buildings and equipment (net)	30,000	20,000	10,000	8,000
Current liabilities	(10,000)	(10,000)	-0-	-0-
Long-term liabilities	(30,000)	(20,000)	(10,000)	(8,000)
	140,000	120,000	20,000	16,000
	×80%	×80%	×80%	
	112,000	96,000	16,000	
Amount of investment	112,000			
Goodwill	-0-			

Equity:	Totals	80% Acquired
Common stock	100,000	80,000
Retained earnings	20,000	16,000
Totals, as above	120,000	96,000

(i) From Exhibit 4.16

EXHIBIT 4.18. Corporation P and Corporation S, Worksheet to Develop Consolidated Balance Sheet, December 31, 19A (just after combination accounted for by the purchase method: 80% acquisition of stock)

	P(i)	S(i)	Eliminations Dr.		Eliminations Cr.		Consolidated Balance Sheet
Cash	500,000	50,000					550,000
Receivables (net)	50,000	20,000		(2)	3,000		67,000
Inventories	100,000	60,000	(1)	16,000			176,000
Buildings and equipment (net)	150,000	20,000	(1)	8,000			178,000
Investment in S	112,000				(1)	112,000	
	912,000	150,000					971,000
Current liabilities	20,000	10,000	(2)	3,000			27,000
Long-term liabilities	140,000	20,000			(1)	8,000	168,000
Common stock	460,000	100,000	(1)	80,000			480,000*
Additional paid-in capital	52,000						52,000
Retained earnings	240,000	20,000	(1)	16,000			244,000**
	912,000	150,000		123,000		123,000	971,000

(i) From Exhibit 4.16
(1) To eliminate intercompany stockholding and adjust S's assets and liabilities to their fair values, from Exhibit 4.17
(2) To eliminate intercompany debt
*Includes $100,000 × 20% = $20,000 of S's common stock owned by outsiders (minority interest)
**Includes $20,000 × 20% = $4,000 of retained earnings attributable to minority interest

P makes this entry:

Investment in Corporation S	112,000	
Common stock		60,000
Additional paid-in capital		52,000

The December 31, 19A, balance sheets of P and S immediately after the combination are as shown in Exhibit 4.16. For its $112,000 investment, P acquired 80% of the fair values of S's assets and liabilities, which equals $112,000. There is no goodwill. Exhibit 4.17 presents calculations of the fair values. P's and S's December 31, 19A, balance sheets are consolidated as shown in Exhibit 4.18.

CHAPTER FIVE

Consolidated Financial Statements after the Date of Business Combination

The financial statements of member companies of a consolidated group after the date of a business combination include elements that represent relationships and the effects of transactions between member companies, which are adjusted or eliminated in consolidation. The items are:

Intercompany stockholdings

Intercompany receivables and payables

Intercompany sales, purchases, fees, rents, interest, and the like

Intercompany profits

Intercompany dividends

Eliminations and adjusting entries are recorded only in the consolidating worksheets, not in the books of any member company.

This chapter illustrates worksheet procedures to prepare consolidated balance sheets, income statements, and statements of changes in retained earnings one year and two years after the date of a business combination under the five different sets of circumstances illustrated in Chapter 4. The consolidated statement of changes in financial position is normally the last financial statement prepared and is ordinarily derived principally from the other consolidated financial statements, as illustrated at the end of this chapter.

In all the following illustrations, the investment in S is accounted for by the cost rather than the equity method, which is discussed in Chapter 6. If P presents the investment at equity in its financial statements, the investment in S is nevertheless kept at cost in the consolidating worksheet. The consolidating entries parallel the entries that would be made in P's investment account to keep it on the equity method.

POOLING OF INTERESTS METHOD: 100% TRANSFER OF STOCK

This section illustrates the procedures to develop consolidated financial statements for the year 19B and the year 19C, one year and two years after a business combination accounted for by the pooling of interests method involving a 100% transfer of stock, using the facts in the related illustration in Chapter 4.

The financial statements of Corporation P and Corporation S for the year 19B are as shown in Exhibit 5.1. During the year 19B, S sold merchandise to P for $25,000, including a profit of $5,000 on inventory on hand at December 31, 19A. S paid a cash dividend of $10,000. At the end of the year, P owed S $15,000.

As illustrated in Exhibit 5.2, the balances from the financial statements of P and S for the year 19B are transferred to the first two columns of a worksheet. The next two columns are for adjustments and eliminations. The last column is for the consolidated income statement, statement of changes in retained earnings, and balance sheet, which contain aggregates of amounts in P's and S's financial statements revised by the adjustments and eliminations.

The financial statements of P and S for the year 19C, two years after the business combination, are as shown in Exhibit 5.3. There were no intercompany sales or dividends in the year 19C. There is no intercompany debt at year-end. The inventory S sold to P at a $5,000 profit the previous year is still on hand at December 31, 19C. The financial statements for the year 19C are consolidated as shown in Exhibit 5.4.

POOLING OF INTERESTS METHOD: 90% TRANSFER OF STOCK

This section illustrates the procedures to develop consolidated financial statements for the year 19B and the year 19C, one year and two years after a business

EXHIBIT 5.1.   Corporation P and Corporation S, Financial Statements for the Year 19B (one year after combination accounted for by the pooling of interests method: 100% transfer of stock)

	P	S
Income Statement		
Sales	$250,000	$150,000
Cost of goods sold	(150,000)	(75,000)
Investment revenue	20,000	
Other expenses	(70,000)	(40,000)
Net income	$ 50,000	$ 35,000
Statement of Changes in Retained Earnings		
Retained earnings, beginning of year	$240,000	$ 20,000
Net income	50,000	35,000
Dividends	(40,000)	(10,000)
Retained earnings, end of year	$250,000	$ 45,000
Balance Sheet		
Cash	$460,000	$ 90,000
Accounts receivable (net)	60,000	35,000
Inventories	100,000	50,000
Buildings and equipment (net)	160,000	15,000
Investment in S	110,000	
	$890,000	$190,000
Current liabilities	$ 30,000	$ 15,000
Long-term liabilities	100,000	30,000
Common stock	510,000	100,000
Retained earnings	250,000	45,000
	$890,000	$190,000

combination accounted for by the pooling of interests method involving a 90% transfer of stock, using the facts in the related illustration in Chapter 4.

The financial statements of P and S for the year 19B, one year after the business combination, are shown in Exhibit 5.5. During the year 19B, P sold merchandise to S for $25,000, including a profit of $5,000 on inventory on hand at December 31, 19B. S paid a cash dividend of $10,000. At the end of the

EXHIBIT 5.2. Corporation P and Corporation S, Worksheet to Develop Consolidated Financial Statements for the Year 19B (one year after combination accounted for by the pooling of interests method: 100% transfer of stock)

	P(i)	S(i)	Adjustments and Eliminations Dr.	Adjustments and Eliminations Cr.	Consolidated Statements
Income Statement					
Sales	250,000	150,000	(2) 25,000		375,000
Cost of goods sold	(150,000)	(75,000)	(3) 5,000	(2) 25,000	(205,000)
Investment revenue	20,000		(4) 10,000		10,000
Other expenses	(70,000)	(40,000)			(110,000)
Net income	50,000	35,000	40,000	25,000	70,000
Statement of Changes in Retained Earnings					
Retained earnings, beginning of year	240,000	20,000			260,000
Merger with S			(1) 10,000		(10,000)
Net income	50,000	35,000	(A) 40,000	(A) 25,000	70,000
Dividends	(40,000)	(10,000)		(4) 10,000	(40,000)
Retained earnings, end of year	250,000	45,000	50,000	35,000	280,000
Balance Sheet					
Cash	460,000	90,000			550,000
Receivables (net)	60,000	35,000		(5) 15,000	80,000
Inventories	100,000	50,000		(3) 5,000	145,000
Buildings and equipment (net)	160,000	15,000			175,000
Investment in S	110,000			(1) 110,000	
	890,000	190,000			950,000
Current liabilities	30,000	15,000	(5) 15,000		30,000
Long-term liabilities	100,000	30,000			130,000
Common stock	510,000	100,000	(1) 100,000		510,000
Retained earnings	250,000	45,000	(B) 50,000	(B) 35,000	280,000
	890,000	190,000	165,000	165,000	950,000

(i) From Exhibit 5.1

(1) To eliminate intercompany stockholding, from Exhibit 4.3: investment of $110,000 in 100% of S's stock charged first against common stock—$100,000—and the excess—$10,000—charged against retained earnings

(2) To eliminate intercompany sales/purchases

(3) To eliminate intercompany profit from inventory

(4) To eliminate intercompany dividends

(5) To eliminate intercompany receivables/payables

(A) From income statements

(B) From statements of changes in retained earnings

EXHIBIT 5.3. Corporation P and Corporation S, Financial Statements for the Year 19C (two years after combination accounted for by the pooling of interests method: 100% transfer of stock)

	P	S
Income Statement		
Sales	$240,000	$140,000
Cost of goods sold	(140,000)	(65,000)
Investment revenue	10,000	
Other expenses	(70,000)	(30,000)
Net income	$ 40,000	$ 45,000
Statement of Changes in Retained Earnings		
Retained earnings, beginning of year	$250,000	$ 45,000
Net income	40,000	45,000
Dividends	(30,000)	
Retained earnings, end of year	$260,000	$ 90,000
Balance Sheet		
Cash	$460,000	$105,000
Accounts receivables (net)	70,000	45,000
Inventories	90,000	60,000
Buildings and equipment (net)	150,000	10,000
Investment in S	110,000	
	$880,000	$220,000
Current liabilities	$ 20,000	$ 10,000
Long-term liabilities	90,000	20,000
Common stock	510,000	100,000
Retained earnings	260,000	90,000
	$880,000	$220,000

year, P owes S $15,000. The financial statements for the year 19B are consolidated as shown in Exhibit 5.6.

The financial statements of P and S for the year 19C, two years after the business combination, are as shown in Exhibit 5.7. There were no intercompany sales or dividends. There is no intercompany debt at year-end. The inventory S sold to P at a $5,000 profit the previous year is still on hand at December 31,

EXHIBIT 5.4. Corporation P and Corporation S, Worksheet to Develop Consolidated Financial Statements for the Year 19C (two years after combination accounted for by the pooling of interests method: 100% transfer of stock)

	P(i)	S(i)	Adjustments and Eliminations Dr.	Cr.	Consolidated Statements
Income Statement					
Sales	240,000	140,000			380,000
Cost of goods sold	(140,000)	(65,000)			(205,000)
Investment revenue	10,000				10,000
Other expenses	(70,000)	(30,000)			(100,000)
Net income	40,000	45,000			85,000
Statement of Changes in Retained Earnings					
Retained earnings, beginning of year	250,000	45,000	(1) 10,000 (2) 5,000		280,000
Net income	40,000	45,000			85,000
Dividends	(30,000)				(30,000)
Retained earnings, end of year	260,000	90,000	15,000		335,000
Balance Sheet					
Cash	460,000	105,000			565,000
Receivables (net)	70,000	45,000			115,000
Inventories	90,000	60,000		(2) 5,000	145,000
Buildings and equipment (net)	150,000	10,000			160,000
Investment in S	110,000			(1) 110,000	
	880,000	220,000			985,000
Current liabilities	20,000	10,000			30,000
Long-term liabilities	90,000	20,000			110,000
Common stock	510,000	100,000	(1) 100,000		510,000
Retained earnings	260,000	90,000	(A) 15,000		335,000
	880,000	220,000	115,000	115,000	985,000

(i) From Exhibit 5.3
(1) To eliminate intercompany stockholding, from Exhibit 4.3
(2) To eliminate intercompany profit from inventory
(A) From statements of changes in retained earnings

EXHIBIT 5.5.   Corporation P and Corporation S, Financial Statements for the Year 19B (one year after combination accounted for by the pooling of interests method: 90% transfer of stock)

	P	S
Income Statement		
Sales	$250,000	$150,000
Cost of goods sold	(150,000)	(75,000)
Investment revenue	20,000	
Other expenses	(70,000)	(40,000)
Net income	$ 50,000	$ 35,000
Statement of Changes in Retained Earnings		
Retained earnings, beginning of year	$250,000	20,000
Net income	50,000	35,000
Dividends	(40,000)	(10,000)
Retained earnings, end of year	$250,000	$ 45,000
Balance Sheet		
Cash	$460,000	$ 90,000
Accounts receivable (net)	60,000	35,000
Inventories	100,000	50,000
Buildings and equipment (net)	160,000	15,000
Investment in S	100,000	
	$880,000	$190,000
Current liabilities	$ 30,000	$ 15,000
Long-term liabilities	100,000	30,000
Common stock	500,000	100,000
Retained earnings	250,000	45,000
	$880,000	$190,000

19C. The financial statements for the year 19C are consolidated as shown in Exhibit 5.8.

PURCHASE METHOD: 100% ACQUISITION OF STOCK

This section illustrates the procedures to prepare consolidated financial statements for the years 19B and 19C, one year and two years after a business combination

EXHIBIT 5.6. Corporation P and Corporation S, Worksheet to Develop Consolidated Financial Statements for the Year 19B (one year after combination accounted for by the pooling of interests method: 90% transfer of stock)

	P(i)	S(i)	Adjustments and Eliminations Dr.	Cr.	Consolidated Statements
Income Statement					
Sales	250,000	150,000 (2)	25,000		375,000
Cost of goods sold	(150,000)	(75,000) (3)	5,000 (2)	25,000	(205,000)
Investment revenue	20,000	(4)	9,000		11,000
Other expenses	(70,000)	(40,000)			(110,000)
Net income	50,000	35,000	39,000	25,000	71,000 *
Statement of Changes in Retained Earnings					
Retained earnings beginning of year	240,000	20,000 (1)	10,000		250,000
Net income	50,000	35,000 (A)	39,000 (A)	25,000	71,000
Dividends	(40,000)	(10,000)	(4)	9,000	(41,000)
Retained earnings, end of year	250,000	45,000	49,000	34,000	280,000 **
Balance Sheet					
Cash	460,000	90,000			550,000
Receivables (net)	60,000	35,000	(5)	15,000	80,000
Inventories	100,000	50,000	(3)	5,000	145,000
Buildings and equipment (net)	160,000	15,000			175,000
Investment in S	100,000		(1)	100,000	
	880,000	190,000			950,000
Current liabilities	30,000	15,000 (5)	15,000		30,000
Long-term liabilities	100,000	30,000			130,000
Common stock	500,000	100,000 (1)	90,000		510,000 ***
Retained earnings	250,000	45,000 (B)	49,000 (B)	34,000	280,000
	880,000	190,000	154,000	154,000	950,000

(i) From Exhibit 5.5
(1) To eliminate intercompany stockholding, from Exhibit 4.6
(2) To eliminate intercompany sales/purchases
(3) To eliminate intercompany profit from inventory
(4) To eliminate intercompany dividends
(5) To eliminate intercompany receivables/payables
(A) From the income statements
(B) From the statements of changes in retained earnings
* Includes $35,000 × 10% = $3,500 of net income attributable to minority interest
** Includes $45,000 × 10% = $4,500 of retained earnings attributable to minority interest
*** Includes $100,000 × 10% = $10,000 of S's common stock owned by outsiders (minority interest)

EXHIBIT 5.7.   Corporation P and Corporation S, Financial Statements for the Year 19C (two years after combination accounted for by the pooling of interests method: 90% transfer of stock)

	P	S
Income Statement		
Sales	$240,000	$140,000
Cost of goods sold	(140,000)	(65,000)
Investment revenue	10,000	
Other expenses	(70,000)	(30,000)
Net income	$ 40,000	$ 45,000
Statement of Changes in Retained Earnings		
Retained earnings, beginning of year	$250,000	$ 45,000
Net income	40,000	45,000
Dividends	(30,000)	
Retained earnings, end of year	$260,000	$ 90,000
Balance Sheet		
Cash	$460,000	$105,000
Receivables (net)	70,000	45,000
Inventories	90,000	60,000
Buildings and equipment (net)	150,000	10,000
Investment in S	100,000	
	$870,000	$220,000
Current liabilities	$ 20,000	$ 10,000
Long-term liabilities	90,000	20,000
Common stock	500,000	100,000
Retained earnings	260,000	90,000
	$870,000	$220,000

accounted for by the purchase method involving a 100% acquisition of stock, using the facts in the related illustration in Chapter 4.

The financial statements of P and S for the year 19B, one year after the business combination, are as shown in Exhibit 5.9. During the year 19B, S sold merchandise to P for $25,000, including a profit of $5,000 on inventory on hand at December 31, 19B. S paid a cash dividend of $10,000. At the end of the

EXHIBIT 5.8. Corporation P and Corporation S, Worksheet to Develop Consolidated Financial Statements for the Year 19C (two years after combination accounted for by the pooling of interests method: 90% transfer of stock)

	P(i)	S(i)	Adjustments and Eliminations Dr.	Cr.	Consolidated Statements
Income Statement					
Sales	240,000	140,000			380,000
Cost of goods sold	(140,000)	(65,000)			(205,000)
Investment revenue	10,000				10,000
Other expenses	(70,000)	(30,000)			(100,000)
Net income	40,000	45,000			85,000*
Statement of Changes in Retained Earnings					
Retained earnings, beginning of year	250,000	45,000	(1) 10,000 (2) 5,000		280,000
Net income	40,000	45,000			85,000
Dividends	(30,000)				(30,000)
Retained earnings, end of year	260,000	90,000	15,000		335,000**
Balance Sheet					
Cash	460,000	105,000			565,000
Receivables (net)	70,000	45,000			115,000
Inventories	90,000	60,000		(2) 5,000	145,000
Buildings and equipment (net)	150,000	10,000			160,000
Investment in S	100,000			(1) 100,000	
	870,000	220,000			985,000
Current liabilities	20,000	10,000			30,000
Long-term liabilities	90,000	20,000			110,000
Common stock	500,000	100,000	(1) 90,000		510,000***
Retained earnings	260,000	90,000	(A) 15,000		335,000
	870,000	220,000	105,000	105,000	985,000

(i) From Exhibit 5.7
(1) To eliminate intercompany stockholding, from Exhibit 4.6
(2) To eliminate prior year's intercompany profit from inventory
(A) From the statements of changes in retained earnings
*   Includes $45,000 × 10% = $4,500 of net income attributable to minority interest
**   Includes $90,000 × 10% = $9,000 of retained earnings attributable to minority interest
*** Includes $100,000 × 10% = $10,000 of S's common stock owned by outsiders (minority interest)

78

EXHIBIT 5.9. Corporation P and Corporation S, Financial Statements for the Year 19B (one year after combination accounted for by the purchase method: 100% acquisition of stock)

	P	S
Income Statement		
Sales	$250,000	$150,000
Cost of goods sold	(150,000)	(75,000)
Investment revenue	20,000	
Other expenses	(70,000)	(40,000)
Net income	$ 50,000	$ 35,000
Statement of Changes in Retained Earnings		
Retained earnings, beginning of year	$240,000	$ 20,000
Net income	50,000	35,000
Dividends	(40,000)	(10,000)
Retained earnings, end of year	$250,000	$ 45,000
Balance Sheet		
Cash	$290,000	$ 90,000
Accounts receivable (net)	60,000	35,000
Inventories	100,000	50,000
Buildings and equipment (net)	160,000	15,000
Investment in S	170,000	
	$780,000	$190,000
Current liabilities	$ 30,000	$ 15,000
Long-term liabilities	100,000	30,000
Common stock	400,000	100,000
Retained earnings	250,000	45,000
	$780,000	$190,000

year, P owed S $15,000. The financial statements for the year 19B are consolidated as shown in Exhibit 5.10.

The financial statements of P and S for the year 19C, two years after the business combination, are as shown in Exhibit 5.11. There were no intercompany sales or dividends. There is no intercompany debt at year-end. The financial statements for the year 19C are consolidated as shown in Exhibit 5.12.

EXHIBIT 5.10. **Corporation P and Corporation S, Worksheet to Develop**

	P(i)	S(i)	Adjustments and Eliminations Dr.		Cr.	Consolidated Statements
Income Statement						
Sales	250,000	150,000	(3)	25,000		375,000
Cost of goods sold	(150,000)	(75,000)	(2)	20,000 (3)	25,000	(225,000)
			(4)	5,000		
Investment revenue	20,000		(5)	10,000		10,000
Other expenses	(70,000)	(40,000)	(2)	1,000		(111,000)
Net income	50,000	35,000		61,000	25,000	49,000
Statement of Changes in Retained Earnings						
Retained earnings, beginning of year	240,000	20,000	(1)	20,000		240,000
Net income	50,000	35,000	(A)	61,000 (A)	25,000	49,000
Dividends	(40,000)	(10,000)		(5)	10,000	(40,000)
Retained earnings, end of year	250,000	45,000		81,000	35,000	249,000

(i) From Exhibit 5.9

(1) To eliminate intercompany stockholding, adjust S's assets and liabilities to their fair values at the date of the combination, and record the difference as goodwill, from Exhibit 4.10

(2) To amortize the excess of the fair values of S's assets and liabilities over their book values and goodwill, from the information derived in Chapter 4:

	Excess Fair Values and Goodwill (ii)	Remaining Life	Attributed to Current Year Cost of Goods Sold	Other Expenses
Inventories	20,000	None	20,000	
Buildings and equipment	10,000	10 years		1,000
Long-term debt	(6,000)	3 years		(2,000)
Goodwill	26,000	13 years		2,000
			20,000	1,000

Consolidated Financial Statements for the Year 19B (one year after combination accounted for by the purchase method: 100% acquisition of stock)

| | P(i) | S(i) | Adjustments and Eliminations | | | | Consolidated Statements |
			Dr.		Cr.		
Balance Sheet							
Cash	290,000	90,000					380,000
Accounts receivable (net)	60,000	35,000		(6)	15,000		80,000
Inventories	100,000	50,000	(1) 20,000	(4)	5,000		145,000
				(2)	20,000		
Buildings and equipment (net)	160,000	15,000	(1) 10,000	(2)	1,000		184,000
Investment in S	170,000			(1)	170,000		
Goodwill			(1) 26,000	(2)	2,000		24,000
	780,000	190,000					813,000
Current liabilities	30,000	15,000	(6) 15,000				30,000
Long-term liabilities	100,000	30,000	(2) 2,000	(1)	6,000		134,000
Common stock	400,000	100,000	(1) 100,000				400,000
Retained earnings	250,000	45,000	(B) 81,000	(B)	35,000		249,000
	780,000	190,000	254,000		254,000		813,000

(ii) From Exhibit 4.9

In each subsequent year, an entry is made to record the cumulative amounts of annual amortization previously recorded, but those subsequent entries affect consolidated retained earnings directly, not consolidated income.

(3) To eliminate intercompany sales/purchases
(4) To eliminate intercompany profit from inventory
(5) To eliminate intercompany dividends
(6) To eliminate intercompany receivables/payables
(A) From the income statements
(B) From the statements of changes in retained earnings

EXHIBIT 5.11.   Corporation P and Corporation S, Financial Statements for the Year 19C (two years after combination accounted for by the purchase method: 100% acquisition of stock)

	P	S
Income Statement		
Sales	$240,000	$140,000
Cost of goods sold	(140,000)	(65,000)
Investment revenue	10,000	
Other expenses	(70,000)	(30,000)
Net income	$ 40,000	$ 45,000
Statement of Changes in Retained Earnings		
Retained earnings, beginning		
of year	$250,000	$ 45,000
Net income	40,000	45,000
Dividends	(30,000)	
Retained earnings, end of year	$260,000	$ 90,000
Balance Sheet		
Cash	$290,000	$105,000
Accounts receivables (net)	70,000	45,000
Inventories	90,000	60,000
Buildings and equipment (net)	150,000	10,000
Investment in S	170,000	
	$770,000	$220,000
Current liabilities	$ 20,000	$ 10,000
Long-term liabilities	90,000	20,000
Common stock	400,000	100,000
Retained earnings	260,000	90,000
	$770,000	$220,000

PURCHASE METHOD: 90% ACQUISITION OF STOCK

This section illustrates the procedures to develop consolidated financial statements for the years 19B and 19C, one year and two years after a business combination accounted for by the purchase method involving a 90% acquisition of stock, using the facts in the related illustration in Chapter 4.

EXHIBIT 5.12. Corporation P and Corporation S, Worksheet to Develop Consolidated Financial Statements for the Year 19C (two years after combination accounted for by the purchase method: 100% acquisition of stock)

	P(i)	S(i)		Adjustments and Eliminations Dr.	Cr.	Consolidated Statements
Income Statement						
Sales	240,000	140,000				380,000
Cost of goods sold	(140,000)	(65,000)				(205,000)
Investment revenue	10,000					10,000
Other expenses	(70,000)	(30,000)	(2)	1,000		(101,000)
Net income	40,000	45,000		1,000		84,000
Statement of Changes in Retained Earnings						
Retained earnings, beginning of year	250,000	45,000	(1)	46,000		249,000
Net income	40,000	45,000	(A)	1,000		84,000
Dividends	(30,000)					(30,000)
Retained earnings, end of year	260,000	90,000		47,000		303,000

(i) From Exhibit 5.11
(1) To eliminate intercompany stockholding, adjust S's assets and liabilities to their fair values at the date of the combination, and record the difference as goodwill, from Exhibit 4.9, reduced by amounts amortized in prior years:

	Excess of Fair Values over Book Values		
	At Date of Combination(ii)	Charged in Prior Years(ii)	Balance at Beginning of Current Year
Inventories	20,000	20,000	-0-
Buildings and equipment (net)	10,000	1,000	9,000
Long-term debt	(6,000)	(2,000)	(4,000)
Goodwill	26,000	2,000	24,000
		21,000	29,000
Intercompany profit still in inventory		5,000	
Retained earnings acquired at date of combination		20,000	
Total charge to retained earnings		46,000	

(ii) From Exhibit 5.10, note (2)

(continued)

EXHIBIT 5.12.   (*Continued*)

	P(i)	S(i)		Adjustments and Eliminations Dr.		Cr.	Consolidated Statements
Balance Sheet							
Cash	290,000	105,000					395,000
Receivables (net)	70,000	45,000					115,000
Inventories	90,000	60,000			(1)	5,000	145,000
Buildings and equipment (net)	150,000	10,000	(1)	9,000	(2)	1,000	168,000
Investment in S	170,000				(1)	170,000	
Goodwill			(1)	24,000	(2)	2,000	22,000
	770,000	220,000					845,000
Current liabilities	20,000	10,000					30,000
Long-term liabilities	90,000	20,000	(2)	2,000	(1)	4,000	112,000
Common stock	400,000	100,000	(1)	100,000			400,000
Retained earnings	260,000	90,000	(B)	47,000			303,000
	770,000	220,000		182,000		182,000	845,000

(ii) From Exhibit 5.10, note (2)
(2) To amortize the excess of the fair values of S's assets and liabilities over their book values and goodwill:

	Excess Fair Values and Goodwill(iii)	Remaining Life#	Charge to Other Expenses
Buildings and equipment	10,000	10 years	1,000
Long-term debt	(6,000)	3 years	(2,000)
Goodwill	26,000	13 years	2,000
			1,000

At time of combination
(A) From income statements
(B) From statements of changes in retained earnings

The financial statements of P and S for the year 19B, one year after the business combination, are as shown in Exhibit 5.13. During the year 19B, S sold merchandise to P for $25,000, including a profit of $5,000 on inventory on hand at December 31, 19B. S paid a cash dividend of $10,000. At the end

EXHIBIT 5.13. Corporation P and Corporation S, Financial Statements for the Year 19B (one year after combination accounted for by the purchase method: 90% acquisition of stock)

	P	S
Income Statement		
Sales	$250,000	$150,000
Cost of goods sold	(150,000)	(75,000)
Investment revenue	20,000	
Other expenses	(70,000)	(40,000)
Net income	$ 50,000	$ 35,000
Statement of Changes in Retained Earnings		
Retained earnings, beginning of year	$240,000	$ 20,000
Net income	50,000	35,000
Dividends	(40,000)	(10,000)
Retained earnings, end of year	$250,000	$ 45,000
Balance Sheet		
Cash	$310,000	$ 90,000
Accounts receivable (net)	60,000	35,000
Inventories	100,000	50,000
Buildings and equipment (net)	160,000	15,000
Investment in S	150,000	
	$780,000	$190,000
Current liabilities	$ 30,000	$ 15,000
Long-term liabilities	100,000	30,000
Common stock	400,000	100,000
Retained earnings	250,000	45,000
	$780,000	$190,000

of the year, P owed S $15,000. The financial statements for the year 19B are consolidated as shown in Exhibit 5.14.

The financial statements of P and S for the year 19C, two years after the business combination, are as shown in Exhibit 5.15. There were no inter-company sales or dividends. There is no intercompany debt at year-end. The financial statements for the year 19C are consolidated as shown in Exhibit 5.16.

EXHIBIT 5.14. Corporation P and Corporation S, Worksheet to Develop method: 90% acquisition of stock)

	P(i)	S(i)		Adjustments and Eliminations Dr.		Cr.	Consolidated Statements
Income Statement							
Sales	250,000	150,000	(3)	25,000			375,000
Cost of goods sold	(150,000)	(75,000)	(2)	18,000	(3)	25,000	(223,000)
			(4)	5,000			
Investment revenue	20,000		(5)	9,000			11,000
Other expenses	(70,000)	(40,000)	(2)	669			(110,669)
Net income	50,000	35,000		57,669		25,000	52,331*
Statement of Changes in Retained Earnings							
Retained earnings, beginning of year	240,000	20,000	(1)	18,000			242,000
Net income	50,000	35,000	(A)	57,669	(A)	25,000	52,331
Dividends	(40,000)	(10,000)			(5)	9,000	(41,000)
Retained earnings, end of year	250,000	45,000		75,669		34,000	253,331**

(i) From Exhibit 5.13
(1) To eliminate intercompany stockholding, adjust S's assets and liabilities to their fair values, and record the difference as goodwill at the date of the combination, from amounts in Exhibit 4.13
(2) To amortize P's proportionate share of the excess of fair values of S's assets and liabilities over their book values and goodwill, from the information derived in Chapter 4:

	90% Excess Fair Values and Goodwill (ii)	Remaining Life	Attributed to Current Year Cost of Goods Sold	Other Expenses
Inventories	18,000	None	18,000	
Buildings and equipment	9,000	10 years		900
Long-term debt	(5,400)	3 years		(1,800)
Goodwill	20,400	13 years		1,569
			18,000	669

Consolidated Financial Statements for the Year 19B (one year after combination

	P(i)	S(i)	Adjustments and Eliminations Dr.		Adjustments and Eliminations Cr.		Consolidated Statements
Balance Sheet							
Cash	310,000	90,000					400,000
Receivables (net)	60,000	35,000			(6)	15,000	80,000
Inventories	100,000	50,000	(1)	18,000	(4)	5,000	145,000
					(2)	18,000	
Buildings and							
equipment (net)	160,000	15,000	(1)	9,000	(2)	900	183,100
Investment in S	150,000				(1)	150,000	
Goodwill	_____	_____	(1)	20,400	(2)	1,569	18,831
	780,000	190,000					826,931
Current liabilities	30,000	15,000	(6)	15,000			30,000
Long-term liabilities	100,000	30,000	(2)	1,800	(1)	5,400	133,600
Common stock	400,000	100,000	(1)	90,000			410,000***
Retained earnings	250,000	45,000	(B)	75,669	(B)	34,000	253,331
	780,000	190,000		229,869		229,869	826,931

(ii) From Exhibit 4.13

In each subsequent year, an entry is made to record the cumulative amounts of annual amortization previously recorded, but those subsequent entries affect consolidated retained earnings directly, not consolidated income.

(3) To eliminate intercompany sales/purchases
(4) To eliminate intercompany profit from inventory
(5) To eliminate intercompany dividends
(6) To eliminate intercompany receivables/payables
(A) From the income statements
(B) From the statements of changes in retained earnings
* Includes $35,000 × 10% = $3,500 of net income attributable minority interest
** Includes $45,000 × 10% = $4,500 of retained earnings attributable to minority interest
***Includes $100,000 × 10% = $10,000 of S's common stock owned by outsiders (minority interest)

EXHIBIT 5.15. Corporation P and Corporation S, Financial Statements for the Year 19C (two years after combination accounted for by the purchase method: 90% acquisition of stock)

	P	S
Income Statement		
Sales	$240,000	$140,000
Cost of goods sold	(140,000)	(65,000)
Investment revenue	10,000	
Other expenses	(70,000)	(30,000)
Net income	$ 40,000	$ 45,000
Statement of Changes in Retained Earnings		
Retained earnings, beginning of year	$250,000	$ 45,000
Net income	40,000	45,000
Dividends	(30,000)	
Retained earnings, end of year	$260,000	$ 90,000
Balance Sheet		
Cash	$310,000	$105,000
Accounts receivable (net)	70,000	45,000
Inventories	90,000	60,000
Buildings and equipment (net)	150,000	10,000
Investment in S	150,000	
	$770,000	$220,000
Current liabilities	$ 20,000	$ 10,000
Long-term liabilities	90,000	20,000
Common stock	400,000	100,000
Retained earnings	260,000	90,000
	$770,000	$220,000

PURCHASE METHOD: 80% ACQUISITION OF STOCK (FOR STOCK)

This section illustrates the procedures to develop consolidated financial statements for the year 19B and the year 19C, one year and two years after a business combination accounted for by the purchase method involving an 80% acquisition of stock (for stock), using the facts in the related illustration in Chapter 4.

EXHIBIT 5.16. Corporation P and Corporation S, Worksheet to Develop Consolidated Financial Statements for the Year 19C (two years after combination accounted for by the purchase method: 90% acquisition of stock)

	P(i)	S(i)	Adjustments and Eliminations Dr.	Cr.	Consolidated Statements
Income Statement					
Sales	240,000	140,000			380,000
Cost of goods sold	(140,000)	(65,000)			(205,000)
Investment revenue	10,000				10,000
Other expenses	(70,000)	(30,000) (2)	669		(100,669)
Net income	40,000	45,000	669		84,331 *
Statement of Changes in Retained Earnings					
Retained earnings, beginning of year	250,000	45,000 (1)	41,669		253,331
Net income	40,000	45,000 (A)	669		84,331
Dividends	(30,000)				(30,000)
Retained earnings, end of year	260,000	90,000	42,338		307,662 **

(i) From Exhibit 5.15

(1) To eliminate intercompany stockholding, adjust S's assets and liabilities to their fair values at the date of the combination, and record the difference as goodwill, from Exhibit 4.13, reduced by amounts amortized in prior years:

	Excess of Fair Values Over Book Values		
	At Date of Combination	Charged in Prior Years	Balance at Beginning of Current Year
Inventories	18,000	18,000	-0-
Buildings and equipment (net)	9,000	900	8,100
Long-term debt	(5,400)	(1,800)	(3,600)
Goodwill	20,400	1,569	18,831
		18,669	23,331
Intercompany profit still in inventory		5,000	
Retained earnings acquired at date of combination		18,000	
Total charge to retained earnings		41,669	

(*continued*)

89

EXHIBIT 5.16. (*Continued*)

	P(i)	S(i)	Adjustments and Eliminations Dr.		Cr.	Consolidated Statements
Balance Sheet						
Cash	310,000	105,000				415,000
Receivables (net)	70,000	45,000				115,000
Inventories	90,000	60,000		(1)	5,000	145,000
Buildings and equipment (net)	150,000	10,000	(1)	8,100 (2)	900	167,200
Investment in S	150,000			(1)	150,000	
Goodwill			(1)	18,831 (2)	1,569	17,262
	770,000	220,000				859,462
Current liabilities	20,000	10,000				30,000
Long-term liabilities	90,000	20,000	(2)	1,800 (1)	3,600	111,800
Common stock	400,000	100,000	(1)	90,000		410,000 ***
Retained earnings	260,000	90,000	(B)	42,338		307,662
	770,000	220,000		161,069	161,069	859,462

(2) To amortize the excess of the fair values of S's assets and liabilities over their book values and goodwill:

	Excess Fair Values and Goodwill	Remaining Life#	Charge to Other Expenses
Buildings and equipment	9,000	10 years	900
Long-term debt	(5,400)	3 years	(1,800)
Goodwill	20,400	13 years	1,569
			669

At time of combination
(A) From income statements
(B) From statements of changes in retained earnings
* Includes $45,000 × 10% = $4,500 of net income attributable minority interest
** Includes $90,000 × 10% = $9,000 of retained earnings attributable to minority interest
*** Includes $100,000 × 10% = $10,000 of S's common owned by outsiders (minority interest)

EXHIBIT 5.17.   Corporation P and Corporation S, Financial Statements for the Year 19B (one year after combination accounted for by the purchase method: 80% acquisition of stock)

	P	S
Income Statement		
Sales	$250,000	$150,000
Cost of goods sold	(150,000)	(75,000)
Investment revenue	20,000	
Other expenses	(70,000)	(40,000)
Net income	$ 50,000	$ 35,000
Statement of Changes in Retained Earnings		
Retained earnings, beginning of year	$240,000	$ 20,000
Net income	50,000	35,000
Dividends	(40,000)	(10,000)
Retained earnings, end of year	$250,000	$ 45,000
Balance Sheet		
Cash	$460,000	$ 90,000
Accounts receivable (net)	60,000	35,000
Inventories	100,000	50,000
Buildings and equipment (net)	160,000	15,000
Investment in S	112,000	
	$892,000	$190,000
Current liabilities	$ 30,000	$ 15,000
Long-term liabilities	100,000	30,000
Common stock	460,000	100,000
Additional paid-in capital	52,000	
Retained earnings	250,000	45,000
	$892,000	$190,000

The financial statements of Corporation P and Corporation S for the year 19B are as shown in Exhibit 5.17. During the year 19B, S sold merchandise to P for $25,000, including a profit of $5,000 on inventory on hand at December 31, 19B. S paid a cash dividend of $10,000. At the end of the year, P owed S $15,000. The financial statements of P and S for the year 19B are consolidated as shown in Exhibit 5.18.

EXHIBIT 5.18. **Corporation P and Corporation S, Worksheet to Develop accounted for by the purchase method: 80% acquisition of stock)**

	P(i)	S(i)		Adjustments and Eliminations Dr.		Cr.	Consolidated Statements
Income Statement							
Sales	250,000	150,000	(3)	25,000			375,000
Cost of goods sold	(150,000)	(75,000)	(2)	16,000	(3)	25,000	(221,000)
			(4)	5,000			
Investment revenue	20,000		(5)	8,000			12,000
Other expenses	(70,000)	(40,000)				1,867	(108,133)
Net income	50,000	35,000		54,000		26,867	57,867*
Statement of Changes in Retained Earnings							
Retained earnings, beginning of year	240,000	20,000	(1)	16,000			244,000
Net income	50,000	35,000	(A)	54,000	(A)	26,867	57,867
Dividends	(40,000)	(10,000)			(5)	8,000	(42,000)
Retained earnings, end of year	250,000	45,000		70,000		34,867	259,867**

(i) From Exhibit 5.17

(1) To eliminate intercompany stockholding, adjust S's assets and liabilities to their fair values, and record the difference as goodwill at the date of the combination, from Exhibit 4.18

(2) To amortize P's proportionate share of the excess of fair values of S's assets and liabilities over their book values, from the information derived in Chapter 4:

	80% Excess Fair Values and Goodwill (ii)	Remaining Life	Attributed to Current Year Cost of Goods Sold	Other Expenses
Inventories	16,000	None	16,000	
Buildings and equipment	8,000	10 years		800
Long-term debt	(8,000)	3 years		(2,667)
			16,000	(1,867)

92

Consolidated Financial Statements for the Year 19B (one year after combination

	P(i)	S(i)	Adjustments and Eliminations Dr.		Adjustments and Eliminations Cr.		Consolidated Statements

	P(i)	S(i)	Dr.		Cr.		Consolidated Statements
Balance Sheet							
Cash	460,000	90,000					550,000
Receivables (net)	60,000	35,000			(6)	15,000	80,000
Inventories	100,000	50,000	(1)	16,000	(4)	5,000	145,000
					(2)	16,000	
Buildings and equipment (net)	160,000	15,000	(1)	8,000	(2)	800	182,200
Investment in S	112,000				(1)	112,000	
	892,000	190,000					957,200
Current liabilities	30,000	15,000	(6)	15,000			30,000
Long-term liabilities	100,000	30,000	(2)	2,667	(1)	8,000	135,333
Common stock	460,000	100,000	(1)	80,000			480,000***
Additional paid-in capital	52,000						52,000
Retained earnings	250,000	45,000	(B)	70,000	(B)	34,867	259,867
	892,000	190,000		191,667		191,667	957,200

(ii) From Exhibit 4.17

In each subsequent year, an entry is made to record the cumulative amounts of annual amortization previously recorded, but those future entries affect consolidated retained earnings directly, not consolidated income.

(3) To eliminate intercompany sales/purchases
(4) To eliminate intercompany profit from inventory
(5) To eliminate intercompany dividends
(6) To eliminate intercompany receivables/payables
(A) From the income statements
(B) From the statements of changes in retained earnings
* Includes $35,000 × 20% = $7,000 of net income attributable minority interest
** Includes $45,000 × 20% = $9,000 of retained earnings attributable to minority interest
***Includes $100,000 × 20% = $20,000 of S's common stock owned by outsiders (minority interest)

EXHIBIT 5.19. Corporation P and Corporation S, Financial Statements for the Year 19C (Two years after combination accounted for by the purchase method: 80% acquisition of stock)

	P	S
Income Statement		
Sales	$240,000	$140,000
Cost of goods sold	(140,000)	(65,000)
Investment revenue	10,000	
Other expenses	(70,000)	(30,000)
Net income	$ 40,000	$ 45,000
Statement of Changes in Retained Earnings		
Retained earnings, beginning		
of year	$250,000	$ 45,000
Net income	40,000	45,000
Dividends	(30,000)	
Retained earnings, end of year	$260,000	$ 90,000
Balance Sheet		
Cash	$460,000	$105,000
Accounts receivable (net)	70,000	45,000
Inventories	90,000	60,000
Buildings and equipment (net)	150,000	10,000
Investment in S	112,000	
	$882,000	$220,000
Current liabilities	$ 20,000	$ 10,000
Long-term liabilities	90,000	20,000
Common stock	460,000	100,000
Additional paid-in capital	52,000	
Retained earnings	260,000	90,000
	$882,000	$220,000

The financial statements of P and S for the year 19C, two years after the business combination, are as shown in Exhibit 5.19. There were no intercompany sales or dividends. There is no intercompany debt at year-end. The inventory S sold to P at a $5,000 profit the previous year is still on hand at December 31, 19C. The financial statements of P and S for the year 19C are consolidated as shown in Exhibit 5.20.

EXHIBIT 5.20. Corporation P and Corporation S, Worksheet to Develop Consolidated Financial Statements for the Year 19C (Two years after combination accounted for by the purchase method: 80% acquisition of stock)

	P(i)	S(i)	Adjustments and Eliminations Dr.	Cr.	Consolidated Statements
Income Statement					
Sales	240,000	140,000			380,000
Cost of goods sold	(140,000)	(65,000)			(205,000)
Investment revenue	10,000				10,000
Other expenses	(70,000)	(30,000)	(2) 1,867		(98,133)
Net income	40,000	45,000		1,867	86,867 *
Statement of Changes in Retained Earnings					
Retained earnings, beginning of year	250,000	45,000	(1) 35,133		259,867
Net income	40,000	45,000		(A) 1,867	86,867
Dividends	(30,000)				(30,000)
Retained earnings, end of year	260,000	90,000	35,133	1,867	316,734 **

(i) From Exhibit 5.19

(1) To eliminate intercompany stockholding, adjust S's assets and liabilities to their fair values at the date of the combination, and record the difference as goodwill, from Exhibit 4.17, reduced by amounts amortized in prior years:

	Excess of Fair Values over Book Values		
	At Date of Combination(ii)	Charged in Prior Years	Balance at Beginning of Current Year
Inventories	16,000	16,000	-0-
Buildings and equipment (net)	8,000	800	7,200
Long-term debt	(8,000)	(2,667)	(5,333)
	16,000	14,133	1,867
Intercompany profit still in inventory		5,000	
Retained earnings acquired at date of combination		16,000	
Total charge to retained earnings		35,133	

(ii) From Exhibit 4.17

(2) To amortize the excess of the fair values of S's assets and liabilities over their book values and goodwill:

(*continued*)

EXHIBIT 5.20. (*Continued*)

	P(i)	S(i)	Adjustments and Eliminations Dr.		Cr.		Consolidated Statements
Balance Sheet							
Cash	460,000	105,000					565,000
Receivables (net)	70,000	45,000					115,000
Inventories	90,000	60,000			(1)	5,000	145,000
Buildings and equipment (net)	150,000	10,000	(1)	7,200	(2)	800	166,400
Investment in S	112,000				(1)	112,000	
	882,000	220,000					991,400
Current liabilities	20,000	10,000					30,000
Long-term liabilities	90,000	20,000	(2)	2,667	(1)	5,333	112,666
Common stock	460,000	100,000	(1)	80,000			480,000 ***
Additional paid-in capital	52,000						52,000
Retained earnings	260,000	90,000	(B)	35,133		1,867	316,734
	882,000	220,000		125,000		125,000	991,400

	Excess Fair Values	Remaining Life#	Charge to Other Expenses
Buildings and equipment	8,000	10 years	800
Long-term debt	(8,000)	3 years	(2,667)
			(1,867)

\# At time of combination
(A) From income statements
(B) From statements of changes in retained earnings
*   Includes $45,000 × 20% = $9,000 of net income attributable to minority interest
**   Includes $90,000 × 20% = $18,000 of retained earnings attributable to minority interest
*** Includes $100,000 × 20% = $20,000 of S's common owned by outsiders (minority interest)

STATEMENT OF CHANGES IN FINANCIAL POSITION

The following illustrates the preparation of consolidated statements of changes in financial position, defining funds as working capital, to accompany the consolidated balance sheets and income statements illustrated earlier in this chapter of Corporation P and its 90% owned subsidiary, Corporation S, for the year 19B, one year after the combination.

Additional information assumed for these statements follows:

$15,000 of equipment was acquired during the year for cash. No equipment was disposed of.

EXHIBIT 5.21.   Corporation P and Corporation S, Consolidated Statement of Changes in Financial Position for the Year 19B (one year after combination accounted for by the pooling of interests method: 90% transfer of stock)

Sources of Working Capital		
Net income before extraordinary items		$67,500
Add items not affecting working capital:		
Depreciation	$10,000	
Income attributable to minority interest	3,500	13,500
Working capital provided by operations		81,000
Uses of Working Capital		
Acquisition of equipment	$15,000	
Retirement of long-term debt	30,000	
Payment of cash dividends	41,000	86,000
Net working capital used		$(5,000)

Increases (decreases) in Elements of Working Capital	Year 19A	Year 19B	
Cash	$550,000	$550,000	$ -0-
Receivables (net)	67,000	80,000	13,000
Inventories	160,000	145,000	(15,000)
Current liabilities	(27,000)	(30,000)	(3,000)
	$750,000	$745,000	
Net decrease in working capital			$(5,000)

Depreciation for the year was $10,000.

Cash was used to retire $30,000 in long-term debt.

There were no extraordinary items.

Pooling of Interests Method

This section illustrates the preparation of the consolidated statement of changes in financial position for the year 19B to accompany the consolidated balance

EXHIBIT 5.22. Corporation P and Corporation S, Statement of Changes in Financial Position for the Year 19B (one year after combination accounted for by the purchase method: 90% acquisition of stock)

Sources of Working Capital		
Net income before extraordinary items		$48,831
Add (subtract) items not affecting working capital:		
Depreciation	$10,900	
Goodwill amortization	1,569	
Amortization of the excess of fair value over book value of long-term debt	(1,800)	
Income attributable to minority interest	3,500	14,169
Working capital provided by operations		63,000
Uses of Working Capital		
Acquisition of equipment	$15,000	
Retirement of long-term debt	30,000	
Payment of cash dividends	41,000	86,000
New working capital used		$(23,000)

Increases (decreases) of Elements of Working Capital

	Year 19A	Year 19B	
Cash	$400,000	$400,000	$ -0-
Receivables (net)	67,000	80,000	13,000
Inventories	178,000	145,000	(33,000)
Current liabilities	(27,000)	(30,000)	(3,000)
	$618,000	$595,000	
Net decrease in working capital			$(23,000)

sheet and income statement of Corporation P and its 90% owned subsidiary, Corporation S, which were combined by the pooling of interests method.

The statement of changes in financial position for the year 19B is shown in Exhibit 5.21. Consolidated net income before extraordinary items for the year 19B is the same as consolidated net income for the year 19B, $67,500, because there are no extraordinary items. The only adjustments to the $67,500 are to add back $10,000 depreciation expense and $3,500 income attributable to minority interest, because they did not affect working capital.

Purchase Method

This section illustrates the preparation of the consolidated statement of changes in financial position for the year 19B to accompany the consolidated balance sheet and income statement of Corporation P and its 90% owned subsidiary, Corporation S, which were combined by the purchase method.

The statement of changes in financial position for the year 19B is shown in Exhibit 5.22. Consolidated net income before extraordinary items for the year 19B is the same as consolidated net income for the year 19B, $48,831, because there are no extraordinary items. The adjustments are made to that amount to arrive at working capital from operations.

CHAPTER SIX

The Equity Method

The *equity method,* which is the focus of APB Opinion 18, is used to account for investments in unconsolidated subsidiaries, corporate joint ventures, and common stock that provide the investor with the ability to exercise significant influence over the operating and financial policies of the investee. Other long-term investments in common stock are accounted for by the method required by FASB Statement No. 12, "Accounting for Certain Marketable Securities," discussed at the end of this chapter.

Under the equity method, an investor initially records an investment at cost. It adjusts the carrying amount of the investment at the end of the period in which it is acquired and in succeeding periods by the investor's proportionate share of changes in the investee's assets and liabilities and for the effects of intercompany profits. The principles for determining the cost of an investment accounted for by the equity method are essentially the same as those for determining the cost of an investment leading to a business combination accounted for by the purchase method, discussed in Chapter 2.

DIFFERENCES BETWEEN CONSOLIDATION AND THE EQUITY METHOD

An investor's net income for a period and its equity at a point in time with its investment accounted for by the equity method are generally the same as they are with the investee consolidated. Application of two statements, FASB Statement No. 12, "Accounting for Certain Marketable Securities," and FASB Statement No. 34, "Capitalization of Interest Cost," cause differences, however.

FASB Statement No. 12

In applying FASB Statement No. 12, the portfolios of marketable equity securities held by investees accounted for by the equity method are kept separate from the portfolios of such securities held by the investor or other investees, for purposes of determining the consolidated lower of cost and market adjustment. In contrast, the portfolios of marketable equity securities held by investees that are consolidated are combined with the portfolios of such securities held by the parent company and other members of the consolidated group for purposes of determining the consolidated lower of cost and market adjustment.

FASB Statement No. 34

Under FASB Statement No. 34, the total amount of interest cost capitalized in a set of consolidated financial statements cannot exceed the total amount of interest cost incurred by all the members of the consolidated group after intercompany amounts are eliminated. With the investments accounted for by the equity method, however, the total amount of interest cost capitalized in the investor's financial statements cannot exceed the total amount of interest cost incurred solely by the investor. That is, interest costs incurred by an investee accounted for by the equity method are excluded in accounting for amounts in the investor's financial statements on which interest is capitalized. Interest cost incurred by the investee can be capitalized only on amounts in the investee's financial statements.

USING THE EQUITY METHOD

An investor generally uses the equity method to account for each of the following types of investments.

Unconsolidated Subsidiaries

If a subsidiary is not consolidated, its financial statement elements are not combined with corresponding elements of the parent company line by line, but are instead reported in the parent company's balance sheet and income statement on one line on each statement, the one called *investment in unconsolidated subsidiary* or the like and the other called *investment revenue* or the like.

Joint Ventures

An enterprise may be formed and operated by a number of other enterprises as a joint venture—a separate business or means to carry out a specific project for the benefit of its investors, also called *venturers*. The venturers pool their resources, knowledge, and talents and share risks for the purpose of ultimately sharing rewards. In many joint ventures, each venturer has more than just a passive interest or investment; each participates—either directly or indirectly—in managing the venture. Investments in joint ventures are generally accounted for by the equity method. Issues concerning that treatment are discussed in Appendix B.

Investments in Common Stock Involving Significant Influence

In the absence of evidence to the contrary, an investor with an investment of from 20% to 50% of the voting common stock of an investee is presumed to have the ability to exercise significant influence over the financial and operating policies of the investee and, because of that, uses the equity method to account for such an investment. Conversely, in the absence of evidence to the contrary, an investor with an investment of less than 20% of the common stock of an investee is presumed not to have the ability to exercise significant influence over the financial and operating policies of the investee and, therefore, does not use the equity method to account for such an investment but uses the method discussed at the end of this chapter.

The ability to exercise significant influence may be inferred from, for example:

Representation on the investee's board of directors

Participation in policy-making processes

Material intercompany transactions

Interchange of managerial personnel

Technological dependency

The inability to exercise significant influence may be inferred from, for example:

Opposition by the investee that challenges the investor's ability to exercise significant influence, such as litigation or complaints to government authorities

An agreement by the investor surrendering significant rights as a stockholder

Concentration of the majority ownership of the investee among a few stockholders, who operate the investee without regard to the views of the investor

Inability of the investor to obtain representation on the investee's board of directors after attempting to do so

Inability of the investor to obtain financial information necessary to apply the equity method after attempting to do so

No one item in either of those lists is the sole determining factor as to whether an investor has the ability to exercise significant influence over the investee. Instead, all items are considered collectively.

If an investor owns two investments of, say, 20% each in unrelated corporations, one investment might qualify for the equity method and the other not, because their circumstances differ. Judgment is always necessary in determining whether an investment gives an investor the ability to exercise significant influence over the investee.

APPLYING THE EQUITY METHOD

Application of the equity method is first discussed and then illustrated.

Under the equity method, the investor's initial investment, in essence, comprises three bundles:

Bundle A.   A proportionate share of the book values of the investee's assets and liabilities on the date of the purchase.

    plus

Bundle B.   A proportionate share of the differences between the book values and the fair values of the investee's assets and liabilities on the date of the initial investment (commonly referred to as *net unrealized appreciation* or *unrealized depreciation*). The principles for determining the fair values of the investee's assets and liabilities parallel the principles in applying the purchase method of accounting for business combinations, discussed in Chapter 2.

plus

Bundle C. Goodwill, which is the excess at the date of purchase of (1) the cost of the investment over (2) the investor's proportionate share of the fair values of the investee's assets and liabilities (the sum of *A* + *B*) at the date of the purchase. If (2) exceeds (1), this bundle is negative goodwill. The principles of accounting for goodwill and negative goodwill under the equity method parallel the principles to account for them in consolidation, discussed in Chapter 2.

The investor adjusts the carrying amount of the investment in succeeding periods by its proportionate share of changes in each bundle and for the effects of intercompany profits.

Bundle A

Changes in the investee's equity are caused by earnings or losses from operations, extraordinary items, prior period adjustments, the payment of cash or property dividends, and other transactions by the investor or the investee in stock of the investee.

The investor charges the investment account for its proportionate share of the investee's earnings from operations and credits investment revenue. If the investee reports a loss, the investor credits the investment account for its proportionate share of the investee's loss from operations and charges investment revenue. A negative balance in the investment revenue account for a reporting period is disclosed as a loss from investment. The investor adjusts its investment account for its proportionate share of the investee's prior period adjustments and extraordinary items and correspondingly charges or credits prior period adjustments and extraordinary items in its own financial statements.

An investor recognizes receipt of a cash dividend by crediting its investment account.

Bundle B

The portion of the investment that represents the investor's proportionate share of the differences between the fair values and the book values of each of the investee's assets and liabilities at the date of the investment (unrealized appreciation or depreciation) is amortized to investment revenue over the remaining estimated useful lives of the underlying assets and liabilities.

Bundle C

The portion of the investment that represents goodwill or negative goodwill is amortized to investment revenue over the period expected to be benefited or 40 years, whichever is shorter.

Intercompany Profit or Loss

Intercompany profit or loss on assets bought from or sold to an investee is eliminated in the period of sale by adjusting the investment and the investment revenue accounts. That entry is reversed in the period in which the asset is sold to unrelated parties. The amount of unrealized profit or loss to be eliminated depends on whether the underlying transactions are considered to be at arm's length. If the transactions are not considered to be at arm's length, all the intercompany profit or loss is eliminated. If, however, the underlying transactions are considered to be at arm's length, only the investor's proportional share of the unrealized profit or loss is eliminated.

Special Considerations

Applying the equity method sometimes involves the following special considerations.

Preferred Dividends

An investor computes its proportionate share of the investee's net income or loss after deducting cumulative preferred dividends, regardless of whether they are declared.

Investee's Capital Transactions

An investor accounts for transactions between the investee and its stockholders (for example, issuances and reacquisitions of its stock) that directly affect the investor's proportionate share of the investee's equity in the same way that such transactions of a consolidated subsidiary are accounted for, discussed in Chapter 7.

Time Lag

An investor's reporting period may differ from that of the investee or the financial statements of the investee may not be available in time for an investor to record in its financial statements the information necessary to apply the equity method currently. In either case, the investor applies the equity method using the investee's most recent available financial statements. The same lag in reporting is used each period for consistency.

Permanent Decline in Value

The recorded amount of an investment accounted for by the equity method is normally not reduced for declines in market value. But if the decline brings that market value below the carrying amount of the investment and is judged to be permanent, the investment is written down to its recoverable amount, usually market value, and a loss is charged to current income. The distinction between a decline that is permanent and one that is not is often not clear. However, evidence of a permanent decline might be demonstrated by, for example, the investor's inability to recover the carrying amount of the investment, the investee's inability to sustain an earnings capacity that would justify the carrying amount of the investment, or a history of losses or market values substantially below cost.

To illustrate: On January 1, 19D, Corporation P accounts for its investment in Corporation S by the equity method. The carrying amount is $24,000 and the market value of the investment is $13,000. If the decline is judged to be permanent, P discontinues applying the equity method and records this entry to reduce the investment to its recoverable amount, in this case market value:

Investment loss	11,000	
Investment in Corporation S		11,000

If the market subsequently recovers, $13,000, not $24,000, is the basis at which to resume applying the equity method.

Excessive Losses

A company that accounts for an investment by the equity method ordinarily discontinues applying that method when the carrying amount of the investment in and net advances to the investee is reduced to zero, unless the investor has guaranteed obligations or is otherwise committed to providing further financial support for the investee. An investor resumes applying the equity method after the investee returns to profitable operations and the investor's proportionate share of the investee's subsequent net income equals the proportionate share of net losses the investor did not recognize during the period application of the equity method was suspended.

Changed Conditions

If an investment no longer qualifies for the equity method because the investor no longer has the ability to exercise significant influence over the investee, the investor stops applying the equity method and starts applying the method described in FASB Statement No. 12 from that point on. The investor does not retroactively adjust the carrying amount of the investment to reflect what the carrying amount of the investment would have been had that method been applied since the the investment was acquired.

To illustrate: On January 1, 19D, Corporation P's investment in Corporation S ceases to give P the ability to exercise significant influence over S. On that date the investment in Corporation S is reported in P's financial statements at $28,000. That becomes the investment's cost for purposes of applying FASB Statement No. 12 from that point on.

If an investment accounted for by the method in FASB Statement No. 12, "Accounting for Certain Marketable Securities," subsequently qualifies for the equity method because the investor subsequently gains the ability to exercise significant influence over the investee, the investor stops applying the Statement No. 12 method and starts applying the equity method from that point on. In that case, in contrast, the investor does retroactively adjust the carrying amount of the investment to what it would have been had it been accounted for by the equity method starting with its first acquisition by the investor, in a manner consistent with the accounting for a step-by-step acquisition of a subsidiary, described in Chapter 7.

To illustrate: P acquired stock of S on January 1, 19C, for $24,000. The investment did not give P the ability to exercise significant influence over S. The investment is reported in P's balance sheet on December 31, 19C, at $24,000, in accordance with FASB Statement No. 12. Had the investment previously qualified for the equity method, the investment in S would have been reported in P's balance sheet at $32,000.

On January 1, 19D, P gains the ability to exercise significant influence over S without a change in its holding of S's stock. P therefore increases its investment account to $32,000, as follows:

Investment in Corporation S	8,000	
Retained earnings		8,000

It applies the equity method from then on the way it would have been applied had P first obtained the ability to exercise significant influence when it first acquired the investment.

COMPREHENSIVE ILLUSTRATION

This section illustrates application of the equity method.

First Year

On January 1, 19A, Corporation P buys 20% of Corporation S's voting stock for $70,000. The 20% investment gives P the ability to exercise significant influence, so the equity method applies. During the year 19A, S pays its stockholders quarterly cash dividends of $5,000, so P receives $1,000 each quarter. S reports income for the year 19A of $100,000. During the year 19A, S sold merchandise to P at a $5,000 profit; the merchandise is held at December 31, 19A.

STEP ONE: Record the investment:

Investment in Corporation S	70,000	
Cash		70,000

STEP TWO: Display the fair values and book values of S's assets and liabilities on the date of the acquisition and compute goodwill, as shown in Exhibit 6.1. The goodwill is amortized over its economic useful life or 40 years, whichever is shorter. P has determined its economic useful life is five years. The information developed in Step Two is used in Step Five below.

EXHIBIT 6.1.   Corporation P and Corporation S, Book Values, Fair Values, and Calculation of Goodwill, January 1, 19A (P's 20% investment in S)

	Fair Values	Book Values	Excess of Fair Values over Book Values	P's 20% Interest in the Excess
Cash	20,000	20,000	-0-	-0-
Receivables	30,000	30,000	-0-	-0-
Inventory	50,000	40,000	10,000	2,000
Buildings and equipment	100,000	90,000	10,000	2,000
Land	300,000	200,000	100,000	20,000
Liabilities	(200,000)	(200,000)	-0-	-0-
	300,000	180,000	120,000	24,000
	× 20%	× 20%	× 20%	
	60,000	36,000	24,000	
Amount of investment	70,000			
Goodwill	10,000			

STEP THREE: Each quarter P makes this entry to record dividends received:

Cash	1,000	
Investment in Corporation S		1,000

STEP FOUR: P records its 20% share of S's income for the year 19A as of December 31, 19A:

Investment in Corporation S	20,000	
Investment revenue		20,000

STEP FIVE: P records the effects of the information developed in Step Two and eliminates intercompany profits at December 31, 19A, as shown in Exhibit 6.2. P reduces investment revenue and investment in S by recording this entry:

Investment revenue	6,000	
Investment in Corporation S		6,000

A summary is presented in Exhibit 6.3.

EXHIBIT 6.2. Corporation P, Amounts to Be Charged to Year 19A Income under the Equity Method

	Investor's Share of Excess of Fair Values over Book Values		Amount to Be Charged to Year 19A Income
Inventory	2,000	Inventory, a current asset, is presumed to have been sold.	2,000
Buildings and equipment	2,000	Remaining service lives of assets at the date of initial investment was two years	1,000
Land	20,000	The $20,000 is eliminated when the land is sold. The land has not yet been sold.	-0-
Goodwill	10,000	Estimated useful life at the date of initial investment was five years.	2,000
Intercompany profit on sales: 20% × $5,000			1,000
			6,000

EXHIBIT 6.3. Corporation P, Summary of Entries to Be Made in Year 19A under the Equity Method

		Dr. (Cr.)		
		Investment in S	Investment Revenue	Cash
Step One:	To record investment	70,000		(70,000)
Step Two:	Information developed in Step Two is used in Step Five			
Step Three:	Records cash dividends	(4,000)		4,000
Step Four:	Records proportionate share of investee's income	20,000	(20,000)	
Step Five:	Amortizes excess fair values and goodwill and eliminates intercompany profit	(6,000)	6,000	
Changes in year 19A		80,000	(14,000)	(66,000)
Balance in investment account, December 31, 19A		80,000		
Net investment revenue for year 19A			(14,000)	

Second Year

During year 19B, S has a net loss of $100,000. It cuts its quarterly cash dividend to $500, so P receives $100 each quarter. S sells merchandise to P at a $10,000 profit; the merchandise is on hand at December 31, 19B.

STEP ONE: On January 1, 19B, the balance of the investment account is $80,000, the same as at December 31, 19A.

STEP TWO: The information determined in year 19A applies also to year 19B and is recorded in Step Five.

STEP THREE: Each quarter P makes this entry to record dividends received:

Cash	100	
Investment in Corporation S		100

STEP FOUR: P records its 20% share of S's loss of $100,000 for the year 19B:

Investment revenue	20,000	
Investment in Corporation S		20,000

STEP FIVE: P amortizes the excess fair values and goodwill from information developed in Step Two, year 19A, and the intercompany profit:

Buildings and equipment	1,000	
Goodwill	2,000	
Intercompany profit	2,000	(20% × $10,000)
	5,000	

P reduces investment revenue and investment in S by recording this entry:

Investment revenue	5,000	
Investment in Corporation S		5,000

A summary is presented in Exhibit 6.4.

EXHIBIT 6.4. Corporation P, Summary of Entries to Be Made in Year 19B under the Equity Method

		Dr.		(Cr.)
		Investment in S	Investment Revenue	Cash
Step One:	Balance	80,000		
Step Two:	Information developed in Step Two is used in Step Five			
Step Three:	Records cash dividends	(400)		400
Step Four:	Records proportionate share of investee's loss	(20,000)	20,000	
Step Five:	Amortizes excess fair values and goodwill and eliminates intercompany profits	(5,000)	5,000	
Changes in year 19B		(25,400)	25,000	400
Balance in investment account		54,600		
Net investment loss for year 19B			25,000 loss	

Third Year

During year 19C, S has a net loss of $200,000. No cash dividends are paid and there is no intercompany profit.

STEP ONE: The January 1, 19C, balance in the investment account, $54,600, is the same as at December 31, 19B.

STEP TWO: The information determined in year 19A applies also to year 19C and is recorded in Step Five. The excess of fair value over book value in Exhibit 6.1 of the land that is sold is written off in Step Five.

STEP THREE: No entry because no dividends were received.

STEP FOUR: P records its proportionate share of S's loss of $200,000 for the year 19C:

Investment revenue	40,000	
Investment in Corporation S		40,000

STEP FIVE: P writes off the excess of the fair value over book value of the land that was sold and amortizes goodwill:

Excess fair value of buildings and equipment	
(now fully depreciated)	-0-
Excess fair value of land	20,000
Goodwill	2,000
Intercompany profit	-0-
Total	22,000

The entry is:

Investment revenue	22,000	
Investment in Corporation S		22,000

A summary is presented in Exhibit 6.5.

If P has guaranteed the debt of S, the investment in S is presented among the liabilities as a $7,400 credit balance. But, if P has not guaranteed the debt of S, the investment is written up to zero and removed from the balance sheet with this entry:

Investment in Corporation S	7,400	
Investment revenue		7,400

P continues to report its investment in S at zero until S reports cumulative earnings great enough for P's proportionate share to exceed its proportionate share of S's cumulative losses, which P has not recorded because application of the equity method was suspended.

Fourth Year

S reports income of $30,000. P's share is $6,000, but the equity method is still not applied, because the $6,000 does not equal the unreported loss of $7,400.

EXHIBIT 6.5.   Corporation P, Summary of Entries to Be Made in Year 19C under the Equity Method

		Dr. (Cr.)		
		Investment in S	Investment Revenue	Cash
Step One:	Balance	54,600		
Step Two:	Information developed in Step Two is used in Step Five			
Step Three:	No entry			
Step Four:	Records proportionate share of investee's loss	(40,000)	40,000	
Step Five:	Amortizes excess fair values and goodwill	(22,000)	22,000	
Changes in year 19C		(62,000)	62,000	-0-
Balance in investment account		(7,400)		
Net investment loss for year 19C			62,000 loss	

Fifth Year

S reports income of $20,000. P's share, $4,000, plus its share of S's income last year, $6,000, now exceeds $7,400, so the equity method is resumed. P's investment in S is reported at $6,000 + $4,000 − $7,400 = $2,600.

DISCLOSURES CONCERNING THE EQUITY METHOD

The following information about investments accounted for by the equity method, as applicable, is disclosed on the face of the financial statements, in the notes to the financial statements, or in supporting schedules or statements:

The names of the investees and the percentages of ownership

Reasons investments of 20% or more of the voting stock of an investee are not accounted for by the equity method

Reasons investments of less than 20% of the voting stock of an investee are accounted for by the equity method

The amounts of net unrealized appreciation or depreciation and how the amounts are amortized

The amounts of goodwill and how they are amortized

The quoted market prices of the investments, if available

Summarized information about the assets, liabilities, and results of operations of investments in unconsolidated subsidiaries or in corporate joint ventures, if they are material individually or collectively in relation to the financial position or results of operations of the investor. The information can be either about each investment accounted for by the equity method or combined information of all investments accounted for by the equity method.

Descriptions of possible conversions, exercises of warrants or options, or other contingent issuances of stock of investees that may significantly affect the investor's shares of reported earnings

Appendix A presents examples of disclosures.

INVESTMENTS NOT QUALIFYING FOR CONSOLIDATION OR THE EQUITY METHOD

Long-term investments in equity securities not qualifying for consolidation or the equity method are ordinarily accounted for in accordance with FASB Statement No. 12, "Accounting for Certain Marketable Securities." Under that statement, an investor initially records an investment at cost but does not subsequently adjust the carrying amount, except for writedowns for permanent impairments in value. The investor charges cash and credits investment revenue when it receives cash dividends from the investee but in no other way reflects its proportionate shares of changes in the investee's equity.

Under Statement No. 12, the aggregate cost of long-term investments in equity securities is compared to their aggregate market value at each reporting date. If the aggregate market value is lower than aggregate cost, an allowance for market declines account is credited and deducted from the cost of the long-term portfolio in the financial statements and a charge is made directly to equity equal to the credit.

The balance in the allowance account is adjusted whenever financial statements are presented, so the net of the aggregate cost and the valuation allowance equals the lower of its aggregate cost and aggregate market value.

If a permanent decline in the value of an individual investment in long-term equity securities is deemed to have occurred, the carrying amount is written down to its recoverable amount, usually market value. Considerations in determining whether to recognize a permanent decline for an investment accounted for in accordance with FASB Statement No. 12 are essentially the same as those for an investment accounted for by the equity method.

CHAPTER SEVEN

Special Topics in Consolidation and the Equity Method

Chapters 2 to 6 discuss and illustrate concepts and procedures that pertain to most sets of consolidated financial statements and investments accounted for by the equity method. Other concepts and procedures in consolidation and the equity method encountered occasionally involve:

Step Acquisition.   Acquisition by an investor of the stock of an investee sufficient to give the investor control or the ability to exercise significant influence in two or more transactions

Stockholding Change.   Change in the percentage of stock of an investee or a subsidiary held by an investor other than to obtain control or the ability to exercise significant influence; a transaction of either the investor or the investee may cause the change

Complex Stockholding.   Holding of stock of a member of a consolidated group by another member of the group that is not the parent company of the group

Subsidiary Preferred Stock.   Treatment in consolidation of a subsidiary having its preferred stock outstanding

Intercompany Tax Allocation.   Allocation of income taxes incurred by a consolidated group to the members of the group

Push Down Accounting.   Presenting in the separate financial statements of a subsidiary the amounts at which its assets and liabilities are recognized in consolidation

STEP ACQUISITION

Two companies sometimes become affiliates or parent company and subsidiary in more than one transaction. The investor may:

First acquire stock less than required to have the ability to exercise significant influence and later acquire stock sufficient to have the ability to exercise significant influence

First acquire stock sufficient to have the ability to exercise significant influence and later acquire stock sufficient for control

First acquire stock less than required to have the ability to exercise significant influence and later acquire stock sufficient for control

The investor may buy the stock on the open market or directly from the investee. Also, the investor can obtain control or the ability to exercise significant influence by the investee's reacquiring some of its stock from entities other than the investor, separately or in combination with purchases of the investee's stock by the investor.

Step acquisitions are first discussed and then illustrated.

Step Acquisition of Control

ARB No. 51, "Consolidated Financial Statements," paragraph 10, requires the difference between (1) the cost to a parent company of stock of a subsidiary acquired in two or more blocks and (2) the book value of the subsidiary's equity related to the stock at the dates of acquisition to be determined and accounted for at each step in the acquisition program by the *step-by-step* basis:

When one company purchases two or more blocks of stock of another company at various dates and eventually obtains control of the other company, the date of acquisition (for the purpose of preparing consolidated statements) depends on the circumstances. If two or more purchases are made over a period of time, the earned surplus of the subsidiary at acquisition should generally be determined on a step-by-step basis.

However, ARB No. 51, paragraph 10, permits a shortcut method of accounting for a step acquisition if control is gained by a number of small purchases of a subsidiary's stock:

> If small purchases are made over a period of time and then a purchase is made which results in control, the date of the latest purchase, as a matter of convenience, may be considered as the date of acquisition.

During the interval between any two such transactions, the parent company's percentage of the subsidiary's stock remains unchanged. The objectives of the step-by-step basis are:

To include in the reported earnings of the consolidated group for such an interval, retroactively if necessary, the portion of the earnings of the subsidiary related to the percentage of the subsidiary's stock held by the parent company during that interval

To include in consolidated income for such an interval the consolidated group's portion of the income of the subsidiary during the interval

To include in consolidated retained earnings the consolidated group's portion of the post-acquisition earnings of the subsidiary

If control is obtained after the ability to exercise significant influence has been obtained, only the difference between the cost of the additional shares and the subsidiary's book value related to those shares needs to be determined. The differences in the earlier acquisitions will have been determined when the ability to exercise significant influence was obtained or while the ability to exercise significant influence was present, discussed below in the sections on step acquisitions of the ability to exercise significant influence and on stockholding changes.

If control is obtained after the parent company acquired an investment in the subsidiary less than that needed to obtain the ability to exercise significant influence, the differences at each date of acquisition of the subsidiary's stock are aggregated the way the differences are aggregated in step acquisitions of the ability to exercise significant influence, discussed next.

Step Acquisition of the Ability to Exercise Significant Influence

APB Opinion 18, "The Equity Method of Accounting for Investments in Common Stock," paragraph 19(m), requires the guidance in ARB No. 51 for step acquisitions of control to be applied to step acquisitions of the ability to exercise significant influence. It requires that when an investor obtains the ability to exercise significant influence in more than one transaction,

> . . . the investment, results of operations (current and prior periods presented), and retained earnings of the investor should be adjusted retroactively in a manner consistent with the accounting for a step-by-step acquisition of a subsidiary.

At the date of each transaction, the difference between the cost of the stock to the investor and the fair values of the investee's assets and liabilities is determined.

However, APB Opinion 18, paragraph 19(n), states that if

> . . . the investor is unable to relate the difference to specific accounts of the investee, the difference should be considered to be goodwill and amortized over a period not to exceed forty years. . . .

Illustrations of Step Acquisition

A step acquisition thus may be:

A step acquisition of the ability to exercise significant influence

A step acquisition of control with an intermediate acquisition of the ability to exercise significant influence

A step acquisition of control without an intermediate acquisition of the ability to exercise significant influence

Step Acquisition of Significant Influence

To illustrate a step acquisition of the ability to exercise significant influence: On January 1, 19A, Corporation P buys 15% of Corporation S's voting stock for $52,500. The investment does not give P the ability to exercise significant influence over S. It makes this entry:

| Investment in Corporation S | 52,500 | |
| Cash | | 52,500 |

During the year 19A, S pays a cash dividend of $20,000, so P receives $3,000 and records it with this entry:

| Cash | 3,000 | |
| Dividend income | | 3,000 |

On January 1, 19B, P buys 5% more of S's voting stock for $23,500 and makes this entry:

| Investment in Corporation S | 23,500 | |
| Cash | | 23,500 |

P now has the ability to exercise significant influence over the financial and operating policies of S and begins accounting for its investment in S by the equity method. P makes calculations for the year 19A to enable it to account retroactively for the investment by the equity method. Additional information is that S reported net income of $100,000 for the year 19A. During the year 19A, S sold merchandise to P at a $1,000 profit. The merchandise is still on hand at year-end.

First, the fair values and book values of S's assets and liabilities on January 1, 19A, are compared and goodwill is computed, as shown in Exhibit 7.1. Second, P's share in S's net income for the year 19A is calculated to be $100,000 × 15% = $15,000. Third, the effects in year 19A of P's proportionate share in the excess of the fair values over book values of S's assets and liabilities, goodwill, and intercompany profit are calculated to be a charge of $4,750, as shown in Exhibit 7.2. Fourth, the difference between P's investment account in S at December 31, 19A, and the amount it would have been had the investment been accounted for by the equity method is calculated. The balance in the account as accounted for is $52,500, the cost of acquisition. The amount it would have been is $59,750, calculated as shown in Exhibit 7.3.

To account for the investment starting on January 1, 19B, by the equity method, P restates its investment account retroactively by the difference of $7,250 between $52,500, the amount at which the investment is recorded, and $59,750, the amount it would be under the equity method:

EXHIBIT 7.1. Corporation P and Corporation S, Book Values, Fair Values, and Calculation of Goodwill, January 1, 19A (P's 15% investment in S)

	Fair Values	Book Values	Excess of Fair Values over Book Values	P's 15% Interest in the Excess
Cash	20,000	20,000	-0-	-0-
Receivables (net)	30,000	30,000	-0-	-0-
Inventory	50,000	40,000	10,000	1,500
Buildings and equipment (net)	100,000	90,000	10,000	1,500
Land	300,000	200,000	100,000	15,000
Liabilities	(200,000)	(200,000)	-0-	-0-
	300,000	180,000	120,000	18,000
	×15%	×15%	×15%	
	45,000	27,000	18,000	
Amount of investment	52,500			
Goodwill	7,500			

Equity:	Totals	15% Acquired
Common stock	100,000	15,000
Retained earnings	80,000	12,000
Totals, as above	180,000	27,000

EXHIBIT 7.2. Corporation P, Amount That Would Be Charged to Year 19A Income under the Equity Method

	P's Share of Excess of Fair Values over Book Values		Amount That Would Be Charged to Year 19A Income
Inventory	1,500	Inventory, a current asset, is presumed to have been sold.	1,500
Buildings and equipment	1,500	Remaining service lives of assets at the date of initial investment was two years.	750
Land	15,000	The $15,000 is eliminated when the land is sold. The land has not yet been sold.	-0-
Goodwill	7,500	Period over which estimated benefits were expected to be derived at the date of initial investment was five years.	1,500
Intercompany profit			1,000
			4,750

EXHIBIT 7.3.   Corporation P, Investment in Corporation S, Reconciliation between Cost and Equity Methods for the Year 19A

	Investment Account
Cost of acquisition, January 1, 19A	52,500
Deduct cash dividend	(3,000)
Add P's share of S's net income for the year 19A	15,000
Deduct charge for excess fair values, goodwill, and intercompany profit	(4,750)
	59,750

Investment in Corporation S	7,250	
Retained earnings		7,250

The investment account on January 1, 19B, after restatement is $52,500 + $23,500 + $7,250 = $83,250.

EXHIBIT 7.4.   Corporation P and Corporation S, Book Values, Fair Values, and Calculation of Goodwill, January 1, 19B (P's 5% investment in S)

	Fair Values	Book Values	Excess of Fair Values over Book Values	P's 5% Interest in the Excess
Cash	30,000	30,000	-0-	-0-
Receivables (net)	35,000	35,000	-0-	-0-
Inventory	60,000	45,000	15,000	750
Buildings and equipment (net)	115,000	100,000	15,000	750
Land	320,000	200,000	120,000	6,000
Liabilities	(150,000)	(150,000)	-0-	-0-
	410,000	260,000	150,000	7,500
	×5%	×5%	×5%	
	20,500	13,000	7,500	
Amount of investment	23,500			
Goodwill	3,000			

Equity:	Totals	5% Acquired
Common stock	100,000	5,000
Retained earnings	160,000	8,000
Totals, as above	260,000	13,000

To account for the investment account thereafter, P determines the share of the excess of the fair values of S's assets and liabilities at January 1, 19B, over their book values related to its acquisition of 5% of S's stock on that date and calculates goodwill to be $3,000, as shown in Exhibit 7.4.

During the year 19B, S has a net loss of $100,000, and cuts its dividend to $2,000. S sells $10,000 of merchandise to P at a $2,000 profit. The merchandise is still on hand at year-end.

The information developed above to account for the fair values and goodwill at January 1, 19A, is used to adjust P's investment account for the year 19B: amortization of excess fair value of buildings and equipment—$750; goodwill amortization—$1,500:

Investment revenue	2,250	
Investment in Corporation S		2,250

The information developed above to account for the fair values and goodwill at January 1, 19B, plus the amount of the intercompany profit is used to adjust

EXHIBIT 7.5.   Corporation P, Amount To Be Charged to Year 19B Income under the Equity Method

	P's Share of Excess of Fair Values over Book Values		Amount to Be Charged to Year 19B Income from Second Investment
Inventory	750	Inventory, a current asset, is presumed to have been sold.	750
Buildings and equipment	750	Remaining service lives of assets at the date of second investment was one year.	750
Land	6,000	The $6,000 is eliminated when the land is sold. The land has not yet been sold.	-0-
Goodwill	3,000	Period over which estimated benefits are expected to be derived at the date of initial investment was five years.	600
Intercompany profit			2,000
			4,100

further the investment account for the year 19B, as shown in Exhibit 7.5. P reduces investment revenue and investment in S by recording this entry:

Investment revenue	4,100	
Investment in Corporation S		4,100

P records receipt of the dividend from S:

Cash	400	
Investment in Corporation S		400

and records its portion of S's loss for the year:

Investment revenue	20,000	
Investment in Corporation S		20,000

A summary is shown in Exhibit 7.6.

EXHIBIT 7.6.   Corporation P, Summary of Entries to Be Made in Year 19B under the Equity Method

	Dr. (Cr.)			
	Investment in S	Investment Revenue	Cash	Retained Earnings
Balance, December 31, 19A	52,500			
Retroactive adjustment, January 1, 19B	7,250			(7,250)
Investment, January 1, 19B	23,500		(23,500)	
Share of S's loss for the year 19B	(20,000)	20,000		
Dividend received	(400)		400	
Amortization of excess fair values and goodwill:				
First investment	(2,250)	2,250		
Second investment	(4,100)	4,100		
Changes in year 19B	4,000	26,350	(23,100)	(7,250)
Balance in investment account	56,500			
Investment loss in year 19B		26,350 loss		

Thereafter, P uses the information calculated as of both investment dates to adjust the investment account each year.

Step Acquisition of Control with Intermediate Acquisition of Significant Influence

To illustrate a step acquisition of control with an intermediate acquisition of the ability to exercise significant influence, the above illustration of a step acquisition of the ability to exercise significant influence is used. On January 1, 19C, P buys 35% of S's voting stock for $125,000. Just before the investment, the balance sheets of P and S are as shown in Exhibit 7.7. P makes this entry to record the investment:

Investment in Corporation S	125,000	
Cash		125,000

P now has control over S and begins to consolidate S's financial statements with its own. The post-investment balance sheets of P and S are as shown in Exhibit 7.8. For its $125,000, P acquired 35% of the fair values of S's assets and liabilities for $116,550, plus $8,450 for goodwill, as shown in Exhibit 7.9. Exhibit 7.10 illustrates consolidation of the January 1, 19C, balance sheets of P and S immediately after the acquisition.

EXHIBIT 7.7. Corporation P and Corporation S, Balance Sheets, January 1, 19C (just before acquisition by P of 35% of S's stock)

	P	S
Cash	$443,500	$ 10,000
Accounts receivable (net)	50,000	15,000
Inventories	100,000	35,000
Buildings and equipment (net)	150,000	75,000
Land		200,000
Investment in S	56,500	
	$800,000	$335,000
Current liabilities	$ 20,000	$ 57,000
Long-term liabilities	140,000	120,000
Common stock	400,000	100,000
Retained earnings	240,000	58,000
	$800,000	$335,000

EXHIBIT 7.8. Corporation P and Corporation S, Balance Sheets, January 1, 19C (just after acquisition by P of 35% of S's stock)

	P	S
Cash	$318,500	$ 10,000
Accounts receivable (net)	50,000	15,000
Inventories	100,000	35,000
Buildings and equipment (net)	150,000	75,000
Land		200,000
Investment in S	181,500	
	$800,000	$335,000
Current liabilities	$ 20,000	$ 57,000
Long-term liabilities	140,000	120,000
Common stock	400,000	100,000
Retained earnings	240,000	58,000
	$800,000	$335,000

EXHIBIT 7.9. Corporation P and Corporation S, Book Values, Fair Values, and Calculation of Goodwill, January 1, 19C (P's 35% investment in S)

	Fair Values	Book Values (i)	Excess of Fair Values over Book Values	P's 35% Interest in the Excess
Cash	10,000	10,000	-0-	-0-
Receivables (net)	15,000	15,000	-0-	-0-
Inventory	45,000	35,000	10,000	3,500
Buildings and equipment (net)	90,000	75,000	15,000	5,250
Land	350,000	200,000	150,000	52,500
Liabilities	(177,000)	(177,000)	-0-	-0-
	333,000	158,000	175,000	61,250
	× 35%	× 35%	× 35%	
	116,550	55,300	61,250	
Amount of investment	125,000			
Goodwill	8,450			

	Total	35% Acquired
Equity:		
Common stock	100,000	35,000
Retained earnings	58,000	20,300
Totals, as above	158,000	55,300

(i) From Exhibit 7.8.

129

EXHIBIT 7.10. **Corporation P and Corporation S, Worksheet to Develop Consolidated Balance Sheet, January 1, 19C (at date of combination)**

	P(i)	S(i)	Eliminations Dr.		Eliminations Cr.		Consolidated Balance Sheet
Cash	318,500	10,000					328,500
Receivables (net)	50,000	15,000					65,000
Inventories	100,000	35,000	(1)	3,500	(A)		138,500
Buildings and equipment (net)	150,000	75,000	(1)	5,250	(B)		230,250
Land		200,000	(1)	73,500	(C)		273,500
Investment in S	181,500				(1)	181,500 (E)	
Goodwill			(1)	15,350	(D)		15,350
	800,000	335,000					1,051,100
Current liabilities	20,000	57,000					77,000
Long-term debt	140,000	120,000					260,000
Common stock	400,000	100,000	(1)	55,000	(E)		445,000*
Retained earnings	240,000	58,000	(1)	28,900	(E)		269,100**
	800,000	335,000		181,500		181,500	1,051,100

(i) From Exhibit 7.8

(1) To eliminate intercompany stockholding, adjust S's assets to fair values, and record goodwill

(A) Excess of fair value of inventory acquired January 1, 19C. Excesses in acquisitions in the years 19A and 19B were realized in those years.

(B) P's share of excess fair value of S's buildings and equipment, from Exhibits 7.1, 7.2, 7.4, 7.5, and 7.9 and entry in text at Exhibit 7.5:

	First Investment	Second Investment	Third Investment	Total
Amounts at dates of investment	1,500	750	5,250	7,500
Amortization				
Year 19A	(750)			(750)
Year 19B	(750)	(750)		(1,500)
Balances	-0-	-0-	5,250	5,250

(C) P's share of excess fair value of S's land, from Exhibits 7.1, 7.4, and 7.9:

First investment	15,000
Second investment	6,000
Third investment	52,500
	73,500

(D) Goodwill, from Exhibits 7.1, 7.2, 7.4, 7.5, and 7.9 and entry in text at Exhibit 7.5:

130

EXHIBIT 7.10. (*Continued*)

	First Investment	Second Investment	Third Investment	Total
Amounts at dates of investment	7,500	3,000	8,450	18,950
Amortization				
Year 19A	(1,500)			(1,500)
Year 19B	(1,500)	(600)		(2,100)
Balances	4,500	2,400	8,450	15,350

(E) Eliminations of investment in S, common stock, and retained earnings:

	Investment in S	Common Stock	Retained Earnings
From investments:			
First investment, from Exhibit 7.1	52,500	15,000	12,000
Second investment, from Exhibit 7.4	23,500	5,000	8,000
Third investment, from Exhibit 7.9	125,000	35,000	20,300
Amounts in excess of fair values realized:			
Inventories acquired in the years 19A and 19B, from Exhibits 7.1 and 7.4	(2,250)		
Buildings and equipment, from (B) above	(2,250)		
Goodwill, from (D) above	(3,600)		
Dividends, from Exhibits 7.3 and 7.6	(3,400)		(3,400)
Eliminations of intercompany profit, from Exhibits 7.2 and 7.5	(3,000)		(3,000)
S's profit, recorded by P, from Exhibits 7.3 and 7.6	(5,000)		(5,000)
	181,500	55,000	28,900

---

* Includes $100,000 × 45% = $45,000 of S's common stock owned by outsiders (minority interest)

** Includes $58,000 × 45% = $26,100 of retained earnings attributable to minority interest

During the year 19C, S had net income of $200,000 and paid cash dividends of $10,000. P records receipt of its share of the dividends:

Cash	5,500	
Investment revenue		5,500

EXHIBIT 7.11.   Corporation P and Corporation S, Financial Statements for the Year 19C

	P	S
Income Statement		
Sales	$250,000	$140,000
Cost of goods sold	(150,000)	(65,000)
Investment revenue	5,500	
Other expenses	(55,000)	(25,000)
Gain on sale of land		150,000
Net income	$ 50,500	$200,000
Statement of Changes in Retained Earnings		
Retained earnings, beginning		
of year	$240,000	$ 58,000
Net income	50,500	200,000
Dividends	(40,000)	(10,000)
Retained earnings, end of year	$250,500	$248,000
Balance Sheet		
Cash	$279,000	$263,000
Accounts receivable (net)	60,000	50,000
Inventories	100,000	45,000
Buildings and equipment (net)	160,000	110,000
Investment in S	181,500	
	$780,500	$468,000
Current liabilities	$ 30,000	$ 40,000
Long-term liabilities	100,000	80,000
Common stock	400,000	100,000
Retained earnings	250,500	248,000
	$780,500	$468,000

EXHIBIT 7.12. **Corporation P and Corporation S, Worksheet to Develop Consolidated Financial Statements for the Year 19C**

	P(i)	S(i)		Adjustments and Eliminations Dr.		Cr.	Consolidated Statements
Income Statement							
Sales	250,000	140,000					390,000
Cost of goods sold	(150,000)	(65,000)					(215,000)
Investment revenue	5,500		(2)	5,500			
Other expenses	(55,000)	(25,000)	(1)	2,625	(A)		(89,915)
			(1)	3,790	(B)		
			(1)	3,500	(C)		
Gain on sale of land		150,000	(1)	73,500	(D)		76,500
Net income	50,500	200,000		88,915			161,585*
Statement of Changes in Retained Earnings							
Retained earnings, beginning of year	240,000	58,000	(3)	28,900	(D)		269,100
Net income	50,500	200,000		88,915	(E)		161,585
Dividends	(40,000)	(10,000)			(2)	5,500	(44,500)
Retained earnings, end of year	250,500	248,000		117,815		5,500	386,185**

(i) From Exhibit 7.11

(1) To eliminate intercompany stockholding, adjust S's assets to fair values, and record amortization of excess fair values and goodwill

(A) P's share of excess fair values of S's buildings and equipment (two-year life at third investment), from Exhibit 7.10:

	First Investment	Second Investment	Third Investment	Total
Amounts at dates of investment	1,500	750	5,250	7,500
Amortization				
Year 19A	(750)			(750)
Year 19B	(750)	(750)		(1,500)
Year 19C	-0-	-0-	(2,625)	(2,625)
Balances	-0-	-0-	2,625	2,625

(*continued*)

133

EXHIBIT 7.12. (*Continued*)

	P(i)	S(i)	Adjustments and Eliminations Dr.	Cr.	Consolidated Statements
Balance Sheet					
Cash	279,000	263,000			542,000
Receivables (net)	60,000	50,000			110,000
Inventories	100,000	45,000			145,000
Buildings and equipment (net)	160,000	110,000	(1) 2,625 (A)		272,625
Investment in S	181,500			(1) 181,500	
Goodwill			(1) 11,560 (B)		11,560
	780,500	468,000			1,081,185
Current liabilities	30,000	40,000			70,000
Long-term liabilities	100,000	80,000			180,000
Common stock	400,000	100,000	(1) 55,000 (D)		445,000***
Retained earnings	250,500	248,000	117,815 (F)	5,500	(F)386,185
	780,500	468,000	187,000	187,000	1,081,185

(B) Goodwill, from Exhibit 7.10:

	First Investment	Second Investment	Third Investment	Total
Amounts at dates of investment (five-year life)	7,500	3,000	8,450	18,950
Amortization				
Year 19A	(1,500)			(1,500)
Year 19B	(1,500)	(600)		(2,100)
Year 19C	(1,500)	(600)	(1,690)	(3,790)
Balances	3,000	1,800	6,760	11,560

(C) Excess fair value of inventories January 1, 19C, which was all sold during the year 19C

(D) From Exhibit 7.10

(E) From income statements

(F) From statements of changes in retained earnings

(2) To eliminate intercompany dividends

* Includes $200,000 × 45% = $90,000 of net income attributable to minority interest

** Includes $248,000 × 45% = $111,600 of retained earnings attributable to minority interest

*** Includes $100,000 × 45% = $45,000 of S's common stock owned by outsiders (minority interest)

134

S sold its land for $350,000. At December 31, 19C, the financial statements of P and S are as shown in Exhibit 7.11. Exhibit 7.12 illustrates consolidation of the financial statements as at December 31, 19C.

Step Acquisition of Control without Intermediate Acquisition of Significant Influence

To illustrate a step acquisition of control without an intermediate acquisition of the ability to exercise significant influence: The initial acquisition by P of 15% of S's voting common stock in the year 19A in the illustration above is used. On January 1, 19B, P buys 40% more of S's voting common stock for $168,000. Just before the investment, the January 1, 19B, balance sheets of P and S are as shown in Exhibit 7.13.

P makes this entry to record the investment:

Investment in Corporation S	168,000	
Cash		168,000

P now controls S and begins to consolidate S's financial statements with its own. The post-investment balance sheets of P and S are as shown in Exhibit 7.14.

EXHIBIT 7.13. Corporation P and Corporation S, Balance Sheets, January 19B (just before additional 40% acquisition)

	P	S
Cash	$427,500	$ 30,000
Accounts receivable (net)	40,000	35,000
Inventories	90,000	45,000
Buildings and equipment (net)	140,000	100,000
Land		200,000
Investment in S	52,500	
	$750,000	$410,000
Current liabilities	$ 15,000	$ 30,000
Long-term liabilities	120,000	120,000
Common stock	400,000	100,000
Retained earnings	215,000	160,000
	$750,000	$410,000

EXHIBIT 7.14. Corporation P and Corporation S, Balance Sheets, January 1, 19B (just after additional 40% acquisition)

	P	S
Cash	$259,500	$ 30,000
Accounts receivable (net)	40,000	35,000
Inventories	90,000	45,000
Buildings and equipment (net)	140,000	100,000
Land		200,000
Investment in S	220,500	
	$750,000	$410,000
Current liabilities	$ 15,000	$ 30,000
Long-term liabilities	120,000	120,000
Common stock	400,000	100,000
Retained earnings	215,000	160,000
	$750,000	$410,000

For its $168,000, P acquired 40% of the fair values of S's assets and liabilities for $164,000, plus $4,000 for goodwill, as shown in Exhibit 7.15. Exhibit 7.16 illustrates consolidation of the January 1, 19B, balance sheets of P and S immediately after the acquisition.

As stated in the illustration above of a step acquisition of the ability to exercise significant influence, S has a net loss of $100,000 during the year 19B, pays a $2,000 dividend, and sells P merchandise for $10,000 at a profit of $2,000. The financial statements of P and S for the year 19B are as shown in Exhibit 7.17. Exhibit 7.18 illustrates consolidation of those financial statements for the year 19B.

STOCKHOLDING CHANGES

After the investor obtains control or the ability to exercise significant influence, the percentage of stock of an investee owned by an investor can change. That can occur in the following types of transactions:

Acquisitions of investee stock from outside entities
   1. Investor acquisitions of additional investee stock
   2. Investee reacquisitions of stock

EXHIBIT 7.15.   Corporation P and Corporation S, Book Values, Fair Values, and Calculation of Goodwill, January 1, 19B (P's 40% investment in S)

	Fair Values	Book Values(i)	Excess of Fair Values over Book Values	P's 40% Interest in the Excess
Cash	30,000	30,000	-0-	-0-
Receivables (net)	35,000	35,000	-0-	-0-
Inventories	60,000	45,000	15,000	6,000
Buildings and equipment (net)	115,000	100,000	15,000	6,000
Land	320,000	200,000	120,000	48,000
Liabilities	(150,000)	(150,000)	-0-	-0-
	410,000	260,000	150,000	60,000
	×40%	×40%	×40%	
	164,000	104,000	60,000	
Amount of investment	168,000			
Goodwill	4,000			

Equity:	Totals	40% Acquired
Common stock	100,000	40,000
Retained earnings	160,000	64,000
Totals, as above	260,000	104,000

(i) From Exhibit 7.14.

Dispositions of investee stock to outside entities
   3. Investor sales of investee stock
   4. Investee issuances of stock

Transactions between investor and investee
   5. Investor acquisitions of investee stock from investee
   6. Investee reacquisitions of stock from investor

Acquisitions of Investee Stock from Outside Entities

Acquisitions of investee stock from outside entities by the investor, the investee, or another member of a consolidated group of which the investee is a member are similar to purchases of assets. No gains or losses are recognized on such transactions.

EXHIBIT 7.16. Corporation P and Corporation S, Worksheet to Develop Consolidated Balance Sheet, January 1, 19B (just after additional 40% acquisition)

	P(i)	S(i)	Eliminations Dr.	Eliminations Cr.	Consolidated Balance Sheet
Cash	259,500	30,000			289,500
Receivables (net)	40,000	35,000			75,000
Inventories	90,000	45,000	(1) 6,000(A)	(2) 1,000	140,000
Building and					
equipment (net)	140,000	100,000	(1) 6,750(B)		246,750
Land		200,000	(1)63,000(C)		263,000
Investment in S	220,500			(1)220,500(E)	
Goodwill			(1)10,000(D)		10,000
	750,000	410,000			1,024,250
Current					
liabilities	15,000	30,000			45,000
Long-term debt	120,000	120,000			240,000
Common stock	400,000	100,000	(1)55,000(E)		445,000*
Retained earnings	215,000	160,000	(1)79,750(E)		294,250**
			(2) 1,000		
	750,000	410,000	221,500	221,500	1,024,250

(i) From Exhibit 7.14
(1) To eliminate intercompany stockholding, adjust asset amounts, and recognize goodwill, from Exhibits 7.1, 7.2, and 7.15:
(A) Excess fair value of inventory at the time of the second investment; excess at the first investment used up during the year 19A
(B) Buildings and equipment

	First Investment	Second Investment	Total
Amounts at dates of investment	1,500	6,000	7,500
Amortization, year 19A	(750)		(750)
Balances	750	6,000	6,750

(C) P's share of excess fair value of S's land

First investment		15,000
Second investment		48,000
		63,000

138

EXHIBIT 7.16. (*Continued*)

(D) Goodwill

	First Investment	Second Investment	Total
Amounts at dates of investment	7,500	4,000	11,500
Amortization, year 19A	(1,500)		(1,500)
Balances	6,000	4,000	10,000

(E) Elimination of investment in S, common stock, and retained earnings:

	Investment in S	Common Stock	Retained Earnings
First investment	52,500	15,000	12,000
Second investment	168,000	40,000	64,000
Realized amounts in excess of			
fair values			
Inventory			1,500
Buildings and equipment			750
Goodwill			1,500
	220,500	55,000	79,750

(2) To eliminate intercompany profit in inventory, from Exhibit 7.2

* Includes $100,000 × 45% = $45,000 of S's common stock owned by outsiders (minority interest)

** Includes $160,000 × 45% = $72,000 of retained earnings of S attributable to minority interest

EXHIBIT 7.17.   Corporation P and Corporation S, Financial Statements for the Year 19B (one year after additional 40% investment)

	P	S
Income Statement		
Sales	$ 240,000	$ 120,000
Cost of goods sold	(145,000)	(95,000)
Investment revenue	1,100	
Other expenses	(50,000)	(125,000)
Net income	$ 46,100	$(100,000)
Statement of Changes in Retained Earnings		
Retained earnings, beginning of year	$ 215,000	$ 160,000
Net income	46,100	(100,000)
Dividends	(30,000)	(2,000)
Retained earnings, end of year	$ 231,100	$ 58,000
Balance Sheet		
Cash	$ 270,600	$ 10,000
Accounts receivable (net)	50,000	15,000
Inventories	100,000	35,000
Buildings and equipment (net)	150,000	75,000
Land		200,000
Investment in S	220,500	
	$ 791,100	$ 335,000
Current liabilities	$ 20,000	$ 57,000
Long-term liabilities	140,000	120,000
Common stock	400,000	100,000
Retained earnings	231,100	58,000
	$ 791,100	$ 335,000

Investor Acquisitions of Additional Investee Stock from Outside Entities

Stockholding changes of type 1, investor acquisitions of additional investee stock from outsiders, are accounted for on the step-by-step basis, the same as in the step acquisition of control or the ability to exercise significant influence, illustrated earlier in this chapter. They are accounted for by the purchase method even if the investor and the investee became parent company and subsidiary in a business combination accounted for by the pooling of interests method.

Investee Reacquisitions of Stock from Outside Entities

Stockholding changes of type 2, reacquisitions of investee stock by the investee, are also accounted for by the purchase method. One effect on the consolidated financial statements in all such reacquisitions by a consolidated subsidiary is an increase in the parent company's stockholding percentage, affecting calculations of minority interest. In addition, if an investee reacquires its stock at other than its book value on the investee's books, the investee's equity is changed. A reacquisition by the investee of its stock at more than book value reduces its equity per share. The investor recognizes that change by reducing its investment and paid-in capital accounts to the extent available and reducing its retained earnings account for any excess. A reacquisition by the investee of its stock at less than book value increases its equity per share. The investor recognizes that change by increasing its investment and paid-in capital accounts.

Illustration Involving the Equity Method

To illustrate reacquisition and immediate retirement of stock from outside entities by an investee accounted for by the equity method by the investor, the above illustration of a step acquisition of the ability to exercise significant influence is used. On January 1, 19C, S reacquires 3% of its voting stock from outside entities. P still has the ability to exercise significant influence over S though P's ownership interest becomes less than 20%, so P continues to account for its investment in S by the equity method. In scenario A, S pays $8,620 and makes this entry:

Common stock	3,000	
Retained earnings	5,620	
Cash		8,620

In scenario B, S pays $1,830 and makes this entry:

Common stock	3,000	
Additional paid-in capital		1,170
Cash		1,830

| | | | Adjustments and Eliminations | | Consolidated |
	P(i)	S(i)	Dr. •	Cr.	Statements
Income Statement					
Sales	240,000	120,000	(2) 10,000		350,000
Cost of goods sold	(145,000)	(95,000)	(1)	1,000(A)	
			(2)	10,000	(235,000)
			(1) 6,000(A)		
Investment revenue	1,100		(3) 1,100		
Other expenses	(50,000)	(125,000)	(1) 6,750(B)		(184,050)
			(1) 2,300(C)		
Net loss	46,100	(100,000)	26,150	11,000	(69,050)*
Statement of Changes in Retained Earnings					
Retained earnings, beginning of year	215,000	160,000	(1) 80,750(D)		294,250
Net loss	46,100	(100,000)	26,150(E)	11,000(E)	(69,050)
Dividends	(30,000)	(2,000)	(3)	1,100	(30,900)
Retained earnings, end of year	231,100	58,000	106,900	12,100	194,300**

(i) From Exhibit 7.17
(1) To eliminate intercompany stockholding, adjust assets amounts, record goodwill, and record amortization of excess fair values and goodwill, from Exhibit 7.16.
(A) Inventories on hand at the dates of investment were sold by December 31, 19B
(B) P's share of excess fair values of S's buildings and equipment (one-year life at date of second investment)

	First Investment	Second Investment	Total
Amounts at dates of investment	1,500	6,000	7,500
Amortization			
Year 19A	(750)		(750)
Year 19B	(750)	(6,000)	(6,750)
Balances	-0-	-0-	-0-

Financial Statements for the Year 19B (one year after 40% additional acquisition)

	$\dot{P}$(i)	S(i)	Adjustments and Eliminations Dr.	Cr.	Consolidated Statements
Balance Sheet					
Cash	270,600	10,000			280,600
Receivables (net)	50,000	15,000			65,000
Inventories	100,000	35,000	(A)		135,000
Buildings and equipment (net)	150,000	75,000	(B)		225,000
Land		200,000	(1) 63,000(D)		263,000
Investment in S	220,500			(1) 220,500(D)	
Goodwill			(1) 7,700(C)		7,700
	791,100	335,000			976,300
Current liabilities	20,000	57,000			77,000
Long-term liabilities	140,000	120,000			260,000
Common stock	400,000	100,000	(1) 55,000(D)		445,000***
Retained earnings	231,100	58,000	106,900(F)	12,100(F)	194,300
	791,100	335,000	232,600	232,600	976,300

(C) Goodwill

	First Investment	Second Investment	Total
Amounts at dates of investment	7,500	4,000	11,500
Amortization			
Year 19A	(1,500)		(1,500)
Year 19B	(1,500)	(800)	(2,300)
	4,500	3,200	7,700

(D) From Exhibit 7.16
(E) From income statements
(F) From statements of changes in retained earnings
(2) To eliminate intercompany sales
(3) To eliminate intercompany dividends: $2,000 \times 55\% = \$1,100$
* Includes $100,000 \times 45\% = \$45,000$ of net loss attributable to minority interest
** Includes $58,000 \times 45\% = \$26,100$ of retained earnings attributable to minority interest
*** Includes $100,000 \times 45\% = \$45,000$ of S's common stock owned by outsiders (minority interest)

Exhibit 7.19 illustrates S's balance sheet at January 1, 19C, just before the reacquisition, after scenario A, and after scenario B. In scenario A, P adjusts its investment account as shown in Exhibit 7.20. P makes this entry:

Retained earnings	800	
Investment in Corporation S		800

In scenario B, P adjusts its investment account as shown in Exhibit 7.21. P makes this entry:

Investment in Corporation S	600	
Additional paid-in capital		600

EXHIBIT 7.19. **Corporation S, Comparison of Balance Sheets before and after Reacquisition, January 1, 19C**

		January 1, 19C	
		After Reacquisition	
		Scenario	
	Before Reacquisition(i)	A	B
Cash	10,000	1,380	8,170
Receivables (net)	15,000	15,000	15,000
Inventories	35,000	35,000	35,000
Buildings and equipment (net)	75,000	75,000	75,000
Land	200,000	200,000	200,000
	335,000	326,380	333,170
Current liabilities	57,000	57,000	57,000
Long-term debt	120,000	120,000	120,000
Common stock	100,000	97,000	97,000
Additional paid-in capital			1,170
Retained earnings	58,000	52,380	58,000
	335,000	326,380	333,170

(i) From Exhibit 7.7

EXHIBIT 7.20.   Corporation P, Adjustment of Investment Account at January 1, 19C, under Scenario A

	Investment in S
Balance January 1, 19C, before reacquisition	56,500
Adjustment for reacquisition	(800)*
Balance, January 1, 19C, after reacquisition	55,700

	S's Equity per Share
*Before reacquisition: ($100,000 + $58,000)/100,000 shares =	$1.58
After reacquisition: ($97,000 + $52,380)/97,000 shares =	$1.54
Decrease	($0.04)
Adjustment to P's investment account: 20,000 shares × ($0.04) a share =	($800)

Illustration Involving Consolidation

To illustrate reacquisition and immediate retirement of stock from outside entities by a consolidated subsidiary, the above illustration of a step acquisition of control with an intermediate acquisition of the ability to exercise significant influence is used. On January 1, 19D, S reacquires and cancels 3,000 of its shares. In scenario A, S pays $13,350 and makes this entry:

EXHIBIT 7.21.   Corporation P, Adjustment of Investment Account at January 1, 19C, under Scenario B

Balance, January 1, 19C, before reacquisition	56,500
Adjustment for reacquisition	600*
Balance, January 1, 19C, after reacquisition	57,100

	S's Equity per Share
*Before reacquisition: ($100,000 + $58,000)/100,000 shares =	$1.58
After reacquisition: ($97,000 + $1,170 + $58,000)/97,000 shares =	$1.61
Increase	$0.03
Adjustment to P's investment account: 20,000 shares × $0.03 a share =	$600

Common stock	3,000	
Retained earnings	10,350	
Cash		13,350

In scenario B, S pays $1,710 and makes this entry:

Common stock	3,000	
Additional paid-in capital		1,290
Cash		1,710

Exhibit 7.22 presents P's and S's balance sheets at January 1, 19D, just before the reacquisition, after scenario A, and after scenario B.

EXHIBIT 7.22. Corporation P and Corporation S, Balance Sheets, January 1, 19D (just before and just after reacquisition under Scenerios A and B)

		S		
			After Reacquisition	
			Scenario	
		Before		
	P	Reacquisition(i)	A	B
Cash	279,000	263,000	249,650	261,290
Receivables (net)	60,000	50,000	50,000	50,000
Inventories	100,000	45,000	45,000	45,000
Buildings and equipment (net)	160,000	110,000	110,000	110,000
Investment in S	181,500			
	780,500	468,000	454,650	466,290
Current liabilities	30,000	40,000	40,000	40,000
Long-term liabilities	100,000	80,000	80,000	80,000
Common stock	400,000	100,000	97,000	97,000
Additional paid-in capital				1,290
Retained earnings	250,500	248,000	237,650	248,000
	780,500	468,000	454,650	466,290

(i) From Exhibit 7.11

EXHIBIT 7.23.   Corporation P and Corporation S, Worksheet to Develop Consolidated Balance Sheet, January 1, 19D (just after reacquisition under scenario A)

	P(i)	S(i)	Eliminations Dr.	Eliminations Cr.	Consolidated Balance Sheet
Cash	279,000	249,650			528,650
Receivables (net)	60,000	50,000			110,000
Inventories	100,000	45,000			145,000
Buildings and equipment (net)	160,000	110,000	(1) 2,625		272,625
Investment in S	181,500			(1)181,500	
Goodwill			(1) 11,560		11,560
	780,500	454,650			1,067,835
Current liabilities	30,000	40,000			70,000
Long-term liabilities	100,000	80,000			180,000
Common stock	400,000	97,000	(1) 55,000		442,000*
Retained earnings	250,500	237,650	(1)117,815	(1) 5,500	375,835**
	780,500	454,650	187,000	187,000	1,067,835

(i) From Exhibit 7.22

(1) To eliminate intercompany stockholding, adjust asset amounts, and record goodwill, from Exhibit 7.12

*   Includes $97,000 × 42/97 = $42,000 of S's common stock owned by outsiders (minority interest)

** Includes $237,650 × 42/97 = $102,900 of retained earnings attributable to minority interest

Exhibit 7.23 illustrates consolidation of the January 1, 19D, balance sheets of P and S immediately after the reacquisition in scenario A. Exhibit 7.24 illustrates consolidation of the January 1, 19D, balance sheets of P and S immediately after the reacquisition in scenario B.

Dispositions of Investee Stock to Outside Entities

Dispositions of investee stock to outside entities by the investor, the investee, or another member of a consolidated group in which the investee is a member are similar to sales. In some such dispositions, gains and losses are recognized. Views and practices are divided.

EXHIBIT 7.24. Corporation P and Corporation S, Worksheet to Develop Consolidated Balance Sheet, January 1, 19D (just after reacquisition under scenario B)

	P(i)	S(i)	Eliminations Dr.	Eliminations Cr.	Consolidated Balance Sheet
Cash	279,000	261,290			540,290
Receivables (net)	60,000	50,000			110,000
Inventories	100,000	45,000			145,000
Buildings and equipment (net)	160,000	110,000	(1) 2,625		272,625
Investment in S	181,500			(1)181,500	
Goodwill			(1) 11,560		11,560
	780,500	466,290			1,079,475
Current liabilities	30,000	40,000			70,000
Long-term liabilities	100,000	80,000			180,000
Common stock	400,000	97,000	(1) 55,000		442,000*
Additional paid-in capital		1,290			1,290**
Retained earnings	250,500	248,000	(1)117,815	(1) 5,500	386,185***
	780,500	466,290	187,000	187,000	1,079,475

(i)   From Exhibit 7.22
(1)   To eliminate intercompany stockholding, adjust asset amounts, and record goodwill, from Exhibit 7.12
*   Includes $97,000 × 42/97 = $42,000 of S's common stock owned by outsiders (minority interest)
**   Includes $1,290 × 42/97 = $559 of additional paid-in capital attributable to minority interest
***   Includes $248,000 × 42/97 = $107,381 of retained earnings attributable to minority interest

Investor Sales of Investee Stock to Outside Entities

Stockholding changes of type 3, investor sales of investee stock to outside entities, can be helpfully considered in two categories: those in which the investment is in an investee accounted for by the equity method and those in which the investee is a consolidated subsidiary.

Sales of Stock Accounted for by the Equity Method

Sales of stock of an investee accounted for by the equity method have counterparts in sales of investments accounted for at cost or at the lower of cost and market.

Both types of investments are carried as assets of the investing entity; in neither is the investee part of the reporting entity. For sales of both types of investments, the proceeds are added to the investor's assets, the carrying amount of the portion of the investment sold is removed from the investor's investment account, and the difference is reported as a gain or loss on sale of an investment. APB Opinion 18, Paragraph 19(f), specifically requires that treatment for investments accounted for by the equity method.

Sales of Stock of a Consolidated Subsidiary

In contrast, sales of stock of a consolidated subsidiary by its parent company or another member of the consolidated group have no counterpart in other areas. The subsidiary is part of the reporting entity in consolidated financial statements, not an investment of the reporting entity. Dealings in its stock could be considered to be dealings between the reporting entity and minority stockholders who have an ownership, not an arm's length, relationship with the reporting entity. If so, the results would be reported solely in consolidated equity, not in consolidated income. That view has been advocated:

> Traditionally, in accounting, gains or losses cannot be recognized on the sale of a company's own corporate securities. . . . an alternative is to report the difference between the book value and the amount received as an adjustment to paid-in capital.[1]

However, the minority stockholders of a subsidiary are not stockholders of the parent company. From the perspective of the users of the consolidated financial statements, who are interested in the fortunes of the parent company, such sales could be considered to result in consolidated income or loss.

The latter view prevails at present. The requirement in APB Opinion 18 to recognize a gain or loss on sale of stock of an investee accounted for by the equity method is also applied to sales by parent companies of stock of consolidated subsidiaries.[2] In such a sale, the proceeds are added to consolidated assets, the consolidated equity pertaining to the stock sold is eliminated, and the difference is reported as a gain or loss in the consolidated income statement.

---

[1] Joe Ben Hoyle, *Advanced Accounting*. (Plano, Texas: Business Publications, Inc., 1984), p. 186.

[2] AICPA Issues Paper, "Accounting in Consolidation for Issuances of a Subsidiary's Stock," June 3, 1980, p. 2.

For a sale by a parent company of stock of a consolidated subsidiary accounted for by the purchase method, the proportionate share of the unamortized amount of positive or negative goodwill is also removed from the consolidated balance sheet.

If all the stock of a subsidiary is sold, the sale may have to be accounted for and presented as a disposal of a segment of a business, in accordance with APB Opinion 30, "Reporting the Results of Operations–Reporting the Effects of Disposal of a Segment of a Business, and Extraordinary, Unusual and Infrequently Occurring Events and Transactions."

Determining Amounts to Be Eliminated

For investor sales of stock of investees accounted for by the equity method or of stock of consolidated subsidiaries, the recorded amounts to be eliminated usually require adjustment to bring them up to date at the time of sale. For investments accounted for by the equity method in the investor's records, all that is required is to make normal equity adjustments for the part of the reporting period in which the stock that was sold was held.

If the investee's stock was acquired in more than one transaction, the amounts pertaining to the stock sold have to be distinguished from the amounts pertaining to the remaining stock held. With the investment accounted for in accordance with the step-by-step basis, those amounts are usually available in the records used to account for the investment or to prepare eliminations in consolidation. If the amounts are not available, they have to be reconstructed.

Management can select any of the stock certificates it pleases to transfer to the purchaser of the stock. Amounts pertaining to those certificates could be used, based on the accounting concept of specific identification. Many authors prefer that method, though they indicate the flow assumptions of FIFO or average are also used. That contrasts with accountants' aversion to using specific identification for inventories, because it could be helpful in manipulating reported income. Because reported income could also be manipulated using specific identification here, it is odd that its use here is not also frowned on.

Illustration of Sale by Investor of Stock of Investee Accounted for by the Equity Method

To illustrate a sale by an investor of stock of an investee accounted for by the equity method, the above illustration of a step acquisition of the ability to exercise significant influence is used. P owns 20,000 shares of S's common stock on January 1, 19C, carried at $56,500 in its investment account. On that date P sold 5,000 shares for $15,000. P retains the ability to exercise influence over S, so it keeps the investment on the equity method.

The average cost method of accounting for shares is used to determine the carrying amount of the shares sold: $56,500 × 5,000/20,000 = $14,125. P records the sale with this entry:

Cash	15,000	
Investment in Corporation S		14,125
Gain on sale of investment		875

After the sale is recorded, the balance in the investment account is $56,500 − $14,125 = $42,375.

Illustration of Sale by Parent Company of Stock of Consolidated Subsidiary

To illustrate a sale by a parent company of stock of a consolidated subsidiary, the above illustration of a step acquisition of control without an intermediate acquisition of the ability to exercise significant influence is used. On January 1, 19C, P sells 3,000 of its 55,000 shares of S's stock for $9,500. The average cost method is used in accounting for the sale: The cost of the shares sold is $220,500 × 3/55 = $12,027. Just before the sale, P's and S's January 1, 19C, balance sheets are as shown in Exhibit 7.25. P records the sale with this entry:

Cash	9,500	
Loss on sale of investment	2,527	
Investment in Corporation S		12,027

Immediately after the sale, P's and S's balance sheets are as shown in Exhibit 7.26. Exhibit 7.27 illustrates consolidation of the financial statements of P and S immediately after the sale.

Subsequent Accounting: Equity Method

If the ability to exercise significant influence is retained after the sale of stock of an investee accounted for by the equity method, the equity method is applied to the date of sale of the stock based on the percentage of stock held to that date and for the remainder of the reporting period at the remaining percentage. If the ability to exercise significant influence is lost, the investment is accounted for by the equity method for the portion of the reporting period to the date of the

EXHIBIT 7.25. Corporation P and Corporation S, Balance Sheets, January 1, 19C (just before sale of S's stock by P)

	P(i)	S(i)
Cash	$270,600	$ 10,000
Accounts receivable (net)	50,000	15,000
Inventories	100,000	35,000
Buildings and equipment (net)	150,000	75,000
Land		200,000
Investment in S	220,500	
	$791,100	$335,000
Current liabilities	$ 20,000	$ 57,000
Long-term liabilities	140,000	120,000
Common stock	400,000	100,000
Retained earnings	231,100	58,000
	$791,100	$335,000

(i) From Exhibit 7.18

EXHIBIT 7.26. Corporation P and Corporation S, Balance Sheets, January 1, 19C (just after sale of S's stock by P)

	P	S
Cash	$280,100	$ 10,000
Accounts receivable (net)	50,000	15,000
Inventories	100,000	35,000
Buildings and equipment (net)	150,000	75,000
Land		200,000
Investment in S	208,473	
	$788,573	$335,000
Current liabilities	$ 20,000	$ 57,000
Long-term liabilities	140,000	120,000
Common stock	400,000	100,000
Retained earnings	228,573*	58,000
	$788,573	$335,000

* Reduced by loss of $2,527 on sale of investment

152

sale and in accordance with FASB Statement No. 12, "Accounting for Certain Marketable Securities," thereafter.

Subsequent Accounting: Subsidiaries

If control is retained after the sale of stock of a consolidated subsidiary, minority interest in consolidated income is determined based on the percentages of its stock held by minority stockholders during periods of the year and on the subsidiary's income during those periods. Minority interest in the equity of the subsidiary is determined based on the percentage of its stock held by minority stockholders at the reporting date. Consolidated income includes the gain or loss on the disposal of the subsidiary's stock, the portion of the income of the subsidiary for the reporting period up to the date of sale pertaining to the stock sold, and the portion of the income of the subsidiary for the entire reporting period pertaining to the stock retained.

If control is lost but the ability to exercise significant influence is retained, the subsidiary is removed from the consolidated reporting entity and is accounted for by the equity method from that point on. The amount of income attributable to the investment for the reporting period is calculated the same way as the contribution to consolidated net income is calculated for a subsidiary whose stock was sold but whose control remained with the parent company, as stated in the preceding paragraph.

If control is lost and the ability to exercise significant influence is not retained, consolidated income includes the amount the subsidiary contributed in the reporting period based on the portion of its stock held by the consolidated group to the date of the sale. Thereafter, the investment is accounted for in conformity with FASB Statement No. 12, with the initial amount stated at the equity of the investor in the subsidiary at the date of sale related to the portion of its stock retained by the parent company. Dividends received from the former subsidiary after that in excess of the investor's share of income earned after that by the former subsidiary are recorded as reductions of the investor's investment, the same as any other investment.

Investee Issuances of Stock to Outside Entities

Stockholding changes of type (4), investee issuances of its stock to outside entities, cause the investor's percentage of the stock of the investee to decrease and the outside interest's percentage to increase. That is reflected in the consolidating adjusting entries at the next reporting date if the investee is a con-

EXHIBIT 7.27. Corporation P and Corporation S, Worksheet to Develop

	P(i)	S(i)	Adjustments and Eliminations Dr.	Cr.	Consolidated Statements
Income Statement					
Gain on sale of investment	(2,527)			(2) 5,171	2,644
Net income for the period	(2,527)			5,171	2,644
Statement of Changes in Retained Earnings					
Retained earnings, beginning of period	231,100	58,000	(1)106,900	(1) 12,100	194,300
Net income for period	(2,527)			5,171(A)	2,644
Retained earnings, end of period	228,573	58,000	106,900	17,271	196,944

(i) From Exhibit 7.26.
* Includes $100,000 × 48% = $48,000 of S's common stock owned by outsiders (minority interest)
** Includes $58,000 × 48% = $27,840 of retained earnings of S attributable to minority interest
(A) From income statements
(B) From statements of retained earnings
(1) Eliminations
(Because 3,000 of the 55,000 shares held December 31, 19B, were sold on January 1, 19C, (55,000–3,000)/55,000 = 52/55 of the amounts of the eliminations at December 31, 19B are eliminated January 1, 19C, after the sale.)

(ii) From Exhibit 7.18
(2) Excess of cost over equity value of investment sold (caused mainly by S's loss of $100,000 in the year 19B, when P owned 55% of S's stock), which turns the $2,527 loss recorded by P in its records with its investment in S carried at cost into a consolidated gain of $2,644.

Consolidated Financial Statements, January 1, 19C

	P(i)	S(i)	Adjustments and Eliminations Dr.	Cr.	Consolidated Statements
Balance Sheet					
Cash	280,100	10,000			290,100
Receivables (net)	50,000	15,000			65,000
Inventories	100,000	35,000			135,000
Buildings and equipment (net)	150,000	75,000			225,000
Land		200,000 (1)	59,564		259,564
Investment in S	208,473			(1)208,473	
Goodwill		(1)	7,280		7,280
	788,573	335,000			981,944
Current liabilities	20,000	57,000			77,000
Long-term liabilities	140,000	120,000			260,000
Common stock	400,000	100,000	(1) 52,000		448,000*
Retained earnings	228,573	58,000	106,900 (B)	17,271 (B)	196,944**
	788,573	335,000	225,744	225,744	981,944

	Eliminations December 31, 19B (ii) Dr.	Cr.	January 1, 19C (52/55 of December 31, 19B) Dr.	Cr.
Retained earnings	94,800		89,629	
Land	63,000		59,564	
Investment in S		220,500		208,473
Goodwill	7,700		7,280	
Common stock	55,000		52,000	
	220,500	220,500	208,473	208,473

solidated subsidiary. If the stock is issued at the book value per share of the existing stock on the investee's books, the investee records the issuance and no entry by the investor is required.

If the investee issues the stock for an amount different from its book value a share, the investor recognizes in its investment account an amount that reflects that difference. Accountants are divided on the other side of the entry: Some support recognition of the amount as a gain or loss; others support recognition of the amount in the parent company's paid-in capital account. For example, the Canadian Institute of Chartered Accountants, in its Handbook, section 1600.47, supports recognition of gain or loss for such transactions by consolidated subsidiaries:

> When a subsidiary company issues shares to interests outside the consolidated group, the effect of the change in the parent's interest as a result of the share issue should enter into determination of consolidated net income.

In contrast,

> Since 1965, the SEC has required that if such differences are increases, they should be recognized in consolidation as credits to paid-in capital rather than as gains.[3]

But,

> The SEC apparently has no guidelines, published or unpublished, for accounting in consolidation for issuances of a subsidiary's stock that cause a decrease in the parent company's equity in the subsidiary.[4]

The Accounting Standards Executive Committee of the American Institute of CPAs has stated an advisory conclusion that for consolidated subsidiaries, such changes should be recognized as gains or losses.[5] The issue is being considered by the FASB in its project on consolidations, discussed in Appendix B.

---

[3]AICPA Issues Paper, "Accounting in Consolidation for Issuances of a Subsidiary's Stock," June 3, 1980, p. 5.

[4]Ibid., p. 5.

[5]Ibid., p. 17.

Illustration of Issuance by Investee

To illustrate issuance of stock to outside entities by an investee in which the investor has the ability to exercise significant influence, the above illustration of a step acquisition of significant influence is used. On January 1, 19C, P owns 20% of S's stock (20,000 shares) carried at equity at $56,500. At that date, S has 100,000 shares outstanding and its stockholders' equity is $158,000, with a book value of $1.58 a share.

Under scenario A, S issues 20,000 shares of stock to outside entities for $31,600. Under scenario B, S issues 20,000 shares for $40,000. Under scenario C, S issues 20,000 shares for $22,000.

Under scenario A, S records the issuance by this entry:

Cash	31,600	
Common stock		31,600

Under scenario B, S records the issuance by this entry:

Cash	40,000	
Common stock		40,000

S's book value a share is changed from $1.58 to ($158,000 + $40,000)/(100,000 + 20,000) = $198,000/120,000 = $1.65, an increase of $.07 a share. P reflects that by increasing its investment account by $0.07 × 20,000 = $1,400.

If P recognizes a gain, it makes this entry:

Investment in Corporation S	1,400	
Investment revenue		1,400

If P does not recognize a gain, it makes this entry:

Investment in Corporation S	1,400	
Additional paid-in capital		1,400

Under scenario C, S records the issuance with this entry:

Cash	22,000	
Common stock		22,000

S's book value a share is changed from $1.58 to ($158,000 + $22,000)/ (100,000 + 20,000) = $180,000/120,000 = $1.50 a share, a decrease of $0.08 a share. P reflects that by decreasing its investment account by $0.08 × 20,000 = $1,600. If P recognizes a loss, it makes this entry:

Investment revenue	1,600	
Investment in Corporation S		1,600

If P does not recognize a loss, it makes this entry:

Additional paid-in capital	1,600	
Investment in Corporation S		1,600

Illustration of Issuance by Consolidated Subsidiary

To illustrate issuance of stock to outside entities by a consolidated subsidiary, the above illustration of a step acquisition of control without an intermediate acquisition of the ability to exercise significant influence is used. On December 31, 19B, P owns 55% (55,000 shares) of S's stock. Exhibit 7.28 is the worksheet consolidating the balance sheets at that date.

Under scenario A, S issues 8,000 shares of its own stock at $1.58 a share for $12,640 on January 1, 19C. Under scenario B, S issues 8,000 shares of its own stock at $2.00 a share for $16,000 on January 1, 19C. Under scenario C, S issues 8,000 shares of its own stock at $1.00 a share for $8,000 on January 1, 19C.

Under scenario A, S records the issuance by this entry:

Cash	12,640	
Common stock		12,640

Because the shares were issued at $1.58 a share, which was the book value a share of previously issued shares, no gain or loss is recognized. Exhibit 7.29 shows the January 1, 19C, consolidating balance sheet immediately after the issuance.

Under scenario B, S records the issuance by this entry:

EXHIBIT 7.28. Corporation P and Corporation S, Worksheet to Develop Consolidated Balance Sheet, December 31, 19B (one year after step acquisition of control without intermediate acquisition of the ability to exercise significant influence)

	P(i)	S(i)	Adjustments and Eliminations(A) Dr.	Cr.	Consolidated Statements
Cash	270,600	10,000			280,600
Receivables (net)	50,000	15,000			65,000
Inventories	100,000	35,000			135,000
Buildings and equipment (net)	150,000	75,000			225,000
Land		200,000	63,000		263,000
Investment in S	220,500			220,500	
Goodwill			7,700		7,700
	791,100	335,000			976,300
Current liabilities	20,000	57,000			77,000
Long-term liabilities	140,000	120,000			260,000
Common stock	400,000	100,000	55,000		445,000*
Retained earnings	231,100	58,000	106,900	12,100	194,300**
	791,100	335,000	232,600	232,600	976,300

(i) From Exhibit 7.17
(A) From Exhibit 7.18
*   Includes $100,000 × 45% = $45,000 of S's common stock owned by outsiders (minority interest)
** Includes $58,000 × 45% = $26,100 of retained earnings attributable to minority interest

Cash	16,000	
Common stock		16,000

If no consolidated gain is recognized, Exhibit 7.30 is the consolidating worksheet immediately after the issuance. If a consolidated gain is recognized, its amount is ($2.00 − $1.58) × 8,000 = $3,360. Exhibit 7.31 is the consolidating worksheet at January 1, 19C, immediately after the issuance.

EXHIBIT 7.29.   Corporation P and Corporation S, Worksheet to Develop Consolidated Balance Sheet, January 1, 19C (no gain or loss on issuance by S of its stock)

	P(i)	S(i)	Adjustments and Eliminations(A) Dr.	Cr.	Consolidated Statements
Cash	270,600	22,640			293,240
Receivables (net)	50,000	15,000			65,000
Inventories	100,000	35,000			135,000
Buildings and equipment (net)	150,000	75,000			225,000
Land		200,000	63,000		263,000
Investment in S	220,500			220,500	
Goodwill			7,700		7,700
	791,100	347,640			988,940
Current liabilities	20,000	57,000			77,000
Long-term liabilities	140,000	120,000			260,000
Common stock	400,000	112,640	55,000		457,640*
Retained earnings	231,100	58,000	106,900	12,100	194,300**
	791,100	347,640	232,600	232,600	988,940

(i)   From Exhibit 7.17 and entry in text.
(A) From Exhibit 7.28
*   Includes $112,640 × 53/108 = $55,277 of S's common stock owned by outsiders (minority interest)
**   Includes $58,000 × 53/108 = $28,463 of retained earnings attributable to minority interest

Under scenario C, S records the issuance by this entry:

Cash	8,000	
Common stock		8,000

If no consolidated loss is recognized, Exhibit 7.32 is the consolidating worksheet immediately after the issuance. If a consolidated loss is recognized, its

EXHIBIT 7.30. Corporation P and Corporation S, Worksheet to Develop Consolidated Balance Sheet, January 1, 19C (issuance above book value— no gain recognized)

| | P(i) | S(i) | Adjustments and Eliminations(A) | | Consolidated Statements |
			Dr.	Cr.	
Cash	270,600	26,000			296,600
Receivables (net)	50,000	15,000			65,000
Inventories	100,000	35,000			135,000
Buildings and equipment (net)	150,000	75,000			225,000
Land		200,000	63,000		263,000
Investment in S	220,500			220,500	
Goodwill			7,700		7,700
	791,100	351,000			992,300
Current liabilities	20,000	57,000			77,000
Long-term liabilities	140,000	120,000			260,000
Common stock	400,000	116,000	55,000		461,000*
Retained earnings	231,100	58,000	106,900	12,100	194,300**
	791,100	351,000	232,600	232,600	992,300

(i) From Exhibit 7.17 and entry in text
(A) From Exhibit 7.28
* Includes $116,000 \times 53/108 = $56,926 of S's common stock owned by outsiders (minority interest)
** Includes $58,000 \times 53/108 = $28,463 of retained earnings attributable to minority interest

amount is ($1.00 − $1.58) × 8,000 = $4,640. Exhibit 7.33 is the consolidating worksheet at January 1, 19C, immediately after the issuance.

Transactions between Investor and Investee

Transactions between an investor and an investee in stock of the investee are not at arm's length, so no gains or losses are recognized on them.

EXHIBIT 7.31. **Corporation P and Corporation S, Worksheet to Develop Consolidated Financial Statements, January 1, 19C (issuance above book value— gain recognized)**

	P(i)	S(i)	Adjustments and Eliminations(A) Dr.	Adjustments and Eliminations(A) Cr.	Consolidated Statements
Income Statement					
Gain on issuance of S's stock				3,360	3,360
Net income				3,360	3,360
Statement of Changes in Retained Earnings					
Retained earnings, beginning of period	231,100	58,000	106,900	12,100	194,300
Net income for period				3,360(B)	3,360
Issuance of S's stock			3,360		(3,360)
Retained earnings, end of period	231,100	58,000	110,260	15,460	194,300*
Balance Sheet					
Cash	270,600	26,000			296,600
Receivables (net)	50,000	15,000			65,000
Inventories	100,000	35,000			135,000
Buildings and equipment (net)	150,000	75,000			225,000
Land		200,000	63,000		263,000
Investment in S	220,500		3,360	223,860	
Goodwill			7,700		7,700
	791,100	351,000			992,300
Current liabilities	20,000	57,000			77,000
Long-term liabilities	140,000	120,000			260,000
Common stock	400,000	116,000	55,000		461,000**
Retained earnings	231,100	58,000	110,260(C)	15,460(C)	194,300
	791,100	351,000	239,320	239,320	992,300

(i) From Exhibit 7.17 and entry in text
(A) From Exhibit 7.28 and amount in text
(B) From income statements
(C) From statements of changes in returned earnings
*   Includes $58,000 × 53/108 = $28,463 of S's retained earnings attributable to minority interest
**   Includes $116,000 × 53/108 = $56,926 of S's common stock owned by outsiders (minority interest)

EXHIBIT 7.32.   Corporation P and Corporation S, Worksheet to Develop Consolidated Balance Sheet, January 1, 19C (issuance below book value—no loss recognized)

	P(i)	S(i)	Adjustments and Eliminations(A) Dr.	Cr.	Consolidated Statements
Cash	270,600	18,000			288,600
Receivables (net)	50,000	15,000			65,000
Inventories	100,000	35,000			135,000
Buildings and					
equipment (net)	150,000	75,000			225,000
Land		200,000	63,000		263,000
Investment in S	220,500			220,500	
Goodwill			7,700		7,700
	791,100	343,000			984,300
Current liabilities	20,000	57,000			77,000
Long-term					
liabilities	140,000	120,000			260,000
Common stock	400,000	108,000	55,000		453,000*
Retained					
earnings	231,100	58,000	106,900	12,100	194,300**
	791,100	343,000	232,600	232,600	984,300

(i)   From Exhibit 7.17 and entry in text
(A) From Exhibit 7.28
*   Includes $108,000 × (45,000 + 8,000)/(100,000 + 8,000) = $108,000 × 53/108 = $53,000
       of S's common stock owned by outsiders (minority interest)
**   Includes $58,000 × 53/108 = $28,463 of retained earnings attributable to minority interest

Investor Acquisitions of Investee Stock from the Investee

Stockholding changes of type 5, investor acquisitions of investee stock from the investee, cause the investor's percentage of the stock of the investee to increase and the outside interests' percentages to decrease. In consolidation, that is reflected in the consolidating adjusting entries at the next reporting date.

EXHIBIT 7.33. Corporation P and Corporation S, Worksheet to Develop Consolidated Financial Statements, January 1, 19C (issuance below book value— loss recognized)

	P(i)	S(i)	Adjustments and Eliminations(A) Dr.	Cr.	Consolidated Statements
Income Statement					
Loss on issuance of S's stock			4,640		(4,640)
Net loss			4,640		(4,640)
Statement of Changes in Retained Earnings					
Retained earnings, beginning of period	231,100	58,000	106,900	12,100	194,300
Net loss for period			4,640(B)		(4,640)
Issuance of S's stock				4,640	4,640
Retained earnings, end of year	231,100	58,000	111,540	16,740	194,300**
Balance Sheet					
Cash	270,600	18,000			288,600
Receivables (net)	50,000	15,000			65,000
Inventories	100,000	35,000			135,000
Buildings and equipment (net)	150,000	75,000			225,000
Land		200,000	63,000		263,000
Investment in S	220,500			215,860	
				4,640	
Goodwill			7,700		7,700
	791,100	343,000			984,300
Current liabilities	20,000	57,000			77,000
Long-term liabilities	140,000	120,000			260,000
Common stock	400,000	108,000	55,000		453,000**
Retained earnings	231,100	58,000	111,540(C)	16,740(C)	194,300
	791,100	343,000	237,240	237,240	984,300

(i) From Exhibit 7.17 and entry in text
(A) From Exhibit 7.28 and amount in text
(B) From income statements
(C) From statements of changes in returned earnings
*   Includes $58,000 × 53/108 = $28,463 of S's retained earnings attributable to minority interest
** Includes $108,000 × 53/108 = $53,000 of S's common stock owned by outsiders (minority interest)

If the investor acquires the stock at less than the book value a share of the existing stock on the investee's books, the increase in the investor's equity at the expense of the outside interest is recognized as an increase in the investor's investment and paid-in capital accounts. If it acquires the stock at more than its book value a share, the decrease in the investor's equity to the benefit of the outside interest is recognized as a decrease in the investor's investment and paid-in capital accounts.

Investee Reacquisitions of Stock from the Investor

Stockholding changes of type 6, investee reacquisition of stock from the investor, are so rare that they are usually mentioned only in passing. If such a transaction occurs, it is accounted for the way other dispositions of investee stock by the investor are accounted for, except that no gain or loss is recognized on the transaction. Because the number of shares of the investee's stock is reduced by such a transaction, the percentage of stock held by outside stockholders is increased. Such a change is reflected in the calculation of minority interest.

COMPLEX STOCKHOLDING

Stockholding in some consolidated groups is complex. Each type of complex stockholding involves holding by a member of the consolidated group, other than the parent company of the group, of stock of another member of the group. Such a stockholding may be:

Indirect Stockholding.   Holding of a controlling amount of stock of a subsidiary by a subsidiary of the parent company or by another subsidiary in linear relationship to the parent company. Such a stockholding is also called *multiple tier stockholding.*

Lateral Stockholding.   Holding of stock of a member of a consolidated group by two or more other members of the group. Such stockholding is also called *connecting stockholding* or *cross holding.*

Reciprocal Stockholding.   Holding of stock of one member of a consolidated group by another member, some of whose stock is held by the first member.

Combination Complex Stockholding.   Holding of stock in a consolidated group that combines two or more of the preceding types of complex stockholdings.

Indirect Stockholding

A member of a consolidated group may be controlled by the parent company of the group by indirect stockholding, in which the member's parent company is itself the subsidiary of the parent company of the group or of another company in the group.

A company may be a member of a consolidated group without the parent company of the group holding, directly or indirectly, a majority of its stock. For example, a parent company may hold 70% of the stock of a daughter subsidiary, which holds 70% of the stock of a granddaughter subsidiary. The parent company of the group holds, directly or indirectly, only 49% (70% × 70%) of the stock of the granddaughter subsidiary; the minority interest in the granddaughter subsidiary (actually a majority interest) is 51%. Nevertheless, the parent company controls the granddaughter subsidiary through its control of the daughter subsidiary, and the granddaughter subsidiary can be included as a member of the consolidated group.

Accounting for complex stockholding is aided by diagrams of the relationships involved. Exhibit 7.34 is a diagram of indirect stockholding.

Consolidation procedures for a consolidated group with indirect stockholding

EXHIBIT 7.34

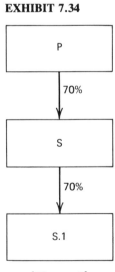

[Diagram A]

begin with the lowest tier, with subsidiaries that own no stock of other member companies. The income of such a subsidiary allocable to its particular parent company is determined and added to its parent company's income. Next, the income of companies one tier up, which are both parent companies and subsidiaries, is determined and added to the income of their parent companies. The process continues until the parent company to which the income is allocated is the parent company of the consolidated group.

Receivables and payables between any two members of the consolidated group are reconciled and eliminated. The excess of the amounts at which inventories or land, buildings, and equipment is stated on the books of one member over their cost to another member from which the first member acquired the assets is eliminated. Only the increased number of accounts that need to be examined

EXHIBIT 7.35. Corporation P and Corporation S, Book Values, Fair Values, and Calculation of Goodwill, January 1, 19A (P's 70% investment in S's stock)

	Fair Values	Book Values	Excess of Fair Values over Book Values	70% of Excess of Fair Values over Book Values
Cash	385,000	385,000	-0-	-0-
Receivables (net)	50,000	50,000	-0-	-0-
Inventories	140,000	100,000	40,000	28,000
Buildings and equipment (net)	200,000	150,000	50,000	35,000
Investment in S	115,000	115,000	-0-	-0-
Current liabilities	(20,000)	(20,000)	-0-	-0-
Long-term liabilities	(140,000)	(140,000)	-0-	-0-
	730,000	640,000	90,000	63,000
	×70%	×70%	×70%	
	511,000	448,000	63,000	
Amount of investment	600,000			
Goodwill	89,000			

Equity:		Total	70% Acquired
Common stock		400,000	280,000
Retained earnings		240,000	168,000
Totals, as above		640,000	448,000

for possible eliminations makes those procedures more involved than in simple consolidations.

To illustrate consolidation involving indirect stockholding, the consolidated group in Exhibit 7.34 is used: On January 1, 19A, P acquired 70% of the S's voting stock (2,800 shares) by paying S's stockholders $600,000. The combination does not qualify for the pooling of interests method, so the purchase method is used. For its $600,000, P acquired 70% of the fair values of S's assets and liabilities for $511,000, plus $89,000 for goodwill, as shown in Exhibit 7.35.

On July 1, 19A, S acquired 70% of the S.1's voting stock (700 shares) by paying S.1's stockholders $115,000. The combination does not qualify for the pooling of interests method, so the purchase method is used. For its $115,000, S acquired 70% of the fair values of S.1's assets and liabilities for $100,800, plus $14,200 for goodwill, as shown in Exhibit 7.36.

During the year 19A, S sold merchandise to P for $25,000. S.1 paid a cash

EXHIBIT 7.36.   Corporation S and Corporation S.1, Book Values, Fair Values, and Calculation of Goodwill, July 1, 19A (S's 70% investment in S.1's stock)

	Fair Values	Book Values	Excess of Fair Values over Book Values	70% of Excess of Fair Values over Book Values
Cash	50,000	50,000	-0-	-0-
Receivables (net)	20,000	20,000	-0-	-0-
Inventories	80,000	60,000	20,000	14,000
Buildings and equipment (net)	30,000	20,000	10,000	7,000
Current liabilities	(10,000)	(10,000)	-0-	-0-
Long-term liabilities	(26,000)	(20,000)	(6,000)	(4,200)
	144,000	120,000	24,000	16,800
	×70%	×70%	×70%	
	100,800	84,000	16,800	
Amount of investment	115,000			
Goodwill	14,200			

			70%
Equity:		Total	Acquired
Common stock		100,000	70,000
Retained earnings		20,000	14,000
Totals, as above		120,000	84,000

dividend of $10,000 and S paid a cash dividend of $40,000 in September 19A. On December 31, 19A, S owed S.1 $4,000 and owed P $3,000.

For a combination accounted for by the purchase method, the results of operations of the acquired company for the portion of the year it is held are included in consolidated results of operations. The financial statements of P and S for the year 19A and of S.1 for the period from July 1, 19A, to December 31, 19A, are as shown in Exhibit 7.37.

EXHIBIT 7.37.   Corporation P, Corporation S, and Corporation S.1, Financial Statements (P and S for the year 19A and S.1 for the period July 1, 19A, to December 31, 19A)

	P	S	S.1
Income Statement			
Sales	$1,400,000	$250,000	$150,000
Cost of goods sold	(790,000)	(150,000)	(75,000)
Investment revenue	28,000	7,000	
Other expenses	(368,000)	(57,000)	(40,000)
Net income	$ 270,000	$ 50,000	$ 35,000
Statement of Changes in Retained Earnings			
Retained earnings, beginning of period	$ 660,000	$240,000	$ 20,000
Net income	270,000	50,000	35,000
Dividends	(80,000)	(40,000)	(10,000)
Retained earnings, end of period	$ 850,000	$250,000	$ 45,000
Balance Sheet			
Cash	$ 150,000	$345,000	$ 90,000
Accounts receivable (net)	400,000	60,000	35,000
Inventories	650,000	100,000	50,000
Buildings and equipment (net)	1,080,000	160,000	15,000
Investments	600,000	115,000	
	$2,880,000	$780,000	$190,000
Current liabilities	$ 160,000	$ 30,000	$ 15,000
Long-term liabilities	750,000	100,000	30,000
Common stock	1,120,000	400,000	100,000
Retained earnings	850,000	250,000	45,000
	$2,880,000	$780,000	$190,000

EXHIBIT 7.38. Corporation S and Corporation S.1, Worksheet to Develop Consolidated Financial Statements (S for the year 19A and S.1 for the period July 1, 19A, to December 31, 19A)

| | | | Adjustments and Eliminations | | Consolidated |
	S(i)	S.1(i)	Dr.	Cr.	Statements
Income Statement					
Sales	250,000	150,000			400,000
Cost of goods sold	(150,000)	(75,000) (2)	14,000		(239,000)
Investment revenue	7,000	(3)	7,000		
Other expenses	(57,000)	(40,000) (2)	360		(97,360)
Net income	50,000	35,000	21,360		63,640 *
Statement of Changes in Retained Earnings					
Retained earnings, beginning of period	240,000	20,000 (1)	14,000		246,000
Net income	50,000	35,000 (A)	21,360		63,640
Dividends	(40,000)	(10,000)	(3)	7,000	(43,000)
Retained earnings, end of period	250,000	45,000	35,360 (B)	7,000	266,640 **
Balance Sheet					
Cash	345,000	90,000			435,000
Receivables (net)	60,000	35,000	(4)	4,000	91,000
Inventories	100,000	50,000 (1)	14,000 (2)	14,000	150,000
Buildings and equipment (net)	160,000	15,000 (1)	7,000 (2)	350	181,650
Investments	115,000		(1)	115,000	
Goodwill			(1) 14,200 (2)	710	13,490
	780,000	190,000			871,140
Current liabilities	30,000	15,000 (4)	4,000		41,000
Long-term liabilities	100,000	30,000 (2)	700 (1)	4,200	133,500
Common stock	400,000	100,000 (1)	70,000		430,000 ***
Retained earnings	250,000	45,000 (B)	35,360 (B)	7,000	266,640
	780,000	190,000	145,260	145,260	871,140

EXHIBIT 7.38. (*Continued*)

(i) From Exhibit 7.37
(1) To eliminate intercompany stockholding, adjust S.1's assets and liabilities to their fair values at the date of the combination, and record the difference as goodwill, from Exhibit 7.36
(2) To amortize the excess of the fair values of S.1's assets and liabilities over their book values and goodwill for the half year S owned its investment in S.1:

	70% Excess Fair Values and Goodwill	Remaining Life	Attributed to Current Year (six months)	
			Cost of Goods Sold	Other Expenses
Inventories	14,000	None	14,000	
Buildings and equipment	7,000	10 years		350
Long-term debt	(4,200)	3 years		(700)
Goodwill	14,200	10 years		710
			14,000	360

(3) To eliminate intercompany dividends
(4) To eliminate intercompany receivables/payables
(A) From the income statements
(B) From the statements of changes in retained earnings
*   Includes $35,000 × 30% = $10,500 of S.1's net income attributable to minority interest
**   Includes $45,000 × 30% = $13,500 of S.1's retained earnings attributable to minority interest
***   Includes $100,000 × 30% = $30,000 of S.1's common stock owned by outsiders (minority interest)

EXHIBIT 7.39. Corporation P, Corporation S, and Corporation S.1, Worksheet

	P(i)	S + S.1(ii)	Adjustments and Eliminations Dr.	Cr.	Consolidated Statements
Income Statement					
Sales	1,400,000	400,000	(3) 25,000		1,775,000
Cost of goods sold	(790,000)	(239,000)	(2) 28,000	(3) 25,000	(1,032,000)
Other expenses	(368,000)	(97,360)	(2) 12,400		(477,760)
Investment revenue	28,000		(5) 28,000		
Net income	270,000	63,640	93,400	25,000	265,240*
Statement of Changes in Retained Earnings					
Retained earnings, beginning of period	660,000	246,000	(1)168,000		738,000
Net income	270,000	63,640	(A) 93,400	(A) 25,000	265,240
Dividends	(80,000)	(43,000)		(5) 28,000	(95,000)
Retained earnings, end of period	850,000	266,640	261,400	53,000	908,240**

(i) From Exhibit 7.37
(ii) From Exhibit 7.38
(1) To eliminate intercompany stockholding, adjust S's assets and liabilities to their fair values at the date of the combination, and record the difference as goodwill, from Exhibit 7.35
(2) To amortize the excess of the fair values of S's assets and liabilities over their book values and goodwill:

	70% Excess Fair Values and Goodwill	Remaining Life	Attributed to Current Year Cost of Goods Sold	Other Expenses
Inventories	28,000	None	28,000	
Buildings and equipment	35,000	10 years		3,500
Goodwill	89,000	10 years		8,900
			28,000	12,400

172

	P(i)	S + S.1(ii)	Adjustments and Eliminations Dr.	Cr.	Consolidated Statements
Balance Sheet					
Cash	150,000	435,000			585,000
Receivables (net)	400,000	91,000		(4) 3,000	488,000
Inventories	650,000	150,000	(1) 28,000	(2) 28,000	800,000
Buildings and					
equipment (net)	1,080,000	181,650	(1) 35,000	(2) 3,500	1,293,150
Investments	600,000			(1)600,000	
Goodwill		13,490	(1) 89,000	(2) 8,900	93,590
	2,880,000	871,140			3,259,740
Current liabilities	160,000	41,000	(4) 3,000		198,000
Long-term					
liabilities	750,000	133,500			883,500
Common stock	1,120,000	430,000	(1)280,000		1,270,000***
Retained					
earnings	850,000	266,640	(B)261,400	(B) 53,000	908,240
	2,880,000	871,140	696,400	696,400	3,259,740

(3) To eliminate intercompany sales/purchases
(4) To eliminate intercompany receivables/payables
(5) To eliminate intercompany dividends
(A) From the income statements
(B) From the statements of changes in retained earnings
* Includes $35,000 × 30% = $10,500 of S.1's net income attributable to minority interest plus $50,000 × 30% = $15,000 of S's net income attributable to minority interest, for a total of $25,500 of consolidated net income attributable to minority interest
** Includes $45,000 × 30% = $13,500 of S.1's retained earnings attributable to minority interest plus $250,000 × 30% = $75,000 of S's retained earnings attributable to minority interest, for a total of $88,500 of consolidated retained earnings attributable to minority interest
*** Includes $100,000 × 30% = $30,000 of S.1's common stock owned by outsiders (minority interest) plus $400,000 × 30% = $120,000 of S's common stock owned by outsiders (minority interest), for a total of $150,000 minority interest in the common stock of the consolidated group

The financial statements of S and S.1 are consolidated first, as shown in Exhibit 7.38. The financial statements of P and the consolidated financial statements of S and S.1 are then consolidated, as shown in Exhibit 7.39.

Lateral Stockholding

The stock of a member of a consolidated group may be held by two or more other members of the group, with a controlling interest held by one or more of the other members. Exhibit 7.40 is a diagram of such a lateral stockholding.

To illustrate consolidation involving lateral stockholding, the consolidated group in Exhibit 7.40 is used: On January 1, 19A, P acquired 70% of S's voting stock (2,800 shares) by paying S's stockholders $600,000. The combination does not qualify for the pooling of interests method, so the purchase method is used. For its $600,000, P acquired 70% of the fair values of S's assets and liabilities for $511,000, plus $89,000 for goodwill, as shown in Exhibit 7.41.

On July 1, 19A, P acquired 40% of the S.1's voting stock (400 shares) by paying S.1's stockholders $66,000, and S acquired 20% of the voting stock (200 shares) of S.1 by paying S.1's stockholders $33,000. Neither transaction qualifies for the pooling of interests method, so the purchase method is used.

For its $66,000, P acquired 40% of the fair values of S.1's assets and liabilities for $57,600 plus $8,400 for goodwill, as shown in Exhibit 7.42. For its $33,000, S acquired 20% of the fair values of S.1's assets and liabilities for $28,800 plus $4,200 for goodwill, as shown in Exhibit 7.43.

EXHIBIT 7.40

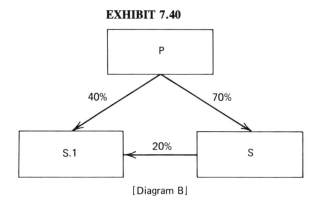

[Diagram B]

EXHIBIT 7.41. Corporation P and Corporation S, Book Values, Fair Values, and Calculation of Goodwill, January 1, 19A (P's 70% investment in S's stock)

	Fair Values	Book Values	Excess of Fair Values over Book Values	70% of Excess of Fair Values over Book Values
Cash	385,000	385,000	-0-	-0-
Receivables (net)	50,000	50,000	-0-	-0-
Inventories	140,000	100,000	40,000	28,000
Buildings and equipment (net)	315,000	265,000	50,000	35,000
Current liabilities	(20,000)	(20,000)	-0-	-0-
Long-term liabilities	(140,000)	(140,000)	-0-	-0-
	730,000	640,000	90,000	63,000
	×70%	×70%	×70%	
	511,000	448,000	63,000	
Amount of investment	600,000			
Goodwill	89,000			

Equity:		Total	70% Acquired
Common stock		400,000	280,000
Retained earnings		240,000	168,000
Totals, as above		640,000	448,000

During the year 19A, S sold merchandise to P for $25,000. S.1 paid a cash dividend of $10,000 and S paid a cash dividend of $40,000 in September 19A. On December 31, 19A, S owed S.1 $4,000 and owed P $3,000.

The financial statements of P and S for the year 19A and of S.1 for the period from July 1, 19A, to December 31, 19A, are as shown in Exhibit 7.44. The financial statements of the common investors in another member of a consolidated group, such as P and S, which both have investments in S.1, are best consolidated together with the other member. For illustrative purposes, P and S are consolidated first, and that set of consolidated financial statements is then consolidated with S.1. The financial statements of P and S are consolidated as shown in Exhibit 7.45. Then the financial statements of S.1 and the consolidated financial statements for P and S are consolidated as shown in Exhibit 7.46.

EXHIBIT 7.42.   Corporation P and Corporation S.1, Book Values, Fair Values, and Calculation of Goodwill, July 1, 19A (P's 40% investment in S.1's stock)

	Fair Values	Book Values	Excess of Fair Values over Book Values	40% of Excess of Fair Values over Book Values
Cash	50,000	50,000	-0-	-0-
Receivables (net)	20,000	20,000	-0-	-0-
Inventories	80,000	60,000	20,000	8,000
Buildings and equipment (net)	30,000	20,000	10,000	4,000
Current liabilities	(10,000)	(10,000)	-0-	-0-
Long-term liabilities	(26,000)	(20,000)	(6,000)	(2,400)
	144,000	120,000	24,000	9,600
	×40%	×40%	×40%	
	57,600	48,000	9,600	
Amount of investment	66,000			
Goodwill	8,400			

Equity:	Total	40% Acquired
Common stock	100,000	40,000
Retained earnings	20,000	8,000
Totals, as above	120,000	48,000

Reciprocal Stockholding

A subsidiary in a consolidated group may hold stock in its parent company, which may be the parent company of the consolidated group or another subsidiary in an indirect or lateral stockholding. Exhibit 7.47 is a diagram of such a reciprocal stockholding.

Such a stockholding presents no problems if the parent company holds all the subsidiary's stock. All related amounts are eliminated in full. If the parent

EXHIBIT 7.43.   Corporation S and Corporation S.1, Book Values, Fair Values, and Calculation of Goodwill, July 1, 19A (S's 20% investment in S.1's stock)

	Fair Values	Book Values	Excess of Fair Values over Book Values	20% of Excess of Fair Values over Book Values
Cash	50,000	50,000	-0-	-0-
Receivables (net)	20,000	20,000	-0-	-0-
Inventories	80,000	60,000	20,000	4,000
Buildings and equipment (net)	30,000	20,000	10,000	2,000
Current liabilities	(10,000)	(10,000)	-0-	-0-
Long-term liabilities	(26,000)	(20,000)	(6,000)	(1,200)
	144,000	120,000	24,000	4,800
	×20%	×20%	×20%	
	28,800	24,000	4,800	
Amount of investment	33,000			
Goodwill	4,200			

Equity:		Total	20% Acquired
Common stock		100,000	20,000
Retained earnings		20,000	4,000
Totals, as above		120,000	24,000

company holds less than all the subsidiary's stock, a view is taken on the nature of the subsidiary's holdings of its parent company's stock.

Two views are taken of such a stockholding—the treasury stock view and the conventional view. Procedures for dealing with such stockholdings depend on the view taken.

The Treasury Stock View

Under the treasury stock view, the stock of the parent company held by the subsidiary is treated as treasury stock of the parent company. That treatment begins when the subsidiary is acquired if it previously held the stock or when it acquires the stock after being acquired. If the subsidiary acquires the stock

EXHIBIT 7.44. Corporation P, Corporation S, and Corporation S.1, Financial Statements (P and S for the year 19A and S.1 for the period July 1, 19A, to December 31, 19A)

	P	S	S.1
Income Statement			
Sales	$1,396,000	$255,000	$150,000
Cost of goods sold	(790,000)	(150,000)	(75,000)
Investment revenue	32,000	2,000	
Other expenses	(368,000)	(57,000)	(40,000)
Net income	$ 270,000	$ 50,000	$ 35,000
Statement of Changes in Retained Earnings			
Retained earnings, beginning of period	$ 660,000	$240,000	$ 20,000
Net income	270,000	50,000	35,000
Dividends	(80,000)	(40,000)	(10,000)
Retained earnings, end of period	$ 850,000	$250,000	$ 45,000
Balance Sheet			
Cash	$ 150,000	$312,000	$ 90,000
Receivables (net)	334,000	125,000	35,000
Inventories	650,000	100,000	50,000
Buildings and equipment (net)	1,080,000	210,000	15,000
Investments	666,000	33,000	
	$2,880,000	$780,000	$190,000
Current liabilities	$ 160,000	$ 30,000	$ 15,000
Long-term liabilities	750,000	100,000	30,000
Common stock	1,120,000	400,000	100,000
Retained earnings	850,000	250,000	45,000
	$2,880,000	$780,000	$190,000

after being acquired, it is seen as buying the parent company's stock on behalf of the parent company.

No income of the parent company is assigned to the subsidiary during consolidation based on the stockholding, and dividends paid on the stock are eliminated in full. The cost of the stock is deducted from consolidated paid-in capital, and, if the parent company itself is a subsidiary, the shares are not considered to be outstanding for the purpose of determining minority interest in that parent company.

The treasury stock view is required by paragraph 13 of ARB No. 51 for holdings of stock of the parent company of a consolidated group: "shares of the parent company held by a subsidiary should not be treated as outstanding stock in the consolidated balance sheet." However, most authorities state that the treasury stock view should not be used if the parent company whose stock is held by its subsidiary is itself a subsidiary in the consolidated group. The reason they give is that no stock of the parent company of the consolidated group is involved.

The Conventional View

Under the conventional view, the stock of a parent company held by its subsidiary is considered to be outstanding stock. The subsidiary's share of the earnings of the parent company is assigned to the subsidiary. As usual, the parent company's share of the earnings of the subsidiary is assigned to the parent company.

The subsidiary's earnings cannot be determined until the parent company's earnings are determined. The parent company's earnings cannot be determined until the subsidiary's earnings are determined. It is therefore impossible to start by determining separately either the subsidiary's earnings or the parent company's earnings. The only possible way to determine them is to determine them at the same time, using simultaneous equations—two equations with two unknowns.

Comparison of Views

The two views can lead to significantly different results. Though the treasury stock view is simpler to apply, it ignores the effect of a holding of stock of a parent company by a subsidiary that has less than 100% of its stock held by the parent company. The effect ignored is the portion of the parent company's earnings attributable to the minority stockholders of the subsidiary.

Illustration of the Treasury Stock View

To illustrate consolidation involving reciprocal stockholding under the treasury stock view, the consolidated group in Exhibit 7.47 is used: On January 1, 19A, P acquired 80% of S's voting stock (800 shares) by paying S's stockholders

EXHIBIT 7.45. Corporation P and Corporation S, Worksheet to Develop Consolidated Financial Statements for the Year 19A

	P(i)	S(i)	Adjustments and Eliminations Dr.		Adjustments and Eliminations Cr.		Consolidated Statements
Income Statement							
Sales	1,396,000	255,000	(4)	25,000			1,626,000
Cost of goods sold	(790,000)	(150,000)	(2)	28,000 (4)	25,000		(943,000)
Investment revenue	32,000	2,000	(5)	28,000			6,000
Other expenses	(368,000)	(57,000)	(2)	12,400			(437,400)
Net income	270,000	50,000		93,400	25,000		251,600
Statement of Changes in Retained Earnings							
Retained earnings, beginning of period	660,000	240,000	(1)	168,000			732,000
Net income	270,000	50,000	(A)	93,400 (A)	25,000		251,600
Dividends	(80,000)	(40,000)		(5)	28,000		(92,000)
Retained earnings, end of period	850,000	250,000		261,400	53,000		891,600
Balance Sheet							
Cash	150,000	312,000					462,000
Receivables (net)	334,000	125,000		(3)	3,000		456,000
Inventories	650,000	100,000	(1)	28,000 (2)	28,000		750,000
Buildings and equipment (net)	1,080,000	210,000	(1)	35,000 (2)	3,500		1,321,500
Investments	666,000	33,000		(1)	600,000		99,000
Goodwill			(1)	89,000 (2)	8,900		80,100
	2,880,000	780,000					3,168,600
Current liabilities	160,000	30,000	(3)	3,000			187,000
Long-term liabilities	750,000	100,000					850,000
Common stock	1,120,000	400,000	(1)	280,000			1,240,000
Retained earnings	850,000	250,000	(B)	261,400 (B)	53,000		891,600
	2,880,000	780,000		696,400	696,400		3,168,600

EXHIBIT 7.45. (*Continued*)

(i) From Exhibit 7.44

(1) To eliminate intercompany stockholding, adjust S's assets and liabilities to their fair values at the date of the combination, and record the difference as goodwill, from amounts in Exhibit 7.41

(2) To amortize the excess of the fair values of S's assets and liabilities over their book values and goodwill:

	70% Excess Fair Values and Goodwill	Remaining Life	Attributed to Current Year	
			Cost of Goods Sold	Other Expenses
Inventories	28,000	None	28,000	
Buildings and equipment	35,000	10 years		3,500
Goodwill	89,000	10 years		8,900
			28,000	12,400

(3) To eliminate intercompany receivables/payables

(4) To eliminate intercompany purchases/sales

(5) To eliminate intercompany dividends

(A) From the income statements

(B) From the statements of changes in retained earnings

	P + S(i)	S.1(ii)	Adjustments and Eliminations Dr.	Cr.	Consolidated Statements
Income Statement					
Sales	1,626,000	150,000			1,776,000
Cost of goods sold	(943,000)	(75,000)	(3) 4,000 (4) 8,000		(1,030,000)
Investment revenue	6,000		(6) 6,000		
Other expenses	(437,400)	(40,000)	(3) 110 (4) 220		(477,730)
Net income	251,600	35,000	18,330		268,270*

Statement of Changes in Retained Earnings					
Retained earnings, beginning of period	732,000	20,000	(1) 4,000 (2) 8,000		740,000
Net income	251,600	35,000	(A) 18,330		268,270
Dividends	(92,000)	(10,000)		(6) 6,000	(96,000)
Retained earnings, end of period	891,600	45,000	30,330	6,000	912,270**

(i) From Exhibit 7.45
(ii) From Exhibit 7.44
(1) To eliminate intercompany stockholding by S of S.1's stock, adjust S.1's assets and liabilities to their fair values at the date of the combination pertaining to S's investment, and record the difference as goodwill, from Exhibit 7.43
(2) To eliminate intercompany stockholding by P of S.1's stock, adjust S.1's assets and liabilities to their fair values at the date of the combination pertaining to P's investment, and record the difference as goodwill, from Exhibit 7.42
(3) To amortize the excess of the fair values of S.1's assets and liabilities over their book values and goodwill pertaining to S's investment for the half year S owned its investment in S.1, from Exhibit 7.43:

	20% Excess Fair Values and Goodwill	Remaining Life	Attributed to Current Year (six months) Cost of Goods Sold	Other Expenses
Inventories	4,000	None	4,000	
Buildings and equipment	2,000	10 years		100
Long-term debt	(1,200)	3 years		(200)
Goodwill	4,200	10 years		210
			4,000	110

Worksheets to Develop Consolidated Financial Statements (P and S for the year

	P + S(i)	S.1(ii)	Adjustments and Eliminations Dr.		Adjustments and Eliminations Cr.		Consolidated Statements
Balance Sheet							
Cash	462,000	90,000					552,000
Receivables (net)	456,000	35,000			(5)	4,000	487,000
Inventories	750,000	50,000	(1) 4,000		(3)	4,000	800,000
			(2) 8,000		(4)	8,000	
Buildings and							
equipment (net)	1,321,500	15,000	(1) 2,000		(3)	100	1,342,200
			(2) 4,000		(4)	200	
Investments	99,000				(1)	33,000	
					(2)	66,000	
Goodwill	80,100		(1) 4,200		(3)	210	92,070
			(2) 8,400		(4)	420	
	3,168,600	190,000					3,273,270
Current liabilities	187,000	15,000	(5) 4,000				198,000
Long-term							
liabilities	850,000	30,000	(3) 200		(1)	1,200	883,000
			(4) 400		(2)	2,400	
Common stock	1,240,000	100,000	(1) 20,000				1,280,000***
			(2) 40,000				
Retained							
earnings	891,600	45,000	(B) 30,330		(B)	6,000	912,270
	3,168,600	190,000	125,530			125,530	3,273,270

(4) To amortize the excess of the fair values of S.1's assets and liabilities over their book values and goodwill pertaining to P's investment for the half year P owned its investment in S.1, from amounts in Exhibit 7.42:

	40% Excess Fair Values and Goodwill	Remaining Life	Attributed to Current Year (six months) Cost of Goods Sold	Attributed to Current Year (six months) Other Expenses
Inventories	8,000	None	8,000	
Buildings and equipment	4,000	10 years		200
Long-term debt	(2,400)	3 years		(400)
Goodwill	8,400	10 years		420
			8,000	220

(5) To eliminate intercompany receivables/payables
(6) To eliminate intercompany dividends
(A) From the income statements
(B) From the statements of changes in retained earnings
* Includes $50,000 × 30% = $15,000 of net income of S attributable to minority interest plus $35,000 × 40% = $14,000 of net income of S.1 attributable to minority interest, for a total of $29,000 of consolidated net income attributable to minority interest
** Includes $250,000 × 30% = $75,000 of S's retained earnings attributable to minority interest plus $45,000 × 30% = $13,500 of S's retained earnings attributable to minority interest, for a total of $88,500 of consolidated retained earnings attributable to minority interest
*** Includes $400,000 × 30% = $120,000 of S's common stock owned by outsiders (minority interest) plus $100,000 × 40% = $40,000 of S.1's common stock owned by outsiders (minority interest), for a total of $160,000 minority interest in the common stock of the consolidated group

EXHIBIT 7.47

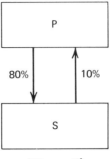

[Diagram C]

EXHIBIT 7.48. Corporation P and Corporation S, Book Values, Fair Values, and Calculation of Goodwill, January 1, 19A (P's 80% investment in S's stock)

	Fair Values	Book Values	Excess of Fair Values over Book Values	80% of Excess of Fair Values over Book Values
Cash	50,000	50,000	-0-	-0-
Accounts receivable (net)	20,000	20,000	-0-	-0-
Inventories	80,000	60,000	20,000	16,000
Buildings and equipment (net)	30,000	20,000	10,000	8,000
Current liabilities	(10,000)	(10,000)	-0- -0-	
Long-term liabilities	(26,000)	(20,000)	(6,000)	(4,800)
	144,000	120,000	24,000	19,200
	×80%	×80%	×80%	
	115,200	96,000	19,200	
Amount of investment	150,000			
Goodwill	34,800			

Equity:		Total	80% Acquired
Common stock		100,000	80,000
Retained earnings		20,000	16,000
Totals, as above		120,000	96,000

$150,000 and S acquired 10% of P's voting stock (200 shares) by paying P's stockholders $64,000, the book value of the stock. The combination does not qualify for the pooling of interests method, so the purchase method is used.

For its $150,000, P acquired 80% of the fair values of S's assets and liabilities for $115,200, plus $34,800 for goodwill, as shown in Exhibit 7.48. During the year 19A, S sold merchandise to P for S's cost of $25,000. S paid a cash dividend of $10,000 and P paid a cash dividend of $40,000 during the year 19A. On December 31, 19A, S owed P $3,000. The financial statements of P and S for the year 19A are as shown in Exhibit 7.49. The financial statements are consolidated as shown in Exhibit 7.50.

EXHIBIT 7.49.   Corporation P and Corporation S, Financial Statements for the Year 19A

	P	S
Income Statement		
Sales	$250,000	$150,000
Cost of goods sold	(150,000)	(79,000)
Investment revenue	8,000	4,000
Other expenses	(58,000)	(40,000)
Net income	$ 50,000	$ 35,000
Statement of Changes in Retained Earnings		
Retained earnings, beginning of year	$240,000	$ 20,000
Net income	50,000	35,000
Dividends	(40,000)	(10,000)
Retained earnings, end of year	$250,000	$ 45,000
Balance Sheet		
Cash	$310,000	$ 61,000
Accounts receivable (net)	60,000	25,000
Inventories	100,000	50,000
Buildings and equipment (net)	160,000	15,000
Investments	150,000	64,000
	$780,000	$215,000
Current liabilities	$ 30,000	$ 40,000
Long-term liabilities	100,000	30,000
Common stock	400,000	100,000
Retained earnings	250,000	45,000
	$780,000	$215,000

EXHIBIT 7.50. Corporation P and Corporation S, Worksheet to Develop

	P(i)	S(i)	Adjustments and Eliminations Dr.	Cr.	Consolidated Statements
Income Statement					
Sales	250,000	150,000	(3) 25,000		375,000
Cost of goods sold	(150,000)	(79,000)	(2) 16,000	(3) 25,000	(220,000)
Investment revenue	8,000	4,000	(5) 12,000		
Other expenses	(58,000)	(40,000)	(2) 2,680		(100,680)
Net income	50,000	35,000	55,680	25,000	54,320*
Statement of Changes in Retained Earnings					
Retained earnings, beginning of year	240,000	20,000	(1) 40,000		220,000
Net income	50,000	35,000	(A) 55,680	(A) 25,000	54,320
Dividends	(40,000)	(10,000)		(5) 12,000	(38,000)
Retained earnings, end of year	250,000	45,000	95,680	37,000	236,320**

(i) From Exhibit 7.49

(1) To eliminate intercompany stockholding, adjust S's assets and liabilities to their fair values, and record the difference as goodwill at the date of the combination, from information in the illustration and in Exhibit 7.48:

	Dr.	Cr.
Excess of fair values in P's purchase of S's stock:		
Inventories	16,000	
Buildings and equipment (net)	8,000	
Long-term debt		4,800
Goodwill	34,800	
Common stock at date of stock purchase		
S's stock bought by P	80,000	
P's stock bought by S	40,000	
Retained earnings at date of stock purchase		
S's retained earnings bought by P	16,000	
P's retained earnings bought by S	24,000	
Investments		
P's investment in S		150,000
S's investment in P		64,000

(2) To amortize P's proportionate share of the excess of fair values of S's assets and liabilities over their book values and goodwill, from Exhibit 7.48:

186

Consolidated Financial Statements for the Year 19A (treasury stock view)

	P(i)	S(i)	Adjustments and Eliminations Dr.	Adjustments and Eliminations Cr.	Consolidated Statements
Balance Sheet					
Cash	310,000	61,000			371,000
Receivables (net)	60,000	25,000		(4) 3,000	82,000
Inventories	100,000	50,000	(1) 16,000	(2) 16,000	150,000
Buildings and equipment (net)	160,000	15,000	(1) 8,000	(2) 800	182,200
Investments	150,000	64,000		(1)214,000	
Goodwill			(1) 34,800	(2) 3,480	31,320
	780,000	215,000			816,520
Current liabilities	30,000	40,000	(4) 3,000		67,000
Long-term liabilities	100,000	30,000	(2) 1,600	(1) 4,800	133,200
Common stock	400,000	100,000	(1)120,000		380,000***
Retained earnings	250,000	45,000	(B) 95,680	(B) 37,000	236,320
	780,000	215,000	279,080	279,080	816,520

	80% Excess Fair Values and Goodwill	Remaining Life	Attributed to Current Year Cost of Goods Sold	Attributed to Current Year Other Expenses
Inventories	16,000	None	16,000	
Buildings and equipment	8,000	10 years		800
Long-term debt	(4,800)	3 years		(1,600)
Goodwill	34,800	10 years		3,480
			16,000	2,680

(3) To eliminate intercompany sales/purchases
(4) To eliminate intercompany receivables/payables
(5) To eliminate intercompany dividends
(A) From the income statements
(B) From the statements of changes in retained earnings
*   Under the treasury stock approach, S's holding of P's shares is treated as retired shares, and the investment revenue recorded by S on those shares is not considered earnings attributable to the minority interest
      Minority interest in net income is determined after investment revenue of S from P is eliminated: ($35,000 − $4,000) × 20% = $6,200
**   Minority interest in retained earnings is determined after dividends by P to S are eliminated: ($45,000 − $4,000) × 20% = $8,200
*** Includes $100,000 × 20% = $20,000 of S's common stock owned by outsiders (minority interest)

EXHIBIT 7.51.   Corporation P and Corporation S, Worksheet to Develop

	P(i)	S(i)	Adjustments and Eliminations Dr.	Cr.	Consolidated Statements
Income Statement					
Sales	250,000	150,000	(3) 25,000		375,000
Cost of goods sold	(150,000)	(79,000)	(2) 16,000	(3) 25,000	(220,000)
Investment revenue	8,000	4,000	(5) 12,000		
Other expenses	(58,000)	(40,000)	(2) 2,680		(100,680)
Net income	50,000	35,000	55,680	25,000	54,320*
Statement of Changes in Retained Earnings					
Retained earnings, beginning of year	240,000	20,000	(1) 40,000		220,000
Net income	50,000	35,000	(A) 55,680	(A) 25,000	54,320
Dividends	(40,000)	(10,000)		(5) 12,000	(38,000)
Retained earnings, end of year	250,000	45,000	95,680	37,000	236,320**

(i) From Exhibit 7.49

  Notes (1) to (5) and (A) and (B) are the same as in Exhibit 7.50

*   Minority interest in net income under the conventional approach is determined by simultaneous equations, using the separate incomes of the parent company and subsidiary, plus each company's allocable share of the other company's income, and exclusive of intercompany dividends

These symbols are used:

  P = P's income from its operations plus its allocable share of S's income

  S = S's income from its operations plus its allocable share of P's income

  *   *   *   *   *   *

  $P = (\$50,000 - \$8,000) + 80\%$ of $S = \$42,000 + 0.8S$

  $S = (\$35,000 - \$4,000) + 10\%$ of $P = \$31,000 + 0.1P$

  so, $P = \$42,000 + 0.8 (\$31,000 + 0.1P) = \$42,000 + \$24,800 + 0.08P = \$66,800 + 0.08P$

Consolidated Financial Statements for the Year 19A (conventional view)

	P(i)	S(i)	Adjustments and Eliminations Dr.	Cr.	Consolidated Statements
Balance Sheet					
Cash	310,000	61,000			371,000
Receivables (net)	60,000	25,000		(4) 3,000	82,000
Inventories	100,000	50,000	(1) 16,000	(2) 16,000	150,000
Buildings and equipment (net)	160,000	15,000	(1) 8,000	(2) 800	182,200
Investments	150,000	64,000		(1)214,000	
Goodwill			(1) 34,800	(2) 3,480	31,320
	780,000	215,000			816,520
Current liabilities	30,000	40,000	(4) 3,000		67,000
Long-term liabilities	100,000	30,000	(2) 1,600	(1) 4,800	133,200
Common stock	400,000	100,000	(1)120,000		380,000***
Retained earnings	250,000	45,000	(B) 95,680	(B) 37,000	236,320
	780,000	215,000	279,080	279,080	816,520

$0.92P = \$66,800$

$P = \$66,800/0.92 = \$72,609$

so, $S = \$31,000 + 0.1(\$72,609) = \$31,000 + \$7,261 = \$38,261$

The outside interest in the income of P is 90% of $\$72,609 = \$65,348$

The outside (minority) interest in the income of S is 20% of $\$38,261 = \$7,652$

*   *   *   *   *   *

The total outside interest is $\$65,348 + \$7,652 = \$73,000$, which is the sum of the incomes of the parent company and subsidiary, exclusive of intercompany dividends, as above: $\$42,000 + \$31,000 = \$73,000$

**   Includes $7,652 of retained earnings attributable to minority interest, based on the net income of S during the period S was a member of the consolidated group

*** Includes $100,000 × 20% = $20,000 of S's common stock owned by outsiders (minority interest)

Illustration of the Conventional View

To illustrate consolidation involving reciprocal stockholding under the conventional view, the facts assumed above in the illustration of the treasury stock view are used. The financial statements are consolidated as shown in Exhibit 7.51.

Combination Complex Stockholding

Any combination of complex stockholding is possible, and examples of any particular combination likely could be found in practice. Exhibit 7.52 is a diagram of a combination stockholding.

No new concepts or procedures are involved in consolidating a consolidated group that combines two or more of the complex stockholdings discussed above. At each connection between members of the consolidated group, the nature of the particular complex stockholding involved is analyzed, and procedures to treat such a stockholding are applied. As in all such complex stockholdings, the members most remote from the parent company of the consolidated group are

EXHIBIT 7.52.

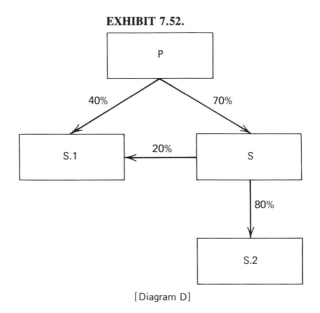

[Diagram D]

treated first, and the procedures are applied up the ladder to the parent company of the consolidated group.

To illustrate consolidation involving combination complex stockholding, the consolidated group in Exhibit 7.52 is used, and the events assumed to illustrate lateral stockholding, above, are assumed here.

On January 1, 19B, S acquired 80% of S.2's voting stock (800 shares) by paying S.2's stockholders $90,000. The combination does not qualify for the pooling of interests method, so the purchase method is used. For its $90,000, S acquired 80% of the fair values of S.2's assets and liabilities for $83,000, plus $7,000 for goodwill, as shown in Exhibit 7.53.

During September 19B, S, S.1, and S.2 paid cash dividends of $12,000, $15,000, and $4,000, respectively. On December 31, 19B, P owed S.2 $2,500.

EXHIBIT 7.53. Corporation S and Corporation S.1, Book Values, Fair Values, and Calculation of Goodwill, January 1, 19B (S's 80% investment in S.1)

	Fair Values	Book Values	Excess of Fair Values over Book Values	80% of Excess of Fair Values over Book Values
Cash	27,000	27,000	-0-	-0-
Receivables (net)	32,000	32,000	-0-	-0-
Inventories	52,000	37,000	15,000	12,000
Buildings and equipment (net)	101,000	78,000	23,000	18,400
Current liabilities	(47,000)	(47,000)	-0-	-0-
Long-term liabilities	(61,250)	(61,250)	-0-	-0-
	103,750	65,750	38,000	30,400
	× 80%	× 80%	× 80%	
	83,000	52,600	30,400	
Amount of investment	90,000			
Goodwill	7,000			

Equity:	Total	80% Acquired
Common stock	50,000	40,000
Retained earnings	15,750	12,600
Totals, as above	65,750	52,600

The financial statements of P, S, S.1, and S.2 for the year 19B are as shown in Exhibit 7.54. The financial statements of S and S.2 are consolidated first, as shown in Exhibit 7.55. Next, the financial statements of P and the consolidated financial statements of S and S.2 are consolidated, as shown in Exhibit 7.56. Finally, the financial statements of S.1 and the consolidated financial statements of P, S, and S.2 are consolidated, as shown in Exhibit 7.57.

EXHIBIT 7.54. Corporation P, Corporation S, Corporation S.1, and Corporation S.2, Financial Statements for the Year 19B

	P	S	S.1	S.2
Income Statement				
Sales	$1,385,600	$250,800	$150,000	$133,000
Cost of goods sold	(750,000)	(129,200)	(70,000)	(63,750)
Investment revenue	14,400	6,200		
Other expenses	(340,000)	(57,800)	(40,000)	(52,000)
Net income	$ 310,000	$ 70,000	$ 40,000	$ 17,250
Statement of Changes in Retained Earnings				
Retained earnings, beginning of year	$ 850,000	$250,000	$ 45,000	$ 15,750
Net income	310,000	70,000	40,000	17,250
Dividends	(90,000)	(12,000)	(15,000)	(4,000)
Retained earnings, end of year	$1,070,000	$308,000	$ 70,000	$ 29,000
Balance Sheet				
Cash	$ 162,000	$204,000	$ 96,000	$ 31,000
Receivables (net)	382,000	125,000	45,000	40,500
Inventories	720,000	186,000	64,000	43,000
Buildings and equipment (net)	1,170,000	240,000	20,000	83,000
Investments	666,000	123,000		
	$3,100,000	$878,000	$225,000	$197,500
Current liabilities	$ 130,000	$ 40,000	$ 25,000	$ 51,500
Long-term liabilities	780,000	130,000	30,000	67,000
Common stock	1,120,000	400,000	100,000	50,000
Retained earnings	1,070,000	308,000	70,000	29,000
	$3,100,000	$878,000	$225,000	$197,500

SUBSIDIARY PREFERRED STOCK

A subsidiary may have capital stock outstanding other than voting common stock, referred to here for convenience as *preferred stock,* though specific issues may be called by other names. No special problem exists if all such preferred stock is held by members of the consolidated group of which the subsidiary is a member. If so, it is all eliminated in consolidation. If some or all is held by outside entities, accounting for the issue of preferred stock requires consideration of the issue's features.

An issue of preferred stock may have special features; for example, it may:

Be cumulative—all undeclared preferred dividends must be declared and paid before dividends may be paid to common stockholders

Be participating—dividends are declared and paid to preferred and common stockholders in a ratio specified in the instruments establishing the issues of stock

Have a call price above its par value

Virtually every combination of those and perhaps other features are possible in an issue of preferred stock. Each issue has to be considered on its own.

The simplest type of issue—noncumulative, nonparticipating preferred stock with no special call or redemption features—presents no special problem. The stock held by outsiders is presented in the consolidated balance sheet at its par value. Dividends declared to outsiders reduce consolidated net income and consolidated retained earnings.

Dividends in arrears on cumulative preferred stock also reduce consolidated net income and consolidated retained earnings. An amount equal to cumulative dividends not declared during the reporting period on stock held by outside entities is charged to consolidated net income just as a declared preferred dividend on such stock is; the amount attributed to minority interest is increased by the undeclared dividend. Consolidated retained earnings is reduced and the amount attributed to minority interest in the balance sheet is increased by cumulative dividends in arrears on such stock.

A participating feature specifies the manner in which dividends on preferred stock are calculated, by reference to dividends on common stock. They are accounted for the same as other cumulative preferred dividends.

EXHIBIT 7.55. Corporation S and Corporation S.2, Worksheet to Develop Consolidated Financial Statements for the year 19B

	S(i)	S.2(i)	Adjustments and Eliminations Dr.		Adjustments and Eliminations Cr.		Consolidated Statements
Income Statement							
Sales	250,800	133,000					383,800
Cost of goods sold	(129,200)	(63,750)	(2)	12,000			(204,950)
Investment revenue	6,200		(3)	3,200			3,000
Other expenses	(57,800)	(52,000)	(2)	2,540			(112,340)
Net income	70,000	17,250		17,740			69,510
Statement of Changes in Retained Earnings							
Retained earnings, beginning of year	250,000	15,750	(1)	12,600			253,150
Net income	70,000	17,250	(A)	17,740			69,510
Dividends	(12,000)	(4,000)			(3)	3,200	(12,800)
Retained earnings, end of year	308,000	29,000		30,340		3,200	309,860
Balance Sheet							
Cash	204,000	31,000					235,000
Receivables (net)	125,000	40,500					165,500
Inventories	186,000	43,000	(1)	12,000	(2)	12,000	229,000
Buildings and equipment (net)	240,000	83,000	(1)	18,400	(2)	1,840	339,560
Investments	123,000				(1)	90,000	33,000
Goodwill			(1)	7,000	(2)	700	6,300
	878,000	197,500					1,008,360
Current liabilities	40,000	51,500					91,500
Long-term liabilities	130,000	67,000					197,000
Common stock	400,000	50,000	(1)	40,000			410,000
Retained earnings	308,000	29,000	(B)	30,340	(B)	3,200	309,860
	878,000	197,500		107,740		107,740	1,008,360

194

EXHIBIT 7.55. (*Continued*)

(i) From Exhibit 7.54

(1) To eliminate intercompany stockholding, adjust S.2's assets and liabilities to their fair values at the date of the combination, and record the difference as goodwill, from amounts in Exhibit 7.53

(2) To amortize the excess of the fair values of S.2's assets and liabilities over their book values and goodwill:

	80% Excess Fair Values and Goodwill	Remaining Life	Attributed to Current Year	
			Cost of Goods Sold	Other Expenses
Inventories	12,000	None	12,000	
Buildings and equipment	18,400	10 years		1,840
Goodwill	7,000	10 years		700
			12,000	2,540

(3) To eliminate intercompany dividends

(A) From the income statements

(B) From the statements of changes in retained earnings

EXHIBIT 7.56.   Corporation P, Corporation S, and Corporation S.2, Worksheet

	P(i)	S + S.2(ii)	Adjustments and Eliminations Dr.	Cr.	Consolidated Statements
Income Statement					
Sales	1,385,600	383,800			1,769,400
Cost of goods sold	(750,000)	(204,950)			(954,950)
Investment revenue	14,400	3,000	(3) 8,400		9,000
Other expenses	(340,000)	(112,340)	(2) 12,400		(464,740)
Net income	310,000	69,510	20,800		358,710
Statement of Changes in Retained Earnings					
Retained earnings, beginning of year	850,000	253,150	(1)208,400		894,750
Net income	310,000	69,510	(A) 20,800		358,710
Dividends	(90,000)	(12,800)		(3) 8,400	(94,400)
Retained earnings, end of year	1,070,000	309,860	229,200	8,400	1,159,060

(i)   From Exhibit 7.54
(ii)   From Exhibit 7.55
(1)   To eliminate intercompany stockholding, adjust S's assets and liabilities to their fair values at the date of the combination, and record the difference as goodwill, reduced by amounts amortized in prior years, from Exhibit 7.41:

	Excess of Fair Values over Book Values		
	At Date of Combination	Charged in Prior Years	Balance at Beginning of Current Year
Inventories	28,000	28,000	-0-
Buildings and equipment	35,000	3,500	31,500
Goodwill	89,000	8,900	80,100
		40,400	111,600
Retained earnings acquired at date of combination		168,000	
Total charge to beginning retained earnings		208,400	

	P(i)	S + S.2(ii)	Adjustments and Eliminations Dr.	Cr.	Consolidated Statements
Balance Sheet					
Cash	162,000	235,000			397,000
Receivables (net)	382,000	165,500		(4) 2,500	545,000
Inventories	720,000	229,000			949,000
Buildings and					
equipment (net)	1,170,000	339,560	(1) 31,500	(2) 3,500	1,537,560
Investments	666,000	33,000		(1)600,000	99,000
Goodwill		6,300	(1) 80,100	(2) 8,900	77,500
	3,100,000	1,008,360			3,605,060
Current liabilities	130,000	91,500	(4) 2,500		219,000
Long-term liabili-					
ties	780,000	197,000			977,000
Common stock	1,120,000	410,000	(1)280,000		1,250,000
Retained earnings	1,070,000	309,860	(B)229,200	(B) 8,400	1,159,060
	3,100,000	1,008,360	623,300	623,300	3,605,060

(2) To amortize the excess of the fair values of S's assets and liabilities over their book values and goodwill, from Exhibit 7.41:

	70% Excess Fair Values and Goodwill	Remaining Life#	Charge to Other Expenses
Buildings and equipment	35,000	10 years	3,500
Goodwill	89,000	10 years	8,900
			12,400

\# At time of combination
(3) To eliminate intercompany dividends: S's dividend to P of $12,000 × 70% = $8,400
(4) To eliminate intercompany receivables/payables
(A) From the income statements
(B) From the statements of changes in retained earnings

	S.1(i)	P + S + S.2(ii)	Adjustments and Eliminations Dr.		Cr.	Consolidated Statements
Income Statement						
Sales	150,000	1,769,400				1,919,400
Cost of goods sold	(70,000)	(954,950)				(1,024,950)
Investment revenue		9,000	(5)	9,000		
Other expenses	(40,000)	(464,740)	(3)	440		(505,400)
			(4)	220		
Net income	40,000	358,710		9,660		389,050*

Statement of Changes in Retained Earnings

	S.1(i)	P + S + S.2(ii)	Dr.		Cr.	Consolidated Statements
Retained earnings, beginning of year	45,000	894,750	(1)	8,000		927,750
			(2)	4,000		
Net income	40,000	358,710	(A)	9,660		389,050
Dividends	(15,000)	(94,400)			(5) 9,000	(100,400)
Retained earnings, end of year	70,000	1,159,060		21,660	9,000	1,216,400**

(i) From Exhibit 7.54
(ii) From Exhibit 7.56
(1) To eliminate intercompany stockholding by P in S.1, adjust S.1's assets and liabilities to their fair values at the date of the combination pertaining to P's investment, and record the difference as goodwill, from Exhibit 7.42
(2) To eliminate intercompany stockholding by S in S.1, adjust S.1's assets and liabilities to their fair values at the date of the combination pertaining to S's investment, and record the difference as goodwill, from Exhibit 7.43
(3) To amortize the excess of the fair values of S's assets and liabilities over their book values and goodwill pertaining to P's investment, from Exhibit 7.42:

	40% Excess Fair Values and Goodwill	Remaining Life#	Charge to Other Expenses
Buildings and equipment	4,000	10 years	400
Long-term debt	(2,400)	3 years	(800)
Goodwill	8,400	10 years	840
			440

\# At time of combination
(4) To amortize the excess of the fair values of S's assets and liabilities over their book values and goodwill pertaining to S's investment, from Exhibit 7.43:

S.2, Worksheet to Develop Consolidated Financial Statements for the Year 19B

	S.1(i)	P + S + S.2(ii)	Adjustments and Eliminations Dr.			Cr.	Consolidated Statements
Balance Sheet							
Cash	96,000	397,000					493,000
Receivables (net)	45,000	545,000					590,000
Inventories	64,000	949,000	(1)	8,000			1,025,000
			(2)	4,000			
Buildings and							
equipment (net)	20,000	1,537,560	(1)	4,000	(3)	400	1,562,960
			(2)	2,000	(4)	200	
Investments		99,000			(1)	66,000	
					(2)	33,000	
Goodwill		77,500	(1)	8,400	(3)	840	88,840
			(2)	4,200	(4)	420	
	225,000	3,605,060					3,759,800
Current liabilities	25,000	219,000					244,000
Long-term							
liabilities	30,000	977,000	(3)	800	(1)	2,400	1,009,400
			(4)	400	(2)	1,200	
Common stock	100,000	1,250,000	(1)	40,000			1,290,000***
			(2)	20,000			
Retained earnings	70,000	1,159,060	(B)	21,660	(B)	9,000	1,216,400
	225,000	3,605,060		113,460		113,460	3,759,800

	20% Excess Fair Values and Goodwill	Remaining Life#	Charge to Other Expenses
Buildings and equipment	2,000	10 years	200
Long-term debt	(1,200)	3 years	(400)
Goodwill	4,200	10 years	420
			220

\#   At time of combination

(5) To eliminate intercompany dividends: S.1's dividend to P of $15,000 × 40% = $6,000 plus S.1's dividend to S of $15,000 × 20% = $3,000, for a total of $9,000

(A) From the income statements

(B) From the statements of changes in retained earnings

*   Includes $70,000 × 30% = $21,000 of S's net income attributable to minority interest, $40,000 × 40% = $16,000 of S.1's net income attributable to minority interest, and $17,250 × 20% = $3,450 of S.2's net income attributable to minority interest, for a total of $40,450 of consolidated net income attributable to minority interest (amounts of net income from Exhibits 7.55 and 7.57)

** Includes $308,000 × 30% = $92,400 of S's retained earnings attributable to minority interest, $70,000 × 40% = $28,000 of S.1's retained earnings attributable to minority interest, and $29,000 × 20% = $5,800 of S.2's retained earnings attributable to minority interest, for a total of $126,200 of consolidated retained earnings attributable to minority interest (amounts of retained earnings from Exhibits 7.55 and 7.57)

*** Includes $400,000 × 30% = $120,000 of S's common stock owned by outsiders (minority interest), $100,000 × 40% = $40,000 of S.1's common stock owned by outsiders (minority interest), and $50,000 × 20% = $10,000 of S.2's common stock owned by outsiders (minority interest), for a total of $170,000 minority interest in the common stock of the consolidated group

A preferred stock issue with a call price above par value is ordinarily presented in the consolidated balance sheet at its par value. That amount is used in the initial consolidation after a business combination or after preferred stock is issued by a company that is already a subsidiary, to establish original goodwill and minority interest.

INTERCOMPANY TAX ALLOCATION

A consolidated group of companies may file a consolidated income tax return, with the taxes paid by the parent company or by other members of the consolidated group. The group may have formal or informal procedures for charging members for the income taxes incurred.

The American Institute of CPAs proposed to the Financial Accounting Standards Board that the board specify the way they should be charged in the absence of a written tax-sharing agreement among the companies and the disclosures that should be made concerning the sharing.[6] The board responded by including filings of consolidated tax returns in the list of examples of related party transactions covered by its Statement No. 57, "Related Party Disclosures," and including the subject of intercompany tax allocation in its project on consolidated financial statements and the equity method, discussed in Appendix B.

PUSH DOWN ACCOUNTING

As discussed and illustrated in Chapters 2, 4, and 5, the assets and liabilities of a subsidiary obtained in a business combination accounted for by the purchase method are presented in consolidation at their fair values at the date of the combination, modified for events since the date of combination, as determined under APB Opinion 16. Those amounts usually differ from their amounts in the records of the subsidiary. The amounts at which they are recognized in consol-

---

[6]American Institute of CPAs, Proposed Statement of Position, "Reporting Intercorporate Tax Allocations," transmitted to the Financial Accounting Standards Board by letter of February 20, 1979.

idation are sometimes assigned—pushed down—to the assets and liabilities of the subsidiary and presented in the separate financial statements of the subsidiary.

The American Institute of CPAs proposed to the Financial Accounting Standards Board that the board require push down accounting after "a transaction that results in a substantial change in ownership."[7] The board is considering that recommendation in its project on consolidated financial statements and the equity method, discussed in Appendix B.

[7]American Institute of CPAs, Issues Paper, "'Push Down' Accounting," October 30, 1979, pp. 25–27.

Examples of Financial Statements and Disclosures from Annual Reports

This appendix presents examples of consolidated financial statements from annual reports and examples of disclosures in notes to financial statements from annual reports.

Consolidated financial statements from annual reports of the following corporations are reproduced here. (The notes to the consolidated financial statements of those corporations, not reproduced here, are integral parts of the corporations' financial presentations.)

The Continental Group, Inc.

Exxon Corporation

National Gypsum Company

Owens-Illinois, Inc.

Sears, Roebuck and Co.

Of particular interest are the following:

In the consolidated financial statements of the Continental Group, the presentation in equity, not in income, of foreign exchange translation adjustments, which conforms to FASB Statement No. 52, "Foreign Currency Translation"

In the consolidated financial statements of the Exxon Corporation, the classification of "Equity of minority shareholders in affiliated companies" as a liability and the classification of "Income applicable to minority interests" with costs and other deductions

In the consolidated financial statements of National Gypsum Company, the classification of "Equity in earnings of affiliate" with net sales and other revenue

In the consolidated financial statements of Owens-Illinois, the classification of "minority shareholders' interests" between liabilities and preferred and common stockholders' equity

In the consolidated financial statements of income of Sears, Roebuck and Co., the combining of equity in net income of unconsolidated companies with income attributed to minority interest

Representative disclosures concerning consolidation, translation, and the equity method in notes to financial statements are presented on pages 224 to 237.

Statement of Consolidated Earnings

The Continental Group, Inc. and Subsidiaries

(in millions, except per share amounts)

years ended December 31	1983	1982	1981
Revenues	**$4,820**	$5,012	$5,194
Other Income	**122**	77	97
	4,942	5,089	5,291
Costs and Expenses			
Cost of goods sold and operating charges	**4,374**	4,427	4,544
Selling and administrative	**309**	323	380
Research and development	**29**	28	41
Interest	**108**	135	123
Interest capitalized	**(30)**	(41)	(26)
Gain on debt retirements	**(5)**	—	(25)
	4,785	4,872	5,037
Earnings Before Income Taxes and Insurance Operations	**157**	217	254
Provision for Income Taxes	**17**	87	69
Earnings Before Insurance Operations	**140**	130	185
Equity Earnings of Insurance Operations	**59**	50	49
Net Earnings	**199**	180	234
Dividends on preferred and preference shares	**23**	23	25
Net earnings applicable to common shares	**$ 176**	$ 157	$ 209
Net Earnings Per Common Share*	**$ 3.66**	$ 3.20	$ 4.24

*Restated for three-for-two stock split.

See Statement of Significant Accounting Policies and Notes to Financial Statements.

Statement of Changes in Consolidated Financial Position

The Continental Group, Inc. and Subsidiaries

(in millions)

years ended December 31	1983	1982	1981
Internally Generated Funds			
Net earnings	$ 199	$180	$234
Items not affecting cash			
Depreciation, depletion and amortization	230	227	234
Writedowns of investments and oil and gas properties	114	—	—
Undistributed equity earnings	(13)	2	(45)
(Decrease) increase in retirement benefits, deferred income taxes, etc.	(55)	42	60
Funds from operations	475	451	483
Disposals of investments and property, plant and equipment	534	63	143
Decrease in working capital, other than changes in cash and short-term debt	72	23	31
Translation adjustments	(26)	(13)	(15)
Other	4	15	(17)
	1,059	539	625
Borrowings and Equity Financings			
Long-term debt borrowings	83	105	159
Long-term debt reductions	(360)	(55)	(157)
Short-term debt reductions, net	(3)	(31)	(21)
Issuances of stock	8	2	11
Purchases of stock	(241)	(12)	(22)
	(513)	9	(30)
Dividends Paid	(105)	(108)	(107)
Capital Expenditures and Investments			
Capital expenditures	(297)	(437)	(406)
Investments and advances	(34)	(158)	(11)
	(331)	(595)	(417)
Increase (Decrease) in Cash	110	(155)	71
Cash, January 1	66	221	150
Cash, December 31	$ 176	$ 66	$221

See Statement of Significant Accounting Policies and Notes to Financial Statements.

Consolidated Balance Sheet
(in millions)

December 31	1983	1982
Assets		
Current Assets		
Cash	$ 176	$ 66
Receivables	477	540
Inventories, at LIFO cost		
Current cost	642	756
Excess over LIFO cost	(332)	(384)
	310	372
Deferred income taxes and other assets	77	67
	1,040	1,045
Investments and Advances		
Insurance Operations	581	548
Unicon Producing Company	181	154
Other	98	166
	860	868
Property, Plant and Equipment, at cost		
Buildings and equipment	1,909	2,716
Accumulated depreciation	(1,092)	(1,422)
	817	1,294
Oil and gas properties, net	576	624
Timberlands, net of timber harvested	138	114
Construction in progress	55	72
Land	17	20
	1,603	2,124
Other Assets	150	162
	$3,653	$4,199

See Statement of Significant Accounting Policies and Notes to Financial Statements.

	1983	1982
Liabilities and Equity		
Current Liabilities		
Accounts payable	**$ 372**	$ 365
Short-term debt	**29**	32
Taxes payable	**36**	74
Accrued payrolls and employee benefits	**174**	160
Other	**121**	147
	732	778
Long-Term Debt, less current portion	**726**	1,006
Other Liabilities		
Retirement benefits	**276**	258
Deferred income taxes	**56**	162
Other	**82**	91
	414	511
Redeemable Preference Shares	**249**	275
Preferred and Common Stockholders' Equity		
$4.25 cumulative preferred stock	**5**	5
Common stock (issued: 1983—49,239,000 shares; 1982—48,940,000 shares adjusted for three-for-two stock split)	**49**	33
Paid-in surplus	**343**	347
Common stock in treasury	**(219)**	—
Net unrealized investment gains	**72**	40
Foreign currency adjustments	**39**	55
Retained earnings	**1,243**	1,149
	1,532	1,629
	$3,653	$4,199

Consolidated Balance Sheet

EXXON CORPORATION

Assets	December 31 1982	December 31 1983
	(thousands of dollars)	
Current assets		
Cash, including time deposits of $1,474,938 and $1,764,021	$ 2,216,262	$ 2,512,287
Marketable securities	1,232,478	1,583,837
Notes and accounts receivable, less estimated doubtful amounts of		
$161,222 and $171,062	8,366,098	7,900,237
Inventories		
Crude oil, products and merchandise	3,798,532	3,598,031
Materials and supplies	1,737,689	1,372,772
Prepaid taxes and expenses	2,441,627	1,628,296
Total current assets	19,792,686	18,595,460
Investments and advances	1,714,484	1,746,620
Property, plant and equipment, at cost, less accumulated depreciation		
and depletion of $19,127,676 and $20,917,407 (Note 1, page 29)	38,981,829	40,868,424
Other assets, including intangibles	1,799,551	1,752,486
Total assets	62,288,550	62,962,990

Liabilities		
Current liabilities		
Notes and loans payable	2,747,685	867,285
Accounts payable and accrued liabilities	11,692,366	11,000,240
Income taxes payable	2,024,689	3,171,163
Total current liabilities	16,464,740	15,038,688
Long-term debt	4,555,580	4,668,915
Annuity reserves and accrued liabilities	2,697,771	3,271,905
Deferred income tax credits	8,676,170	9,012,594
Deferred income	268,170	315,150
Equity of minority shareholders in affiliated companies	1,185,928	1,212,643
Total liabilities	33,848,359	33,519,895

Shareholders' equity		
Capital stock issued (Note 3, page 30)	2,822,254	2,822,254
Earnings reinvested	27,211,257	29,515,384
Cumulative foreign exchange translation adjustments	(531,620)	(1,070,397)
	29,501,891	31,267,241
Less capital stock reacquired (Note 3, page 30)	1,061,700	1,824,146
Total shareholders' equity	28,440,191	29,443,095
Total liabilities and shareholders' equity	$62,288,550	$ 62,962,990

The information on pages 28 through 35 is an integral part of these statements

Consolidated Statement of Income and Earnings Reinvested

EXXON CORPORATION

Revenue	1981	1982	1983
		(thousands of dollars)	
Sales and other operating revenue, including excise taxes	$113,220,300	$102,058,895	$ 93,446,663
Earnings from equity interests and other revenue	1,702,261	1,499,650	1,287,308
	114,922,561	103,558,545	94,733,971

Costs and other deductions			
Crude oil and product purchases	64,383,105	56,083,520	46,709,473
Operating expenses	11,693,327	10,705,840	10,450,376
Selling, general and administrative expenses	5,232,793	5,253,148	4,948,385
Depreciation and depletion	2,898,920	3,333,455	3,527,817
Exploration expenses, including dry holes	1,650,214	1,773,318	1,408,009
Income, excise and other taxes	23,342,745	21,443,070	21,805,511
Interest expense	779,688	669,595	748,758
Income applicable to minority interests	115,554	110,667	157,685
	110,096,346	99,372,613	89,756,014

Net Income	$ 4,826,215	$ 4,185,932	$ 4,977,957
Per share	$5.58	$4.82	$5.78

Earnings reinvested			
Balance at beginning of year	$ 23,397,835	$ 25,629,781	$ 27,211,257
Net income	4,826,215	4,185,932	4,977,957
Dividends ($3.00 per share in 1981 and 1982 and $3.10 in 1983)	(2,594,269)	(2,604,456)	(2,673,830)
Balance at end of year	$ 25,629,781	$ 27,211,257	$ 29,515,384

Analysis of Change in Cumulative Foreign Exchange Translation Adjustments

	1981	1982	1983
		(thousands of dollars)	
Balance at beginning of year	$ 1,534,582	$ 287,062	$ (531,620)
Adjustments for the year	(1,247,520)	(818,682)	(538,777)
Balance at end of year	$ 287,062	$ (531,620)	$ (1,070,397)

The information on pages 28 through 35 is an integral part of these statements.

Consolidated Statement of Funds Provided and Utilized

EXXON CORPORATION

	1981	1982	1983
		(thousands of dollars)	
Funds from operations			
Net income			
Accruing to Exxon shareholders	$ 4,826,215	$ 4,185,932	$ 4,977,957
Accruing to minority interests	115,554	110,667	157,685
Costs charged to income not requiring funds			
Depreciation and depletion	2,898,920	3,333,455	3,527,817
Deferred income tax charges	1,740,939	1,789,029	777,822
Annuity and accrued liability provisions	225,879	780,943	724,375
Dividends received in excess of/(less than) equity in			
current earnings of equity companies (Note 1, page 29)	39,921	(43,815)	(112,132)
Funds provided from operations	9,847,428	10,156,211	**10,053,524**
Funds from other sources, excluding financing activities			
Sales of property, plant and equipment	278,785	402,715	417,348
Other reductions/(increases) in investments and advances	103,260	(27,440)	79,996
All other (increases) in long-term items-net	(58,586)	(424,911)	(22,901)
Changes in working capital, excluding cash and debt			
Reduction/(increase) in notes and accounts receivable	183,879	1,298,790	465,861
Reduction/(increase) in inventories	(512,940)	1,648,906	565,418
Reduction/(increase) in prepaid taxes and expenses	(429,858)	67,085	813,331
Increase/(reduction) in accounts payable	237,574	(1,024,568)	(692,126)
Increase/(reduction) in income taxes payable	(872,404)	32,111	1,146,474
Funds from other sources, excluding short-term			
debt, cash and marketable securities	(1,070,290)	1,972,688	**2,773,401**
Funds from /(used in) financing activities			
Additions to long-term debt	905,070	1,526,247	911,283
Reductions in long-term debt	(468,756)	(2,124,111)	(797,948)
Net additions/(reductions) in short-term debt	1,494,959	(284,658)	(1,880,400)
Funds from/(used in) financing activities	1,931,273	(882,522)	**(1,767,065)**
Less: changes due to foreign exchange translation			
Change in working capital, debt and other items-net	(177,602)	134,360	264,911
Total funds provided, excluding cash items	10,530,809	11,380,737	**11,324,771**
Utilization of funds			
Additions to property, plant and equipment	9,002,949	9,039,881	7,123,710
Cash dividends to Exxon shareholders	2,594,269	2,604,456	2,673,830
Cash dividends to minority interests	107,202	105,712	117,401
Acquisition/(disposition) of Exxon shares-net	(131,067)	65,469	762,446
Funds utilized	11,573,353	11,815,518	**10,677,387**
Changes due to foreign exchange translation			
Reduction in property, plant and equipment	1,679,229	1,556,452	1,245,086
Reduction in deferred income tax credits	(609,311)	(603,410)	(441,398)
Change in working capital, debt and other items-net	177,602	(134,360)	(264,911)
Total adjustments in shareholders' equity	(1,247,520)	(818,682)	(538,777)
Funds provided or utilized	—	—	—
Increase /(decrease) in cash and marketable securities	$ (1,042,544)	$ (434,781)	$ **647,384**

The information on pages 28 through 35 is an integral part of these statements.

Consolidated Statements of Earnings and Retained Earnings *National Gypsum Company and Subsidiaries*

	Year Ended December 31		
	1983	1982	1981
	(Thousands except per share amounts)		
Net sales	$1,130,868	$929,506	$965,665
Equity in earnings of affiliate	2,900	2,736	3,511
Other revenue	5,828	6,868	11,757
	1,139,596	939,110	980,933
Expenses:			
Cost of products sold	885,717	764,416	793,510
Selling, administrative and general	148,209	135,820	133,053
Interest	15,888	18,589	12,531
Sundry	3,735	5,092	1,782
	1,053,549	923,917	940,876
Income from continuing operations before taxes and extraordinary item	86,047	15,193	40,057
Taxes on income	36,700	1,100	7,660
Earnings from continuing operations before extraordinary item	49,347	14,093	32,397
Extraordinary item – nontaxable gain on exchange of long-term debt for common stock	4,445	—	—
Adjustment to estimated cost of disposal of Cement Division	—	—	6,427
NET EARNINGS	$ 53,792	$ 14,093	$ 38,824
EARNINGS PER COMMON SHARE			
Earnings from continuing operations before extraordinary item	$ 3.01	$ .89	$ 2.01
Net earnings	$ 3.29	$ .89	$ 2.41
RETAINED EARNINGS			
Balance beginning of year	$ 338,066	$347,480	$332,415
Net earnings for the year	53,792	14,093	38,824
	391,858	361,573	371,239
Cash dividends	24,836	23,507	23,759
BALANCE END OF YEAR	$ 367,022	$338,066	$347,480

See notes to financial statements.

C onsolidated Balance Sheets   *National Gypsum Company and Subsidiaries*

	December 31	
ASSETS	*1983*	*1982*
	(Thousands)	
CURRENT ASSETS		
Cash and short-term investments	$ 40,753	$ 17,994
Trade and sundry receivables, less		
allowances (1983 – $18,804,000;		
1982 – $13,750,000)	182,642	147,803
Inventories:		
Finished goods	68,230	70,098
Products in process	28,475	24,669
Materials and supplies	62,809	56,262
	159,514	151,029
Refundable income taxes	—	11,083
Other	13,176	13,505
TOTAL CURRENT ASSETS	396,085	341,414
PROPERTY, PLANT AND EQUIPMENT – BASED ON COST		
Plant sites	13,162	12,839
Mineral deposits	11,855	11,808
Buildings	171,223	171,579
Machinery and equipment	663,235	654,639
	859,475	850,865
Less allowances for depreciation and depletion	455,211	421,796
	404,264	429,069
INVESTMENTS AND OTHER ASSETS	65,569	63,297
	$865,918	$833,780

LIABILITIES AND STOCKHOLDERS' EQUITY	December 31	
	1983	1982
	(Thousands)	
CURRENT LIABILITIES		
Accounts payable	$ 49,519	$ 45,180
Accrued liabilities	48,338	40,931
Taxes on income	14,354	—
Commercial paper	—	9,061
Current portion of long-term debt	6,683	8,801
TOTAL CURRENT LIABILITIES	118,894	103,973
LONG-TERM DEBT	134,658	180,953
DEFERRED ITEMS		
Income taxes	67,199	60,641
Other	20,683	16,699
STOCKHOLDERS' EQUITY		
Common stock	9,175	8,747
Additional paid-in capital	197,502	171,579
Retained earnings	367,022	338,066
Equity adjustment from foreign currency translation	(13,440)	(11,103)
	560,259	507,289
Cost of treasury stock	35,775	35,775
	524,484	471,514
	$865,918	$833,780

See notes to financial statements.

Consolidated Statements of Changes in Financial Position   *National Gypsum Company and Subsidiaries*

	1983	1982	1981
	Year Ended December 31		
	(Thousands)		
SOURCE OF FUNDS			
From operations:			
Earnings from continuing operations before extraordinary item	$ 49,347	$ 14,093	$ 32,397
Depreciation, depletion and deferred taxes	50,690	51,975	42,731
Undistributed equity in earnings of affiliate	(1,312)	(1,500)	(3,511)
TOTAL FROM OPERATIONS	98,725	64,568	71,617
Extraordinary gain on exchange of long-term debt for common stock:			
Extraordinary gain	$ 4,445		
Value of common stock issued in exchange for debt and related interest	25,646		
Reduction of principal amount of long-term debt	(27,500)	2,591	—	—
Proceeds from long-term borrowings		50,000	129	61,000
Proceeds from capital construction funds		190	919	13,673
Carrying value of properties sold or retired		1,445	1,537	6,013
Increase (Decrease) in other deferred items		3,984	8,144	(6,868)
		156,935	75,297	145,435
USE OF FUNDS			
Additions to property, plant and equipment		18,630	35,421	117,691
Cash dividends		24,836	23,507	23,759
Purchase of treasury stock		—	—	21,892
Investment in oil and gas properties		3,606	9,046	15,491
Reduction of long-term debt		68,795	8,462	6,306
Other		1,318	(6,059)	2,917
		117,185	70,377	188,056
INCREASE (DECREASE) IN WORKING CAPITAL		$ 39,750	$ 4,920	$(42,621)
INCREASE (DECREASE) IN WORKING CAPITAL, BY COMPONENT			
Cash and short-term investments		$ 22,759	$ 3,386	$(64,339)
Trade and sundry receivables		34,839	13,175	(2,240)
Inventories		8,485	(21,867)	28,405
Refundable income taxes		(11,083)	8,871	2,212
Other		(329)	913	(3,477)
Accounts payable		(4,339)	(3,016)	(1,203)
Accrued liabilities		(7,407)	9,266	(6,648)
Taxes on income		(14,354)	—	8,767
Commercial paper		9,061	(4,985)	(4,076)
Current portion of long-term debt		2,118	(823)	(22)
INCREASE (DECREASE) IN WORKING CAPITAL		$ 39,750	$ 4,920	$(42,621)

See notes to financial statements.

Consolidated Earnings Owens-Illinois, Inc.

Millions of dollars, except per-share amounts Years ended December 31,	1983	1982	1981
Revenues:			
Net sales	$3,422.1	$3,552.9	$3,943.3
Interest and dividends	32.7	43.8	42.7
Royalties and net technical assistance	28.7	38.0	34.6
Equity in earnings of associates	15.9	16.9	4.0
Other	23.9	16.4	40.4
	3,523.3	3,668.0	4,065.0
Costs and expenses:			
Manufacturing, shipping and delivery	2,912.8	3,061.5	3,300.7
Research and development	28.1	24.6	28.8
Engineering	33.8	36.6	38.3
Selling and administrative	320.4	328.6	334.9
Interest	55.4	66.0	77.0
Other	35.8	15.1	10.2
	3,386.3	3,532.4	3,789.9
Earnings before capacity curtailment adjustments and divestitures, provision for income taxes, minority shareholders' interests, and cumulative effect of changes in methods of accounting	137.0	135.6	275.1
Capacity curtailment adjustments and divestitures	36.5	95.7	3.2
Earnings before provision for income taxes, minority shareholders' interests, and cumulative effect of changes in methods of accounting	100.5	39.9	271.9
Provision for income taxes	27.3	(6.0)	114.0
	73.2	45.9	157.9
Minority shareholders' interests in earnings of subsidiaries	4.1	6.2	3.8
Earnings before cumulative effect of changes in methods of accounting	69.1	39.7	154.1
Cumulative effect on prior years (to December 31, 1981) of changes in methods of accounting for furnace rebuilding costs and mold costs, net of applicable income taxes		51.0	
Net earnings	$ 69.1	$ 90.7	$ 154.1
Earnings per common share:			
Primary:			
Earnings before cumulative effect of changes in methods of accounting	$ 2.48	$ 1.36	$ 5.15
Cumulative effect of changes in methods of accounting		1.82	
Net earnings	$ 2.48	$ 3.18	$ 5.15
Fully diluted:			
Earnings before cumulative effect of changes in methods of accounting	$ 2.41	$ 1.35	$ 4.84
Cumulative effect of changes in methods of accounting		1.72	
Net earnings	$ 2.41	$ 3.07	$ 4.84

See Statement of Significant Accounting Policies and Financial Review on pages 29-36.

Consolidated Balance Sheet Owens-Illinois, Inc.

Millions of dollars December 31,	1983	1982
Assets		
Current assets:		
Cash (including time deposits of $34.3 in 1983 and $38.0 in 1982)	$ 65.7	$ 74.9
Short-term investments (at cost, which approximates market)	152.6	105.8
Receivables, less allowances for losses and discounts ($16.0 million in 1983 and $18.9 million in 1982)	491.1	401.2
Inventories	353.6	392.1
Prepaid expenses	8.4	23.4
Total current assets	1,071.4	997.4
Investments and other assets:		
Foreign investments and advances	156.7	206.4
Domestic investments	27.8	40.2
Repair parts inventories	103.5	119.0
Deferred charges	24.4	26.5
Deposits, receivables and other assets	68.6	62.0
Total investments and other assets	381.0	454.1
Property, plant and equipment:		
Land and timberlands, at cost less depletion	95.4	95.3
Buildings and equipment, at cost	2,617.1	2,681.8
	2,712.5	2,777.1
Less accumulated depreciation and amortization	1,229.0	1,232.8
Total property, plant and equipment	1,483.5	1,544.3
Total assets	$2,935.9	$2,995.8
Liabilities and Shareholders' Equity		
Current liabilities:		
Short-term loans and notes payable	$ 22.1	$ 46.3
Accounts payable	217.7	197.7
Salaries and wages	87.3	90.1
U.S. and foreign income taxes	12.6	11.7
Other accrued liabilities	207.1	192.2
Long-term debt due within one year	28.7	21.9
Total current liabilities	575.5	559.9
Long-term debt	544.8	591.3
Deferred taxes and other credits:		
Deferred taxes	260.1	247.2
Obligations under foreign pension plans	72.8	74.5
Other liabilities and reserves	103.3	72.6
Total deferred taxes and other credits	436.2	394.3
Minority shareholders' interests	52.9	62.9
Redeemable preferred shares	4.8	5.4
Shareholders' equity (excluding redeemable preferred shares):		
Preference shares (liquidation preference, $18.7 million in 1983 and $25.7 million in 1982)	3.7	5.1
Common shares	86.7	84.2
Capital in excess of stated value	154.7	136.9
Retained earnings	1,178.3	1,155.8
Cumulative foreign currency translation adjustment	(101.7)	
Total shareholders' equity (excluding redeemable preferred shares)	1,321.7	1,382.0
Total liabilities and shareholders' equity	$2,935.9	$2,995.8

See Statement of Significant Accounting Policies and Financial Review on pages 29-36.

Consolidated Capital in Excess of Stated Value Owens-Illinois, Inc.

Millions of dollars Years ended December 31,	1983	1982	1981
Balance at beginning of year	$ 136.9	$ 137.2	$ 113.7
Issuance of common shares	17.6	9.2	25.9
Purchase of common shares for treasury		(9.9)	(3.3)
Retirement of preferred shares	.2	.4	.9
Balance at end of year	$ 154.7	$ 136.9	$ 137.2

Consolidated Retained Earnings Owens-Illinois, Inc.

Millions of dollars, except per-share amounts Years ended December 31,	1983	1982	1981
Balance at beginning of year	$1,155.8	$1,179.1	$1,100.9
Adjustment due to change in method of accounting for foreign currency translation	.7		
Balance at beginning of year, as adjusted	1,156.5	1,179.1	1,100.9
Net earnings	69.1	90.7	154.1
	1,225.6	1,269.8	1,255.0
Deduct:			
Cash dividends:			
Preferred—$4.00 per share	.2	.3	.3
Preference—$4.75 per share	1.1	1.4	2.1
Common—$1.68 per share in 1983 and 1982; and $1.56 per share in 1981	46.0	47.0	45.8
	47.3	48.7	48.2
Purchase of common shares for treasury		65.3	27.7
	47.3	114.0	75.9
Balance at end of year	$1,178.3	$1,155.8	$1,179.1

See Statement of Significant Accounting Policies and Financial Review on pages 29-36.

Consolidated Changes in Financial Position Owens-Illinois, Inc.

Millions of dollars
Years ended December 31,

	1983	1982	1981
Sources:			
Cash provided by operations:			
Earnings before cumulative effect of changes in methods of accounting	$ 69.1	$ 39.7	$154.1
Charges not affecting working capital in the current period:			
Depreciation, depletion and amortization	162.5	169.5	144.5
Gain on divestitures	(41.1)		
Undepreciated cost of property, plant and equipment disposals	28.5	15.5	10.9
Capacity curtailment costs (non-current portion)	18.2	46.8	
Increase in deferred taxes, etc.	22.4	6.3	29.2
Working capital provided by operations (a)	259.6	277.8	338.7
Changes in components of working capital related to operations:			
Decrease (increase) in current assets:			
Receivables (exclusive of divestiture proceeds in 1983)	(26.1)	20.6	16.7
Inventories and prepaid expenses	55.0	4.5	82.8
Increase (decrease) in current liabilities:			
Accounts payable and accrued liabilities	34.9	19.3	22.2
U.S. and foreign income taxes	.9	(39.2)	(2.1)
Salaries and wages	(2.8)	(10.7)	(6.5)
Related cash effects from Lily divestiture			(71.7)
	61.9	(5.5)	41.4
Cash provided by operations (a)	321.5	272.3	380.1
Increase in deferred taxes and other credits	10.3		
Decrease (increase) in other assets	10.2	(29.6)	(2.7)
Cash proceeds from Lily divestiture			145.6
	342.0	242.7	523.0
Applications:			
Investment transactions:			
Additions to property, plant and equipment (excluding cumulative effect of changes in methods of accounting)	201.6	231.6	181.6
Increase in foreign investments and advances	9.1	11.9	
	210.7	243.5	181.6
Other transactions:			
Cash dividends	47.3	48.7	48.2
Issuance of common shares	(18.7)	(9.0)	(27.1)
Purchase of common shares for treasury		84.5	34.8
Other	.4	1.1	2.7
	29.0	125.3	58.6
Foreign currency translation adjustments—net (excluding amounts related to investments and property, plant and equipment)	.8		
	240.5	368.8	240.2
Increase (decrease) in net liquidity position	$101.5	$(126.1)	$282.8
Changes in elements of net liquidity position:			
Increase (decrease) in cash and short-term investments	$ 37.6	$(135.9)	$153.1
Decrease (increase) in total debt:			
Short-term loans and notes payable and long-term debt due within one year	17.4	(10.0)	64.0
Long-term debt:			
Borrowings	(21.4)	(25.0)	(18.3)
Reductions	67.9	44.8	84.0
Change in total debt	63.9	9.8	129.7
Increase (decrease) in net liquidity position	$101.5	$(126.1)	$282.8

(a) Recognition in 1982 of the cumulative effect on prior years of changes in methods of accounting did not affect working capital or cash provided by operations.
See Statement of Significant Accounting Policies and Financial Review on pages 29-36.

Sears, Roebuck and Co.
Consolidated Statements of Income

millions, except per share data			Year Ended December 31
	1983	1982	1981
Revenues	**$35,882.9**	$30,019.8	$27,357.4
Expenses			
Costs and expenses	**32,415.5**	27,382.2	25,375.4
Interest	**1,701.4**	1,627.0	1,519.9
Total expenses	**34,116.9**	29,009.2	26,895.3
Operating income	**1,766.0**	1,010.6	462.1
Realized capital gains and other	**126.2**	70.7	183.6
Income before income taxes, equity in net income of unconsolidated companies and minority interest	**1,892.2**	1,081.3	645.7
Income taxes (note 4)	**571.3**	231.6	10.1
Equity in net income of unconsolidated companies and minority interest	**21.3**	11.5	14.5
Net income	**$ 1,342.2**	$ 861.2	$ 650.1
Income per share	**$3.80**	$2.46	$2.06
Average shares outstanding	**353.1**	350.3	315.6

See accompanying notes which include the summarized Group financial statements.

Sears, Roebuck and Co.
Consolidated Statements of Financial Position

millions		December 31
	1983	1982
Assets		
Investments		
Bonds and redeemable preferred stocks, at amortized cost (market $7,252.9 and $5,862.0)	$ 8,237.2	$ 7,188.1
Mortgage loans	4,396.2	3,587.3
Common and preferred stocks, at market (cost $1,457.5 and $1,545.7)	1,808.3	1,786.6
Real estate	992.6	934.8
Total investments	15,434.3	13,496.8
Receivables		
Retail customers	10,978.6	7,859.2
Brokerage clients	2,300.0	1,767.9
Insurance premium installments	793.2	724.9
Finance installment notes	494.9	481.5
Other	839.6	603.2
Total receivables	15,406.3	11,436.7
Property and equipment, net	3,938.3	3,396.4
Merchandise inventories	3,620.5	3,146.0
Securities purchased under agreements to resell	2,343.0	1,004.7
Trading account securities owned, at market	1,756.4	758.5
Cash and invested cash (note 6)	1,502.5	1,307.6
Investments in unconsolidated companies	301.7	434.9
Other assets	1,873.1	1,559.0
Total assets	46,176.1	36,540.6
Liabilities		
Long-term debt (note 7)	7,405.3	5,816.1
Insurance reserves	6,252.8	5,667.1
Short-term borrowings (note 6)	4,595.6	2,820.1
Accounts payable and other liabilities	4,334.6	3,372.8
Savings accounts and advances from Federal Home Loan Bank	4,319.8	3,132.8
Securities sold under repurchase agreements	3,106.9	1,332.9
Unearned revenues	2,918.6	2,695.7
Deferred income taxes (note 4)	2,054.8	1,571.8
Payables to brokerage clients	1,400.8	1,318.9
Total liabilities	36,389.2	27,728.2
Commitments and contingent liabilities (notes 1, 8, 9 and 10)		
Shareholders' equity (note 10)		
Common shares ($.75 par value, 354.6 and 351.4 shares outstanding)	271.4	269.4
Capital in excess of par value	1,245.5	1,163.3
Retained income	8,231.3	7,426.1
Treasury stock (at cost)	(133.0)	(143.5)
Unrealized net capital gains on marketable equity securities	254.0	171.5
Cumulative translation adjustments	(82.3)	(74.4)
Total shareholders' equity	$ 9,786.9	$ 8,812.4

See accompanying notes which include the summarized Group financial statements.

Consolidated Statements of Shareholders' Equity

	Year Ended December 31					
	1983	1982	1981	**1983**	1982	1981
	millions			shares in thousands		
Preferred shares—$1.00 par value, 50 million shares authorized, none issued						
Common shares—$.75 par value, 500 million shares authorized, issued as follows:						
Balance, beginning of year	$ **269.4**	$ 268.5	$ 244.0	**359,230.5**	357,995.2	325,335.0
Issued for acquired companies	—	—	24.5	—	—	32,619.3
Issued under incentive compensation plan	—	.3	—	**30.1**	351.2	27.0
Stock options exercised and other changes	**2.0**	.6	—	**2,562.5**	884.1	13.9
Balance, end of year	**271.4**	269.4	268.5	**361,823.1**	359,230.5	357,995.2
Capital in excess of par value						
Balance, beginning of year	**1,163.3**	1,143.9	640.5			
Issued for acquired companies	—	—	508.8			
Issued under incentive compensation plan	**1.1**	6.5	.4			
Stock options exercised and other changes	**81.1**	12.9	(5.8)			
Balance, end of year	**1,245.5**	1,163.3	1,143.9			
Retained income						
Balance, beginning of year	**7,426.1**	7,041.2	6,820.2			
Net income	**1,342.2**	861.2	650.1			
Dividends ($1.52 per share in 1983 and $1.36 per share in 1982 and 1981)	**(537.0)**	(476.3)	(429.1)			
Balance, end of year	**8,231.3**	7,426.1	7,041.2			
Treasury stock (at cost)						
Balance, beginning of year	**(143.5)**	(186.7)	(192.4)	**(7,820.8)**	(10,107.3)	(10,167.6)
Purchased	—	—	(5.1)	—	—	(299.8)
Exchanged for Sears debt (note 7)	—	25.3	30.3	—	1,341.4	1,606.0
Issued to subsidiary in connection with acquisition	—	—	(37.8)	—	—	(2,216.4)
Reissued under dividend reinvestment plan	**10.5**	17.9	18.3	**564.5**	945.1	970.5
Balance, end of year	**(133.0)**	(143.5)	(186.7)	**(7,256.3)**	(7,820.8)	(10,107.3)
Unrealized net capital gains on marketable equity securities						
Balance, beginning of year	**171.5**	48.5	152.4			
Net increase (decrease)	**82.5**	123.0	(103.9)			
Balance, end of year	**254.0**	171.5	48.5			
Cumulative translation adjustments						
Balance, beginning of year	**(74.4)**	(46.5)	—			
Initial application of SFAS No. 52	—	—	(29.3)			
Net increase in unrealized losses	**(7.9)**	(36.9)	(17.2)			
Realized on sale of subsidiaries	—	9.0	—			
Balance, end of year	**(82.3)**	(74.4)	(46.5)			
Total shareholders' equity and shares outstanding	**$9,786.9**	$8,812.4	$8,268.9	**354,566.8**	351,409.7	347,887.9

See accompanying notes which include the summarized Group financial statements.

Sears, Roebuck and Co.
Consolidated Statements of Changes in Financial Position

millions		Year Ended December 31	
	1983	1982	1981
Sources of operating funds			
Net income	**$1,342.2**	$ 861.2	$ 650.1
Increase in insurance reserves	**596.1**	529.0	654.7
Deferred income taxes	**454.7**	97.2	(18.4)
Depreciation	**375.6**	336.5	308.8
Increase in unearned revenues	**210.9**	186.2	212.1
Amortization of debt discount and other non-cash items	**19.0**	103.8	(16.4)
From operations	**2,998.5**	2,113.9	1,790.9
Increase in savings accounts and advances from Federal Home Loan Bank	**1,187.0**	349.2	87.5
Increase in accounts payable and other liabilities	**689.5**	681.0	378.9
Total available operating funds	**4,875.0**	3,144.1	2,257.3
Uses of operating funds			
Increase in receivables, before sales of accounts	**2,501.9**	1,124.0	651.9
Net investment additions	**1,030.7**	863.2	817.7
Increase (decrease) in trading account securities owned	**997.9**	(515.7)	—
Net additions to mortgage loans and finance installment notes	**822.3**	244.9	49.7
Net additions to property and equipment	**542.3**	406.4	347.9
Increase in other assets	**220.0**	287.2	36.2
Increase in merchandise inventories	**63.0**	161.1	388.6
Total operating funds used	**6,178.1**	2,571.1	2,292.0
Net funds generated from operations before dividends, acquisitions and financing transactions	**(1,303.1)**	573.0	(34.7)
Dividends paid to shareholders, net of reinvested amounts	**(502.3)**	(458.4)	(410.8)
Cost of acquired companies, net of cash acquired	**(172.5)**	—	(790.0)
Common stock issued for acquired companies	**—**	—	495.5
Common stock issued for employee stock plans	**74.6**	20.3	(5.4)
Increase (decrease) in customer receivable balances sold	**(859.4)**	177.1	315.2
Proceeds from long-term debt	**1,162.8**	1,104.0	439.9
Repayment of long-term debt	**(288.3)**	(647.3)	(127.5)
Net increase (decrease) in short-term borrowings	**1,589.6**	(266.0)	264.8
Net change in securities agreements to repurchase or resell	**435.7**	(404.0)	—
Treasury stock reissued, net of purchases	**—**	25.3	25.2
Net assets of subsidiaries sold	**57.8**	12.9	—
Dividends, acquisitions and financing transactions	**1,498.0**	(436.1)	206.9
Increase in cash and invested cash	**$ 194.9**	$ 136.9	$ 172.2

See accompanying notes which include the summarized Group financial statements.

CORNING GLASS WORKS (DEC)

NOTES TO CONSOLIDATED FINANCIAL STATE-MENTS

Note 10 (in part): Stockholders' Equity

Poolings of Interests

On February 26, 1982 the businesses of the company and MetPath Inc., a New Jersey based clinical laboratory services company, were combined in a transaction accounted for as a pooling of interests. This transaction involved the combining of the account balances of the two companies and the exchange, at .4488 share of Corning common stock for each outstanding share of MetPath, of 2,915,955 shares of Corning common stock for all outstanding shares of MetPath not previously owned by Corning. Financial statements for all years presented have been restated to include the accounts and operations of MetPath Inc. MetPath's previously reported financial results have been changed to conform to Corning's fiscal year end. Separate results of operations of the combined entities for the years ended January 3, 1982 and December 28, 1980 are as follows:

	1981	1980
Net Sales		
Corning (as previously reported)	$1,598.5	$1,529.7
MetPath Inc.	115.6	92.8
Combined	$1,714.1	$1,622.5
Net Income		
Corning (as previously reported)	$ 97.4	$ 114.7
MetPath Inc.	6.3	5.8
Combined	$ 103.7	$ 120.5

POOLINGS OF INTERESTS

CHESEBROUGH-POND'S INC. (DEC)

NOTES TO CONSOLIDATED FINANCIAL STATE-MENTS

3. Acquisition

On June 30, 1982 the company acquired Prince Manufacturing, Inc. and certain royalty rights ("Prince") for 1,903,497 shares of stock valued at $62.4 million. Prince manufactures and markets tennis racquets and tennis equipment. This acquisition has been accounted for on a pooling-of-interests basis and, accordingly, the accompanying consolidated financial statements for years prior to 1982 have been restated to include the accounts and operations of Prince. Combined and separate results of Chesebrough-Pond's Inc. and Prince for the periods prior to the acquisition were as follows:

(in thousands)	Six Months Ended June 30, 1982 (unaudited)	Year Ended December 31, 1981	Year Ended December 31, 1980
Net Sales			
Chesebrough-Pond's Inc.	$759,875	$1,522,272	$1,375,282
Prince	28,597	35,376	18,039
Combined	$788,472	$1,557,648	$1,393,321
Net Income			
Chesebrough-Pond's Inc.	$56,563	$112,418	$97,788
Prince	3,207	5,003	$1,950
Combined	$59,770	$117,421	$99,738

DOYLE DANE BERNBACH INTERNATIONAL INC. (DEC)

NOTES TO CONSOLIDATED FINANCIAL STATE-MENTS

Note C (in part):

On March 16, 1982, the Registrant consummated its merger of Fletcher/Mayo/Associates, Inc. ("FMA"), an advertising agency in St. Joseph, Missouri, specializing in agricultural and industrial advertising, into a wholly-owned subsidiary of the Registrant. Under the terms of the Merger Agreement, the shareholders of FMA received an aggregate of 199,962 shares of the Registrant's common stock. The merger has been accounted for as a pooling of interests and, accordingly, the consolidated financial statements for prior years have been restated to reflect the accounts of FMA. The Registrant's results of operations for the calendar years 1980 and 1981 have been restated to include FMA's results for its fiscal years ended September 30, 1980 and 1981, respectively. FMA's net income of $196,000 ($.03 per share) generated from commissions and fees of $1,457,000) for the three months ended December 31, 1981 was credited to consolidated retained earnings in 1982.

A reconciliation of commissions and fees, net income and net income per share as originally reported and as restated follows (in thousands of dollars):

	1980	1981
Commissions and fees:		
Doyle Dane Bernbach International Inc.	$145,070	$161,793
Fletcher/Mayo/Associates, Inc.	3,486	4,448
As Restated	$148,556	$166,241
Net income:		
Doyle Dane Bernbach International Inc.	$ 10,728	$ 10,735
Fletcher/Mayo/Associates, Inc.	185	267
As Restated	$ 10,913	$ 11,002
Net income per share:		
As previously reported	$2.02	$1.94
As restated	$1.98	$1.92

Purchases

ANHEUSER-BUSCH COMPANIES, INC. (DEC)

NOTES TO CONSOLIDATED FINANCIAL STATE-MENTS

2 (in part): Acquisitions and Disposition

On November 2, 1982 the company acquired all of the outstanding common stock of Campbell Taggart, Inc. (Campbell Taggart). Campbell Taggart, through its operating subsidiaries, is engaged in the production and sale of food and food-related products. The cost of the acquisition was $560.0 million, consisting of $275.0 million paid in cash for approximately 50% of Campbell Taggart's outstanding common stock and 7.5 million shares of Anheuser-Busch Convertible Redeemable Preferred Stock with an estimated fair value of $285.0 million issued in exchange for the remaining Campbell Taggart common stock. The estimated fair value of the convertible redeemable preferred stock was determined on August 19, 1982.

The acquisition has been accounted for using the purchase method of accounting. Campbell Taggart's assets and liabilities have been recorded in the company's financial statements at their estimated fair values at the acquisition date. The excess cost of the acquisition over the estimated fair value of the net assets is amortized on a straight-line basis over 40 years. The Consolidated Statement of Income includes the operations of Campbell Taggart from November 2, 1982 through December 28, 1982.

Following are pro forma combined results of operations for the years ended December 31, 1982 and 1981, assuming the acquisition of Campbell Taggart had occurred on January 1, 1981. The results are not necessarily indicative of what would have occurred had the acquisition been consummated as of January 1, 1981, or of future operations of the combined companies. The results are based on purchase accounting adjustments recognized on consolidating Campbell Taggart, and include additional interest expense as if funds borrowed in connection with the acquisition had been outstanding from the beginning of each year.

	Pro Forma (unaudited) Year ended December 31,	
	1982	1981
	(In millions, except per share data)	
Net sales	$5,623.0	$5,097.2
Net income	299.0	233.4
Net income per share (fully diluted)	5.65	4.49

AMERICAN HOME PRODUCTS CORPORATION (DEC)

NOTES TO CONSOLIDATED FINANCIAL STATEMENTS

Note 2. In March, 1982, the Company acquired for $425,000,000 and expenses the Sherwood Medical Group of companies (Sherwood). The acquisition has been accounted for as a purchase; the excess of cost over the fair value of the net assets acquired was approximately $71,115,000 and is being amortized over 40 years on the straight-line method. Sherwood's results of operations since the acquisition date are included in the consolidated financial statements. The following table summarizes, on an unaudited pro-forma basis, the combined results of operations as though Sherwood had been acquired on January 1, 1982 and 1981 (in thousands of dollars except per share amounts):

	1982	1981
	---	---
Net sales	$4,627,574	$4,390,994
Net income	$ 555,568	$ 484,101
Net income per share	$ 3.56	$ 3.10

BAKER INTERNATIONAL CORPORATION (SEP)

NOTES TO CONSOLIDATED FINANCIAL STATEMENTS

2 (in part): Acquisitions:

Effective March 2, 1982, the Company acquired Envirotech Corporation, a manufacturer of mining and industrial processing machinery and equipment. The purchase price of $64,789,000 consisted of $13,688,000 in cash and 1,825,000 shares of Baker common stock with a market value of $51,101,000.

This acquisition has been accounted for as a purchase, and the results of operations of Envirotech have been included with those of the Company since the date of acquisi-

tion. The excess of the total acquisition cost over the fair value of net assets acquired was $75,404,000 and is being amortized on the straight-line basis over forty years.

The unaudited pro forma consolidated results of operations which follow assume that the merger had occurred as of October 1, 1980. The pro forma data do not include the results of operations discontinued by Envirotech prior to the March 2, 1982 acquisition date.

	Year Ended September 30,	
(In thousands of dollars except per share amounts)		
	1982	1981
Revenues	$2,679,530	$2,520,872
Net income	242,545	220,202
Net income per share	3.48	3.20

Prior to March 2, 1982, Envirotech discontinued operations in certain of its business segments. At the acquisition date, the Company provided for estimated future costs to be incurred in closing down these businesses and resolving customer claims. At September 30, 1982, these discontinued segments are included in the consolidated balance sheet as follows: other current assets, $22,500,000; other long-term assets, $5,100,000; other current liabilities, $30,400,000; and other long-term liabilities, $43,873,000.

BUCKBEE-MEARS COMPANY (DEC)

NOTES TO CONSOLIDATED FINANCIAL STATEMENTS

(in thousands, except share amounts)

2. Acquisitions

In June 1982, the Company acquired Camelot Industries Corporation ("Camelot"), a producer of optical products, for $13,500 in cash. The transaction has been accounted for as a purchase and the financial statements include the results of operation of Camelot from the date of purchase. The acquisition cost has been allocated to the acquired net assets based on their relative values. The excess of aggregate value of the acquired net assets over the acquisition cost was applied to noncurrent assets reducing them to zero. The remaining excess of $8,864 has been recorded as a deferred credit to be amortized into income on an accelerated basis over a period of five years. Included as a reduction of cost of products sold in the operating results for the year ended December 31, 1982 is $1,933 of amortization.

The following unaudited pro forma information shows the results of operations for the years ended December 31, 1982 and 1981 as though the purchase of Camelot were made at the beginning of each period presented. In addition to combining the historic results of Camelot with the Company, the pro forma calculations include adjustments for the estimated effect on Camelot's historical results of operations of certain changes in asset and liability values and additional interest expense as if debt incurred in connection with the purchase had been outstanding from the beginning of each period.

	1982	1981
	---	---
Revenues	$142,022	$141,378
Net Earnings	$ 5,889	$ 8,170
Earnings per Share	$1.73	$2.58

The pro forma financial information is not necessarily indicative either of results of operations that would have occurred had the purchase been made at the beginning of the period, or of future results of operations of the combined companies.

During the second quarter of 1982, the Company acquired three contact lens manufacturers for cash and notes payable and formed a subsidiary, the Vision-Ease Contact Lens Company. On September 1, 1981, a subsidiary of the Company acquired substantially all of the assets of Electronics Stamping Corporation, a California manufacturer of precision metal stampings and proprietary connector components, for cash and notes payable. These acquisitions, accounted for as purchases, did not have a material effect on operating results and financial position of the Company.

MARRIOTT CORPORATION (DEC)

NOTES TO CONSOLIDATED FINANCIAL STATE-MENTS

Acquisitions and Dispositions

In 1982, subsidiaries of the company acquired the outstanding common stock of Host International, Inc. (Host) and Gino's Inc. (Gino's) for cash. Both acquisitions were financed through the company's available revolving bank loan commitments and were accounted for as purchases. The aggregate purchase price and long-term liabilities assumed were $151,300,000 and $53,425,000 for Host and $48,119,000 and $64,606,000 for Gino's, respectively. Excess of cost over values assigned (goodwill) of $8,576,000 for Host is being amortized on a straight line basis over 40 years.

Host is a diversified company operating a number of airline terminals, specialty restaurants and retail merchandising facilities. In connection with the acquisition, the company honored option agreements granted by Host to DFS Group Limited and sold certain of Host's duty-free operations for $20,000,000 plus $11,857,000 for inventories. The results of operations for Host are included in the consolidated financial statements from the date of acquisition, March 3, 1982. Operating results of Host have been identified with the company's existing businesses and are included within the Contract Food Services and Restaurant segments. Summarized below are the unaudited pro forma consolidated results from continuing operations as if Host had been acquired at the beginning of 1981 (in thousands except per share amounts):

	1982	1981
Sales	$2,590,555	$2,294,448
Net Income	93,175	79,988
Earnings per share (fully diluted)	3.39	2.97

The above unaudited pro forma results of operations pertaining to the periods prior to the acquisition include adjustments to reflect the interest expense on borrowed funds used to finance the acquisition, additional depreciation on revalued purchased assets and the elimination of results from discontinued operations.

Gino's was a fast food and restaurant company acquired primarily to obtain prime real estate sites and to convert them into Roy Rogers Restaurants. Operating profits for Gino's are recorded as a reduction in the cost of units being converted to Roy Rogers. Gino's assets that will be sold have been recorded at their estimated net realizable value as of the acquisition date, February 5, 1982. By the end of 1983, the company plans to convert 175 of Gino's 540 restaurants into Roy Rogers and to sell a significant portion of the remaining Gino's restaurants and operations. On August 6, 1982, the company sold 69 Gino's units to KFC Corporation for $15,077,000. Additionally, an agreement in principle was signed on December 10, 1982 for the sale of 108 of Gino's Rustler Restaurants. Closing on the sale is anticipated in 1983.

"Assets from acquisitions held for sale" at fiscal year-end includes primarily Gino's restaurants to be disposed of, at net realizable value, net of related capital lease obligations of $27,357,000.

On March 9, 1982, the company sold its Farrell's Ice Cream Parlour Restaurant Division for $15,000,000 plus $1,886,000 for inventories. Farrell's sales and operating income for 1982 through the disposition date were $8,376,000 and $970,000 (including gain on sale) and were $50,531,000 and $3,646,000 for 1981, and $51,646,000 and $2,770,000 for 1980.

All Subsidiaries Consolidated

ALLIED STORES CORPORATION (JAN)

NOTES TO CONSOLIDATED FINANCIAL STATE-MENTS

Significant Accounting Policies (in part)

Principles of Consolidation: The consolidated financial statements of Allied Stores Corporation include the accounts of all the Corporation's subsidiaries, which are the merchandising subsidiaries, Allied Stores Credit Corporation and Alstores Realty Corporation. Condensed financial statements of the credit and real estate subsidiaries are presented on page 25.

AMERICAN STANDARD INC. (DEC)

NOTES TO FINANCIAL STATEMENTS

Note 1 (in part): Accounting Policies

Consolidation The financial statements include on a consolidated basis the results of all majority-owned operating subsidiaries. All material intercompany transactions are eliminated. Investments in associated companies are included at cost plus the Company's equity in their net income.

JAMES RIVER CORPORATION OF VIRGINIA

NOTES TO CONSOLIDATED FINANCIAL STATE-MENTS

1 (in part): Summary of Significant Accounting Policies:

A) Consolidation and Segment Reporting:

The accompanying financial statements include the accounts of James River Corporation of Virginia ("James River") and its subsidiaries (collectively, the "Company"), all of which are wholly-owned except James River-Pepperell, Inc. which is 80% owned. All material intercompany accounts and transactions are eliminated in consolidation.

The Company is predominantly engaged in one business segment: the development, manufacture and marketing of specialty and other papers.

NL INDUSTRIES, INC. (DEC)

SUMMARY OF ACCOUNTING POLICIES

Basis of Consolidation. The consolidated financial statements include the accounts of the Company and all majority-owned domestic and foreign subsidiaries. The effect of changes in companies included in the consolidation during the three years ended December 31, 1982 did not have a material effect on net income during such years.

The Company's investments in unconsolidated partially-owned domestic and foreign companies are stated at cost, adjusted for subsequent changes in equity. The Company includes in income its equity in the net income of such companies.

OUTBOARD MARINE CORPORATION

NOTES TO CONSOLIDATED FINANCIAL STATE-MENTS

(2) Basis of Consolidation

The accounts of all subsidiaries are included in the Consolidated Financial Statements. Intercompany accounts, transactions and earnings have been eliminated in consolidation. All subsidiary companies are wholly owned except Outboard Marine Australia Pty. Limited which is 75% owned; the minority interest in this subsidiary's earnings of $160,000, $451,000 and $669,000 in 1982, 1981 and 1980, respectively, is included in other expense in the Statement of Consolidated Earnings.

J.P. STEVENS & CO., INC.

NOTES TO FINANCIAL STATEMENTS

Note A—Summary of Significant Accounting Policies

Principles of Consolidation: The consolidated financial statements include the accounts of the Company and its subsidiaries, including the accounts of Children's Publishers Corporation from April 16, 1981, Stevens Color Concepts Inc. from April 28, 1981 and Oxmoor Press Inc. from February 29, 1980, the dates of acquisition. The three aforementioned companies are printing companies; the assets (net of certain liabilities) of which were acquired by purchase. In 1980, the Company sold substantially all the assets of one foreign subsidiary and a 50% interest in another foreign subsidiary. These transactions did not have a material effect on the consolidated financial statements.

Intercompany items and transactions have been eliminated in consolidation.

All Significant Subsidiaries Consolidated

AMERADA HESS CORPORATION (DEC)

NOTES TO CONSOLIDATED FINANCIAL STATE-MENTS

1 (in part): Summary of Significant Accounting Policies

Principles of Consolidation: The consolidated financial statements include the accounts of Amerada Hess Corporation and all significant subsidiaries (the "Corporation").

Investments in affiliated companies owned 20% to 50% inclusive, are stated at cost of acquisition plus the Corporation's equity in undistributed net income since acquisition.

The change in the equity in net income of these affiliated companies is included in other revenues in the Statement of Consolidated Income.

Inter-company items are eliminated in consolidation.

BEATRICE FOODS CO. (FEB)

NOTES TO CONSOLIDATED FINANCIAL STATE-MENTS

1: Summary of Significant Accounting Policies

Principles of Consolidation—The consolidated financial statements include all significant majority owned subsidiaries. Intercompany transactions and balances have been eliminated in consolidation. Investments in 20% to 50% owned companies and joint ventures (affiliated companies) are carried on the equity method. Subsidiaries operating outside the United States are included on the basis of fiscal years generally ending on December 31.

COLLINS & AIKMAN CORPORATION (FEB)

NOTES TO CONSOLIDATED FINANCIAL STATE-MENTS

(dollar amounts in thousands, except per share data)

1 (in part): Accounting Policies

Basis of consolidation

The consolidated financial statements include the accounts of all domestic and Canadian subsidiaries. The Company's European subsidiaries, which are not material, are accounted for on an equity basis. All intercompany transactions and profits have been eliminated.

MINNESOTA MINING AND MANUFACTURING COMPANY (DEC)

NOTES TO FINANCIAL STATEMENTS

Accounting Policies (in part)

Consolidation: All significant subsidiaries are consolidated. Subsidiaries outside the United States are included in consolidation on the basis of their fiscal years ended October 31. Unconsolidated affiliates are included on the equity basis.

PIONEER HI-BRED INTERNATIONAL, INC. (AUG)

NOTES TO FINANCIAL STATEMENTS

Note 1 (in part): Significant Accounting Policies

Principles of consolidation:

The consolidated financial statements include the accounts of the Company, its wholly-owned domestic subsidiaries and its Canadian subsidiaries. All significant intercompany balances and transactions have been eliminated in consolidation.

The Company carries its investment in thirteen foreign subsidiaries, which in the aggregate do not constitute a significant subsidiary, at cost plus (less) equity in undistributed net income (loss).

Finance-Related Subsidiaries Not Consolidated

AMERICAN BRANDS, INC. (DEC)

SUMMARY OF SIGNIFICANT ACCOUNTING POLICIES

Principles of Consolidation:

The consolidated financial statements include the accounts of the Company and all subsidiaries other than The Franklin Life Insurance Company, a wholly owned subsidiary, which is accounted for by the equity method. Fiscal year-ends of certain subsidiaries of Gallaher Limited range from September 30 to November 30 to facilitate Gallaher's year-end closing.

The 1981 and 1980 consolidated statements of changes in financial position have been restated to conform to the 1982 presentation.

ARCHER DANIELS MIDLAND COMPANY (JUN)

SUMMARY OF SIGNIFICANT ACCOUNTING POLICIES

Principles of Consolidation:

The consolidated financial statements include the accounts of the Company and all majority-owned subsidiaries except ADM Leasco, Inc. (see Note 11). Investments in ADM Leasco, Inc. and 50%-owned companies are carried at cost plus equity in undistributed earnings since acquisition.

NOTES TO CONSOLIDATED FINANCIAL STATEMENTS

Note 11—ADM Leasco, Inc.

The Company's wholly-owned leasing subsidiary, ADM Leasco, Inc., is engaged primarily in leasing transportation equipment within the United States. At June 30, 1982, ADM Leasco, Inc. had equipment with a net book value of approximately $53,000,000 and long-term debt of approximately $50,000,000. Annual operating income during each of the three years ended June 30, 1982 approximated $8,000,000 and earnings, which were not material, are included in other income.

THE BENDIX CORPORATION (OCT)

NOTES TO CONSOLIDATED FINANCIAL STATEMENTS

Summary of Significant Accounting Policies (in part)

CONSOLIDATED FINANCIAL STATEMENTS AND RELATED MATTERS—The consolidated financial statements comprise those of the Corporation and all of its subsidiaries, except for a finance subsidiary. The equity method of accounting is used for the finance subsidiary and for other investments in nonconsolidated companies where the Corporation is able to exercise significant influence over operating and financial policies.

The financial statements of subsidiaries outside the U.S. and Canada generally are included in the consolidated financial statements on the basis of fiscal years ending August 31. Certain amounts for years prior to 1982 have been reclassified for comparative purposes.

THE DOW CHEMICAL COMPANY (DEC)

SUMMARY OF SIGNIFICANT ACCOUNTING POLICIES

CONSOLIDATION—The accompanying consolidated financial statements include the assets, liabilities, revenues and expenses of all significant subsidiaries except for banks and insurance companies. Because of the nature of their operations, the accounts of these companies are not consolidated. However, their earnings are included in consolidated net income under the equity method of accounting.

THE FIRESTONE TIRE & RUBBER COMPANY (OCT)

NOTES TO FINANCIAL STATEMENTS

Significant Accounting Policies (in part)

Principles of consolidation—The financial statements include the accounts of all significant subsidiaries in which the Company owns 50 percent or more of the voting stock, except Firestone Credit Corporation (FCC), a wholly-owned subsidiary which is accounted for based on the equity method. Pre-tax income of FCC is included in the Statements of Income as a reduction of interest and debt expense and the income taxes thereon are included in income taxes.

Intercompany accounts and transactions of consolidated subsidiaries have been eliminated in consolidation.

Investments in companies in which ownership interests range from 20% to 50% and the Company exercises significant influence over operating and financial policies are accounted for on the equity method. Other investments are accounted for on the cost method.

PORTEC, INC. (DEC)

NOTES TO CONSOLIDATED FINANCIAL STATEMENTS

Note 1 (in part): Accounting Policies

Consolidation—The consolidated financial statements include the accounts of all subsidiaries except Portec Lease Corp., which is accounted for under the equity method of accounting. Portec Lease Corp. is a lease financing subsidiary which is 100% owned by the Company. Condensed financial information for Portec Lease Corp. is shown in Note 4. The United Kingdom subsidiary is consolidated on the basis of a November 30 fiscal year.

Note 4. Investments in and Advances to Portec Lease Corp.

Investment in and advances to Portec Lease Corp. at December 31, 1982 and 1981, were $13,588,000 and $5,432,000, respectively. The Company's equity in net income from Portec Lease Corp. for 1982, 1981 and 1980, was $1,000,0000, $537,000 and $628,000, respectively.

Condensed financial information for Portec Lease Corp. as of December 31, is as follows:

Condensed Balance Sheet

	1982	1981
	(In thousands of dollars)	
Assets		
Cash and marketable securities	$ 8,331	$ 154
Receivables under lease contract—net	3,825	2,331
Notes receivable	541	1,083
Investment in leveraged leases...................	2,398	531
Equipment under operating leases—net	9,886	6,436
Other assets.......................................	131	92
	$25,112	$10,627
Liabilities and Stockholders' Equity		
Amounts payable to Parent......................	$ 3,001	$ 1,284
Other liabilities....................................	56	58
Deferred income taxes	2,054	853
Advances from Parent............................	7,156	—
Revolving credit agreement......................	3,300	3,000
Long-term debt....................................	3,113	—
Total Liabilities................................	18,680	5,195
Stockholders' equity		
Common stock, $100 par value authorized 60,000 shares 40,000 shares issued and outstanding....................................	4,000	4,000
Retained earnings.................................	2,432	1,432
	6,432	5,432
	$25,112	$10,627

Condensed Statements of Income year ended December 31,

	1982	1981	1980
	(In thousands of dollars)		
Revenues	$1,794	$845	$597
Expenses			
Interest	956	324	31
Depreciation.............................	588	321	151
General and administrative	233	193	78
	1,777	838	260
Income before income taxes........................	17	7	337
Income taxes and investment tax credits—net ...	(983)	(530)	(291)
Net income	$1,000	$537	$628

Business: Portec Lease Corp. is a wholly owned subsidiary of Portec, Inc. which leases and finances to third parties, equipment manufactured by divisions of the Parent and outside suppliers.

Portec Lease Corp.'s balance sheet, in accordance with industry practice, does not classify the assets and liabilities as current or noncurrent.

Foreign Subsidiaries Not Consolidated

HARNISCHFEGER CORPORATION (OCT)

FINANCIAL NOTES

Note 1 (in part): Summary of Significant Accounting Policies

Consolidation—The consolidated financial statements include the accounts of all majority-owned subsidiaries except a wholly-owned domestic finance subsidiary, a subsidiary organized in 1982 as a temporary successor to a distributor, both of which are accounted for under the equity method, and a wholly-owned Brazilian subsidiary, which is carried at estimated net realizable value due to economic uncertainty. A 9% investment in an associated company is accounted for under the equity method. Intercompany transactions have been eliminated in the consolidated financial statements.

Financial statements of certain consolidated subsidiaries, principally foreign, are included on the basis of their fiscal years ending July 31 through September 30. Such fiscal periods have been adopted by the subsidiaries in order to provide for a timely consolidation with the Corporation.

Other Nonconsolidated Subsidiaries

COLT INDUSTRIES INC (DEC)

NOTES TO FINANCIAL STATEMENTS

1 (in part): Summary of Accounting Policies

Principles of Consolidation—Investments in which the company's ownership of common voting stock is over 50 percent are consolidated in the financial statements except for its finance business and Colt Canada Inc which are accounted for on the equity basis. The finance business is not consolidated since its operations are not similar to the operations of the consolidated group. Colt Canada Inc is not consolidated due to its pending sale early in 1983. Investments in which the company has stock ownership of at least 20 percent but not over 50 percent are accounted for on the equity basis. Intercompany accounts and transactions are eliminated.

A.E. STALEY MANUFACTURING COMPANY (SEP)

SUMMARY OF ACCOUNTING POLICIES

Principles of Consolidation

The consolidated financial statements include the accounts of the Company and all subsidiaries which are more than 50% owned, except for the Company's wholly owned commodity futures trading subsidiary. All material intercompany transactions have been eliminated.

Investments in the commodity futures trading subsidiary and in affiliates 50% or less owned are accounted for by the equity method and are referred to as equity companies. The consolidated financial statements include in net earnings the Company's share of the net earnings of equity companies, and the Company's investments in such companies are stated at cost plus equity in undistributed net earnings.

Effective with 1982, the Company adopted Financial Accounting Standards Board Statement No. 52 for translating foreign currency in accounting for its foreign subsidiaries and equity companies.

FOREIGN CURRENCY TRANSLATION

Effective for fiscal years beginning on or after December 15, 1982, FASB *Statement of Financial Accounting Standards No. 52* will supersede FASB *Statement of Financial Accounting Standards No. 8* as the authoritative pronouncement on foreign currency translation. *SFAS No. 52* requires translation adjustments to be reported separately and accumulated in a separate component of equity; whereas, *SFAS No. 8* requires translation adjustments to be included in determining net income. Table 1-8 shows that 309 survey companies (142 in 1981 and 167 in 1982) disclosed early compliance with *SFAS No. 52*. Examples of foreign currency translation disclosures follow.

ALUMINUM COMPANY OF AMERICA (DEC)

NOTES TO FINANCIAL STATEMENTS
(In millions)

D. Accounting Change–Foreign Currency Translation

In 1982 Alcoa adopted Statement of Financial Accounting Standards No. 52, Foreign Currency Translation. For the company's significant foreign operations, the U.S. dollar continues to be the functional currency under the new standard. Retroactive application of this standard would not have been material to Alcoa's 1981 and 1980 results.

The following table is an analysis of the translation adjustment component of shareholders' equity at December 31, 1982.

Translation adjustment as of January 1, 1982	$ 1,7
Translation adjustments during the year	(15.9)
Income tax effect	7.3
Translation adjustment at December 31, 1982	$ (6.9)

Foreign currency transaction gains (losses) included in net income follows.

	1982	1981	1980
Consolidated companies	$ 2.1	$ 7.5	$ .9
Equity companies:			
Alcoa of Australia	9.5	1.0	1.3
Other	(7.1)	(3.9)	(4.0)
	$ 4.5	$ 4.6	$(1.8)

BORG-WARNER CORPORATION (DEC)

NOTES TO FINANCIAL STATEMENTS

Operations Outside the United States

Borg-Warner's equity in net earnings of consolidated subsidiaries outside the U.S. was $29.9 million in 1982, a net loss of $3.3 million in 1981 and net earnings of $2.7 million in 1980.

Borg-Warner's equity in the net assets of these companies at December 31 is summarized as follows:

(millions of dollars)	1982	1981	1980
Current assets	$308.7	$352.9	$302.3
Non-current assets	156.6	155.7	207.0
Total assets	465.3	508.6	509.3
Current liabilities	162.2	152.6	138.3
Non-current liabilities	93.9	132.8	120.6
Net assets before minority interests	209.2	223.2	250.4
Minority interests	24.2	23.8	20.9
Borg-Warner's equity in net assets	$185.0	$199.4	$229.5

In 1981, Borg-Warner consolidated the majority of its Mexican and South American subsidiaries. Borg-Warner's equity in underlying net assets of its Mexican and South American subsidiaries at December 31, 1980, translated at the exchange rate in effect at year-end, exceeded the carrying value of these companies by $13.0 million.

Consolidated net earnings include foreign exchange charges of $5.4 million in 1982 resulting primarily from the recognition of Mexico as a hyperinflationary economy. Net losses of consolidated Mexican operations were not material. Foreign exchange charges of $5.2 million were included in consolidated earnings for 1980.

Current translation adjustment

In 1981 Borg-Warner Corporation adopted Statement of Financial Accounting Standards No. 52, whereby adjustments resulting from the translation of foreign currency financial statements are excluded from the determination of income and accumulated in a separate component of shareholders' equity. Following is an analysis of the change in the currency translation adjustment for the years ended December 31:

(millions of dollars)	1982	1981
Currency translation adjustment at January 1	$(14.0)	$15.8
Current translation adjustments and net asset hedges	(24.5)	(26.7)
Amounts allocated to income tax liabilities	(2.0)	(3.1)
Currency translation adjustment at December 31	$(40.5)	$(14.0)

The currency translation effect on working capital included in the Statement of Changes in Financial Position reflects the net effect of currency translation resulting from the application of FASB Statement 52 to the elements of the balance sheet.

ELI LILLY AND COMPANY (DEC)

Consolidated Statements of Income and Retained Earnings

	1982	1981	1980
		(Dollars in thousands)	
Net sales	$2,962,711	$2,773,205	$2,558,637
Operating costs and expenses:			
Manufacturing costs of products sold	1,129,094	1,083,734	1,023,515
Research and development	267,365	234,809	200,700
Marketing	561,129	507,516	463,756
Shipping	58,343	58,657	57,736
General administrative	275,842	271,880	247,623
	2,291,773	2,156,596	1,993,330
Operating Income	670,938	616,609	565,307
Other income (deductions):			
Interest income	50,212	58,070	39,560
Interest expense	(40,055)	(45,450)	(35,595)
Interest expense capitalized	13,365	23,276	17,153
Foreign exchange losses	(18,495)	(25,209)	(14,008)
Other—net	8,192	18,694	17,924
Income Before Taxes	684,157	645,990	590,341

NOTES TO CONSOLIDATED FINANCIAL STATEMENTS

Accounting Change

Foreign Currency Translation: Effective January 1, 1981, the Company adopted the provisions of Financial Accounting Standards Board Statement No. 52. In the application of this Statement, exchange adjustments resulting from foreign currency transactions generally are recognized currently in income, whereas adjustments resulting from translation of financial statements generally are reflected as a separate component of shareholders' equity. This accounting change had the effect of increasing net income for 1981 by $13 million ($.17 per share). The effect on net income for 1980 would not have been material. An analysis of currency translation adjustments reflected in shareholders' equity is shown on page 37.

Currency Translation Adjustments

Following is an analysis of currency translation adjustments reflected in shareholders' equity:

	1982	1981
	(Thousands)	
Balance (negative amount) at January 1.......	$(45,663)	$ (5,708)
Translation adjustments and gains and losses from hedging and intercompany transactions	(43,470)	(40,712)
Allocated income taxes.........................	4,273	757
Balance at December 31.....................	$(84,860)	$(45,663)

JOHNSON & JOHNSON (DEC)

NOTES TO CONSOLIDATED FINANCIAL STATE-MENTS

Note 4. Foreign Currency Translation

In 1981, the Company adopted FAS No. 52, Foreign Currency Translation, which replaced FAS No. 8. The financial statements for 1980 have not been restated for the change as the effect of FAS No. 52 in that year was immaterial. Under FAS No. 8, net earnings would have been reduced by $58.6 million or $.32 per share in 1981. Net currency transaction gains and losses included in net earnings were a gain of $4.6 million in 1982 and losses of $.7 million and $.1 million in 1981 and 1980.

Under FAS No. 52, balance sheet currency effects are recorded in a separate component of stockholders' equity. This equity account includes the results of translating all balance sheet assets and liabilities at current exchange rates except for those located in highly inflationary economies, principally Argentina, Brazil, Colombia and Mexico.

An analysis of the changes during 1982 and 1981 in the separate component of stockholders' equity for cumulative currency translation adjustments follows:

(Dollars in Millions)	1982	1981
Beginning of year......................................	$ (85.7)	(5.0)
Translation adjustments	(76.8)	(78.6)
Income taxes allocated to translation adjustments	(1.0)	(2.1)
End of year...	$(163.5)	(85.7)

Translation adjustments relate primarily to inventories and property, plant and equipment and do not exist in terms of functional currency cash flows. FAS No. 52 provides that these translation adjustments should not be reported as part of operating results since realization is remote unless such international businesses were sold or liquidated.

NL INDUSTRIES, INC. (DEC)

SUMMARY OF ACCOUNTING POLICIES

Translation of Foreign Currencies: In 1982, the Company adopted FAS No. 52 (Foreign Currency Translation) which replaces FAS No. 8. Accordingly, since January 1, 1982, the balance sheets of foreign subsidiaries have been translated at year end rates of exchange and income statements at weighted average rates of exchange, a change from FAS No. 8 which required translation of fixed assets and related de-

preciation, inventories, cost of sales and applicable deferred income tax accruals at historical rates of exchange. In addition, gains and losses from translation, certain intercompany balances, hedging net foreign investments and their related tax effects have been accumulated in a separate section of shareholders' equity which, in prior years, were included in net income. These changes apply to all foreign entities except those in highly inflationary economies, for which translation rules remain essentially unchanged and which are not material.

NOTES TO FINANCIAL STATEMENTS

3: Foreign Exchange

Effective January 1982, the Company adopted FAS No. 52 (See Summary of Accounting Policies). Foreign currency exchange gains and losses included in the determinations of income for the years 1982, 1981 and 1980 were as follows:

	1982	1981	1980
		(in thousands)	
Transaction gains	$321	$1,174	$2,241
Translation gains.........................	—	4,892	1,207
Included in other income	321	6,066	3,448
Effects of translating fixed assets, depreciation and inventories at historical rates of exchange (included in cost of sales)...........................		(14,887)	(1,674)
	$321	$(8,821)	$1,774

The impact of adopting the new method of 1982 is estimated to have increased net income $13,000,000 ($.20 per share of common stock).

The changes in the "Translation Adjustments" component of shareholders' equity during 1982 were as follows:

(in thousands)	1982
Balance at January 1, 1982...................................	$ (319)
Translation adjustments, gains (losses) from hedging and certain intercompany balances	(29,286)
Income taxes related to hedges and intercompany balances	433
Balance at end of year......................................	$(29,172)

OWENS-CORNING FIBERGLAS CORPORATION (DEC)

Consolidated Statement of Income

	1982	1981	1980
	(In thousands of dollars)		
Costs and Expenses:			
Cost of sales	$1,888,551	$1,924,535	$1,851,734
Marketing and administrative expenses	293,733	285,750	251,060
Science and technology expenses	72,479	67,697	58,278
Cost of borrowed funds	32,808	37,041	32,715
Cash discounts	20,576	21,142	20,553
State and local income and franchise taxes	5,214	4,855	6,845
Foreign currency exchange (gain) loss (Note 3)	5,836	(2,768)	164
Gain on sale of investment in affiliates....	—	(4,665)	—
Gain on repurchase of debt	(3,910)	(1,064)	(939)
Other	46,404	21,093	38,604
	$2,361,691	$2,353,616	$2,259,014

Consolidated Statement of Stockholders' Equity

	1982	1981	1980
	(In thousands of dollars)		
Common Stock			
Balance Beginning of Year........	$120,552	$119,818	$117,167
Add:			
Proceeds from issuance of shares under stock option plan	257	690	2,464
Tax benefits arising from employees' disqualifying disposition of common stock purchased under stock option plan	12	44	187
Balance End of Year	$120,821	$120,552	$119,818
Retained Earnings			
Balance Beginning of Year........	$653,035	$639,957	$622,339
Add—Net income for the year ...	29,686	49,849	54,321
Deduct—Cash dividends declared on common stock ($1.20 per share).............................	36,787	36,771	36,703
Balance End of Year	$645,934	$653,035	$639,957
Foreign Currency Translation Adjustments (Note 3)			
Initial adjustment January 1, 1982	$ (4,946)	$ —	$ —
Current year effect of translation adjustments (net of income taxes of $1,469,000)..........	(9,080)	—	—
Balance End of Year	$(14,026)	$ —	$ —
Treasury Stock			
Purchase of 3,000,000 common shares at cost	$(97,888)	$ —	$ —
Stockholders' Equity	$654,841	$773,587	$759,775

SUMMARY OF SIGNIFICANT ACCOUNTING POLICIES

Foreign Operations

Accounts of foreign subsidiaries and affiliates are maintained in the currencies of the countries in which they operate and beginning January 1982 are translated into U.S. dollars in conformity with FASB Statement 52. Years prior to 1982 are translated into U.S. dollars in conformity with FASB Statement 8.

Forward exchange contracts are purchased to hedge against currency fluctuations affecting operations of certain foreign subsidiaries. Realized and unrealized gains and losses on these contracts are recorded in income currently except that gains and losses on contracts to hedge specific foreign currency commitments are deferred and accounted for as part of the commitment transaction.

NOTES TO CONSOLIDATED FINANCIAL STATEMENTS

3: Foreign Currency Translations and Exchange Loss

The accounts of foreign subsidiaries and affiliates are translated in accordance with FASB Statement 8 for 1981 and 1980. If 1981 and 1980 had been translated in accordance with FASB Statement 52, net income and earnings per share would have been $42,314,000 and $1.38 in 1981, and $53,288,000 and $1.74 in 1980 respectively. The adjustment as of January 1, 1982, to reflect the conversion to FASB Statement 52 is a reduction of stockholders' equity of $4,946,000.

During the fourth quarter of 1982, losses due to unauthorized speculation in foreign currency contracts were detected which reduced 1982 net income by $5,800,000, or $.19 per share.

UNIROYAL, INC. (DEC)

NOTES TO CONSOLIDATED FINANCIAL STATEMENTS

Translation of Foreign Currencies

In 1981 the company adopted Statement of Financial Accounting Standards No. 52, "Foreign Currency Translation," which generally provides for the exclusion of foreign exchange translation adjustments from net income and requires the use of current exchange rates for translating the foreign currency denominated financial position and the results of operations in countries which are not considered to be highly inflationary. The company has subsidiary or affiliate operations of varying significance in Argentina, Brazil, Colombia and Mexico which are considered to be highly inflationary economies and, therefore, the translation procedures applicable to these operations generally remained unchanged. The effect of the adoption on 1980 net income was not considered significant and, therefore, 1980 was not restated.

An analysis of the change in accumulated translation adjustment follows:

	1982	1981
	In thousands	
Beginning balance	$(24,631)	(6,809)
Translation adjustments and gains and losses from certain hedges	(14,084)	(17,996)
Applicable income taxes	(205)	174)
Realization of losses applicable to divestments	4,232	—
Ending balance	$(34,688)	(24,631)

Other income, net consisted of:

	1982	1981	1980
	In thousands		
Interest income	$15,441	16,636	15,189
Equity in net income of affiliated companies.................................	2,644	8,588	7,203
Dividends and stock redemptions from PASA...................................	1,952	1,181	3,364
Royalty income...........................	2,227	2,784	2,952
Gain on sale of assets	2,668	166	10,199
Gain on Monochem and Rubicon restructing	24,568	—	—
Minority interest.........................	549	391	(2,160)
Foreign exchange........................	(2,868)	(1,441)	3,295
Other	3,430	(508)	(834)
Total	$50,611	27,797	39,208

Equity Method

DOW JONES & COMPANY, INC.

Consolidated Balance Sheets

December 31, 1982 and 1981

	1982	1981
Total current assets	$166,906	$150,246
Investments in Associated Companies, at equity (Note 4)...............................	126,019	126,274

Consolidated Statements of Income
For the years ended December 31, 1982, 1981 and 1980

(in thousands except per share amounts)	1982	1981	1980
Other Income (Deductions):			
Investment income	$5,970	$10,958	$7,900
Interest expense	(6,282)	(1,884)	(1,514)
Equity in earnings of associated companies (Note 4)	5,549	6,575	2,724
Gain on disposition of investments	4,239	—	3,812
Write-down of excess of cost over net assets of businesses acquired	(1,800)	(9,400)	—
Other, net	(563)	185	1,580

Note 4. Investments in Associated Companies

Investments comprise ownership interests which are accounted for by the equity method.

In November and December 1981, the company invested $78,675,000 for a 24.5% interest in Continental Cablevision, Inc., the country's 10th largest cable TV operator. At December 31, 1981, $20,495,000 of the purchase price was payable to former stockholders and was included in the Balance Sheet caption "Other Payables." The company's interest was increased to 24.7% as a result of a capital change by Continental Cablevision in 1982.

In August and September 1981, the company invested $8,581,000 for a 20.1% interest in Press-Enterprise Company of Riverside, California. The company publishes the morning Enterprise, the evening Press and the Sunday Press-Enterprise.

During the three years ended December 31, 1982 the company has invested an additional $12,885,000 in Bear Island Paper Company in which the company has a 33.3% interest.

In November 1980 the company sold its interest in 25% of the outstanding stock of Extel Corporation and in February 1982 sold the remaining 10% for gains, net of income taxes, of $2,000,000 and $713,000, respectively.

The operating results of the principal associated companies accounted for by the equity method have been included in the accompanying consolidated financial statements on the following basis:

	% of Ownership	Twelve Months Ended
Bear Island Paper Company.......	33.3	December 31, 1982 and 7 months ended December 31, 1981
	30	5 months ended May 31, 1981 December 31, 1980
Continental Cablevision, Inc. ...	24.7	9 months ended September 30, 1982
Extel Corporation	35	11 months ended October 31, 1980
F.F. Soucy Inc. and Partners ..	40	December 31

The excess cost of the investments over the applicable net assets is approximately $65 million, net of amortization, which is reflected in the investment account.

Market quotations are not available for any of the aforementioned investments.

Summarized financial information pertaining to major equity investments was as follows:

Continental Cablevision, Inc.
(unaudited) for the years ended September 30:

(in thousands)	1982	1981	1980
Income Statements:			
Revenues	$ 98,680	$ 65,685	$ 43,195
Operating income before depreciation and amortization .	37,405	27,392	19,553
Net income	11,067	3,784	4,655
Balance Sheets:			
Property, plant and equipment, net of accumulated depreciation............................	$186,996	$120,394	
Other assets.....................	49,484	36,818	
	236,480	157,212	
Less:			
Debt.............................	129,389	114,154	
Other liabilities.................	27,050	22,367	
Shareholders' equity...............	$ 80,041	$ 20,691	

F.F. Soucy Inc. and Partners (Soucy) and Bear Island Paper Company (Bear Island), operators of newsprint mills, for the years ended December 31:

(in thousands)	1982	1981	1980
Soucy Income Statements:			
Net sales	$ 45,453	$ 50,154	$ 45,381
Operating income	15,289	19,140	17,059
Net income	12,056	15,336	14,277
Bear Island Income Statements:			
Net sales	$ 68,382	$ 63,540	$ 41,672
Operating income (loss)	6,662	5,133	(7,052)
Net (loss)	(1,864)	(3,748)	(15,527)
Combined Balance Sheets:			
Current assets, principally cash, accounts receivable and inventories	$ 36,211	$ 28,829	
Property, plant and equipment, net of accumulated depreciation............................	167,997	174,042	
	204,208	202,871	
Less:			
Current liabilities, principally notes and accounts payable and accrued expenses.......	28,309	19,252	
Long-term debt.................	78,985	88,547	
Partners' equity and loan capital .	$ 96,914	$ 95,072	

INTERNATIONAL MULTIFOODS CORPORATION

Consolidated Balance Sheets

February 28, 1982 and 1981 (dollars in thousands)	1982	1981
Other assets:		
Intangibles, less accumulated amortization, $3,126 in 1982; $2,841 in 1981	$16,812	$17,387
Investments in affiliated companies (page 21) .	11,329	12,835
Miscellaneous receivables and other assets....	19,549	14,305
Total other assets	$47,690	$44,527

Consolidated Statements of Earnings

Three years ended February 28, 1982
(dollars in thousands
except amounts per share)

	1982	1981	1980
Costs and expenses, net:			
Cost of sales	$ 952,004	$ 910,881	$849,315
Selling, general and administrative expenses .	138,206	122,211	109,539
Interest expense	16,580	17,123	14,383
Other income, net (page 17)	(10,286)	(6,166)	(3,885)
Total	$1,096,504	$1,044,049	$969,352

Other income (expense) is as follows (in thousands):

	1982	1981	1980
Interest income	$ 4,443	$2,824	$2,228
Equity in earnings of unconsolidated affiliates	4,523	2,162	1,657
Foreign exchange	299	1,295	(139)
Gain on property disposals, net	1,241	51	583
Other......................................	(220)	(166)	(444)
Total	$10,286	$6,166	$3,885

Investments in 20-50 percent owned unconsolidated affiliates at February 28, 1982, which are accounted for by the equity method, consist of:

Mexicana de Inversiones Femac, SA. de C.V. (Mexico)	45%
Misr Food Company (Egypt)	25%
Kinsman Lines, Inc. (U.S.)	25%

Summarized financial information for the unconsolidated affiliates as at February 28, 1982 and 1981 and for the three years ended February 28, 1982 is as follows (in thousands):

	1982	1981	1980
Current assets	$ 29,505	$27,592	
Noncurrent assets	6,894	8,504	
Current liabilities	(11,362)	(11,805)	
Noncurrent liabilities	(3,917)	(989)	
Net assets	$ 21,120	$23,302	
Net sales	$145,680	$90,333	$84,841
Cost of sales	115,031	73,423	70,290
Net earnings	13,110	4,804	3,682
Multifoods' equity in net earnings	$ 4,523*	$ 2,162	$ 1,657
Multifoods' equity in undistributed earnings	$ 7,761	$ 8,205	$ 6,043
Dividends received by Multifoods	$ 452	—	—
Intangibles included in Multifoods' consolidated assets........................	$ 931	$ 1,372	—

*Includes provision for loss on disposal of joint venture in Brazil.

EXXON CORPORATION

Consolidated Balance Sheet

(Millions of Dollars)

	Dec 31, 1981	Dec 31, 198
Total current assets	$23,242	$19,79
Investments and advances	1,643	1,714
Property, plant and equipment, at cost, less accumulated depreciation and depletion of $17,519 and $19,127.	35,285	38,98.
Other assets, including intangibles	1,404	1,79
Total assets	$61,574	$62,28

Consolidated Statement of Income and Earnings Reinvested

(Millions of Dollars)

Revenue	1980	1981	198.
Sales and other operating revenue, including excise taxes....	$108,412	$113,220	$102,05
Earnings from equity interests and other revenue	1,778	1,702	1,49
	$110,190	$114,922	$103,55

NOTES TO FINANCIAL STATEMENTS

1 (in part): Summary of Accounting Policies

Principles of consolidation The consolidated financia statements include the accounts of those significant sub sidiaries owned directly or indirectly more than 50 percent.

Amounts representing the corporation's percentage inter est in the underlying net assets of less than majority-owned companies in which a significant equity ownership interest is held are included in "Investments and advances." The corpo ration's share of the net income of these companies is in cluded in the consolidated statement of income caption "Earnings from equity interests and other revenue."

Investments in all other less than majority-owned com panies, none of which is significant, are included in "Invest ments and advances" at cost or less. Dividends from these companies are included in income as received.

3. Equity Company Information

The summarized financial information below includes those less than majority-owned companies, except Aramco for which Exxon's share of net income is included in consoli dated net income (see Note 1, page 25). Exxon's earnings from these companies consist in large part of earnings from natural gas production and distribution companies in the Netherlands and West Germany.

These data exclude Aramco, in which the government o Saudi Arabia acquired during 1980 the beneficial interest ir substantially all of the assets and operations. Aramco con tinues to have access to a significant volume of Saudi Ara bian crude oil. Exxon's share of earnings of Aramco, after application of adjustments related to crude oil purchased totaled $205 million, $244 million and $62 million in 1980. 1981 and 1982, respectively.

	1980 Total	1980 Exxon share	1981 Total	1981 Exxon share	1982 Total	1982 Exxon share
			(millions of dollars)			
Total revenues, of which 16%, 15% and 15% in 1980, 1981 and 1982, respectively, were from companies included in the Exxon consolidation	$20,574	$6,395	$24,166	$7,416	$21,999	$6,816
Earnings before income taxes	$ 3,647	$1,634	$ 4,145	$1,825	$ 3,694	$1,660
Less: Related income taxes	(1,706)	(765)	(1,986)	(864)	(1,740)	(777)
Earnings	1,941	869	2,159	961	1,954	883
Less: Interest expense	(408)	(131)	(761)	(238)	(510)	(169)
Related income taxes on interest expense	333	109	367	113	227	74
Net income	$ 1,866	$ 847	$ 1,765	$ 836	$ 1,671	$ 788
Current assets	$ 7,489	$2,561	$ 8,220	$2,752	$ 7,401	$2,476
Property, plant and equipment, less accumulated depreciation	6,111	2,267	5,830	2,213	5,907	2,327
Other long-term assets	424	165	512	209	610	261
Total assets	14,024	4,993	14,562	5,174	13,918	5,064
Short-term debt	3,060	1,001	2,921	951	2,968	964
Other current liabilities	4,735	1,789	5,387	1,983	4,675	1,739
Long-term debt	2,623	844	2,509	807	2,387	832
Other long-term liabilities	807	314	999	409	999	417
Net assets	$ 2,799	$1,045	$ 2,746	$1,024	$ 2,889	$1,112

LEE ENTERPRISES, INCORPORATED

Consolidated Balance Sheets

	September 30, 1982	1981	1980
Total current assets	$45,201,000	$36,643,000	$26,814,000
Investments, associated companies (Note 2)	$18,128,000	$18,429,000	$16,638,000

Consolidated Statements of Income

	Years Ended September 30, 1982	1981	1980
Operating Revenue:			
Newspaper advertising	$ 76,923,000	$ 75,066,000	$ 67,785,000
Newspaper circulation	26,944,000	24,809,000	21,827,000
Broadcasting	43,205,000	39,124,000	35,512,000
Associated companies (Note 2):			
Editorial service and management fees	6,394,000	6,004,000	5,172,000
Equity in net income	3,074,000	4,217,000	2,945,000
Other	4,040,000	3,841,000	3,717,000
	$160,580,000	$153,061,000	$136,958,000

NOTES TO CONSOLIDATED FINANCIAL STATEMENTS

Note 1 (in part): Significant Accounting Policies

Investments in Associated Companies:

Investments in the common stock of associated companies are reported at cost plus the Company's share of undistributed earnings since acquisition, less amortization of goodwill.

Note 2. Investments in Associated Companies

The Company has an effective 50% ownership interest in NAPP Systems (USA) Inc., a manufacturer of specialized graphic products, and three newspaper publishing companies operating at Lincoln, Nebraska (Journal-Star Printing Co.), Madison, Wisconsin (Madison Newspapers, Inc.) and Bismarck, North Dakota (Bismarck Tribune Company).

Summarized financial information of these companies is as follows:

Combined Associates	1982	1981	1980
Assets			
Current assets	$ 31,826,000	$ 27,604,000	$31,768,000
Investments and other assets	2,980,000	2,782,000	1,605,000
Property and equipment, net	26,222,000	27,924,000	29,585,000
	$ 61,028,000	$ 58,310,000	$62,958,000
Liabilities and Stockholders' Equity			
Current liabilities	$ 24,877,000	$ 20,789,000	$20,051,000
Long-term debt	3,966,000	4,238,000	13,237,000
Deferred items	3,414,000	4,077,000	4,223,000
Stockholders' equity	28,771,000	29,206,000	25,447,000
	$ 61,028,000	$ 58,310,000	$62,958,000
Revenue	$105,316,000	$110,835,000	$99,524,000
Operating income	11,547,000	17,432,000	10,930,000
Net income	6,319,000	8,620,000	6,093,000

Certain information relating to Company investments in these associated companies is as follows:

Share of:			
Stockholders' equity	$ 14,511,000	$ 14,703,000	$12,805,000
Undistributed earnings	11,316,000	11,617,000	9,826,000
Net income	3,074,000	4,217,000	2,945,000

LEGGETT & PLATT, INCORPORATED

Consolidated Balance Sheets

	December 31	
(Dollar amounts in thousands)	1982	1981
Other Assets		
Investment in and advances to associated companies	$ 7,259	$6,538
Excess of cost of purchased companies over net assets acquired, less accumulated amortization of $636 in 1982 and $532 in 1981....	2,166	1,893
Restricted funds—bonds proceeds	1,324	36
Sundry	5,112	725
	$15,861	$9,192

Consolidated Statements of Earnings

	Year Ended December 31		
(Dollar amounts in thousands, except per share data)	1982	1981	1980
Earnings from majority-owned operations	$ 8,573	$11,280	$7,683
Equity in earnings of associated companies, net of income taxes	559	673	712
Net Earnings............................	$ 9,132	$11,953	$8,395

NOTES TO CONSOLIDATED FINANCIAL STATEMENTS

A (in part): Summary of Accounting Policies

Investments in Associated Companies: Investments in associated companies are accounted for by the equity method of accounting. Associated companies include entities in which the Company has at least 20%, but not more than a 50% interest.

B–Investment in Associated Companies

The Company's investment in associated companies at December 31, 1982 consisted of 50% interests in Adcom Wire (a partnership), Globe Spring and Cushion Company, Ltd., LSF Manufacturing Co., and RLP Marketing Co.

Combined financial data for these companies as of December 31, 1982, 1981 and 1980 and for the years then ended, is as follows:

Balance Sheet Data

(in thousands)	1982	1981	1980
Current assets	$10,268	$ 9,807	$ 9,404
Property, plant and equipment	11,369	11,925	11,328
Other assets.............................	401	534	653
	22,038	$22,266	$21,385
Liabilities	$11,989	$12,943	$12,800
Equity	10,049	9,323	8,585
	$22,038	$22,266	$21,385

Statement of Earnings Data

(in thousands)	1982	1981	1980
Net sales	$44,269	$42,658	$35,937
Operating expenses	(42,423)	(40,136)	(34,272)
Income taxes.............................	(88)	(207)	(203)
Net earnings before tax on partnership earnings	$ 1,758	$ 2,315	$ 1,462

The Company's investment in associated companies and its equity in their net earnings as of December 31, 1982, 1981 and 1980 and for the years then ended, is as follows:

Investment in Associated Companies

(in thousands)	1982	1981	1980
Equity	$4,898	$4,516	$4,207
Advances	1,878	1,525	748
Excess of cost over net assets	483	497	511
Investment in and advances to associated companies...................	$7,259	$6,538	$5,466

Equity in Net Earnings of Associated Companies

(in thousands)	1982	1981	1980
Net earnings of associated companies before tax on partnership earnings .	$ 881	$ 1,148	$ 757
Income tax on partnership earnings ...	(322)	(475)	(45)
Net earnings	$ 559	$ 673	$ 712

Distributions received from associated companies were $397,000, $900,000 and $1,700,000 for 1982, 1981 and 1980, respectively.

MILTON ROY COMPANY

Consolidated Balance Sheet

	As of December 31,	
	1982	1981
Total current assets	$33,407,000	$33,246,000
Investments in joint ventures, at equity	2,851,000	3,040,000

Consolidated Statement of Income

For the year ended December 31,	1982	1981	1980
Income before equity in net income of joint ventures .	$3,164,000	$3,350,000	$2,565,000
Equity in net income of joint ventures	588,000	669,000	808,000
Net income	$3,752,000	$4,019,000	$3,373,000

NOTES TO CONSOLIDATED FINANCIAL STATEMENTS

Note 6—Investments in Joint Ventures, at Equity:

The Company's interests in joint ventures in each of the three years ended December 31, 1982 were as follows:

	December 31,		
	1982	1981	1980
Dosapro-Milton Roy, S.A.	50%	50%	50%
Ichibishi Company, Ltd.	50%	50%	50%
Applied Science Europe, B.V.	—	50%	50%
DosiSistemas, S.A. de C.V.	49%	—	—

These investments are stated at cost of acquisition plus the Company's equity in the undistributed net income since acquisition, adjusted for deferred foreign currency translation losses of $1,419,000. A summary of the combined financial position and results of operations of joint venture companies follows:

Summary Financial Position

	(Thousands) December 31,	
	1982	1981
Current assets	$14,022	$15,561
Property, plant and equipment	1,347	1,767
Goodwill	356	450
Other assets	185	204
Total assets	15,910	17,982
Current liabilities	7,961	9,697
Other liabilities	272	438
Long term debt	1,975	1,766
Total liabilities	10,208	11,901
Net assets	$ 5,702	$ 6,081
Company's equity in net assets	$ 2,851	$ 3,040

Summary Statement of Income

	(Thousands) For the year ended December 31,		
	1982	1981	1980
Net revenues	$24,721	$26,418	$25,506
Costs and expenses	22,661	24,042	23,121
Provision for income taxes	885	1,038	769
Net income	$ 1,175	$ 1,338	$ 1,616
Company's equity in net income	$ 588	$ 669	$ 808
Company's portion of dividends declared and paid	$ 187	$ 35	$ 32

The Company engages in various transactions with its joint venture companies. Agreements with these companies generally provide for a price structure projected to result in a reasonable return to the respective parties. Transactions with the companies that are accounted for on the equity method for each of the three years ended December 31, 1982 were insignificant.

STAUFFER CHEMICAL COMPANY

Consolidated Balance Sheet

December 31	1982	1981
	(Dollars in thousands)	
Investments and Other Assets		
Investments and Advances—Associated Companies	$ 41,846	$ 49,985
Intangibles Arising from Business Acquisitions	18,923	20,084
Other Assets	90,574	69,709
Total Investments and Other Assets	$151,343	$139,778

Statement of Consolidated Earnings

Year ended December 31	1982	1981	1980
	(Dollars in thousands except per-share amounts)		
Earnings from Consolidated Operations	$133,543	$162,372	$146,061
Minority Interest	13,103	21,960	23,116
Equity in Earnings of Associated Companies	3,107	9,512	13,256
Net Earnings	$123,547	$149,924	$136,201

SUMMARY OF SIGNIFICANT ACCOUNTING POLICIES

CONSOLIDATION—The consolidated financial statements include those of the Company and its subsidiaries. Investments in associated companies (20 to 50 percent owned) are stated at cost plus equity in undistributed earnings since acquisition. All significant intercompany transactions and balances have been eliminated.

NOTES TO FINANCIAL STATEMENTS

Associated Companies

Operations of associated companies (20 to 50 percent owned) are summarized as follows:

	1982	1981	1980
	(Dollars in thousands)		
Net sales	$175,101	$231,170	$228,387
Net earnings	7,280	16,363	26,191
Assets	162,358	191,592	181,668
Liabilities	71,772	85,875	80,367
Total Equity	$ 90,586	$105,717	$101,301
Stauffer share:			
Net earnings	$ 3,107	$ 9,512	$ 13,256
Dividends	4,916	5,067	7,674
Undistributed earnings	33,617	36,756	33,743
Equity, including advances	$ 41,846	$ 49,985	$ 46,972
Number of associates	15	14	14

Contemporary Issues in Consolidation, Translation, and the Equity Method

Generally accepted accounting principles are always in flux. In its current project on consolidation and the equity method,[1] the Financial Accounting Standards Board is restudying most concepts and procedures in consolidation and the equity method. The FASB is not restudying translation now, having recently revised translation rules, but, if the past is a guide, translation may be changed again.

This appendix describes issues concerning those concepts and procedures, with some of our views on the issues. Understanding challenges to present concepts and procedures, and changes that have been proposed, contributes to enlightened application of present generally accepted accounting principles and facilitates adaptation to change when it comes.

MERITS OF CONSOLIDATION

Consolidated financial statements have for many years been the primary financial statements for most groups of parent companies and subsidiaries in the United States. However, it has been difficult to obtain universal agreement that consolidated financial statements are essential or even helpful in reporting to the users of financial reports. For example, consolidated financial statements are just

---

[1]FASB *Status Report*, July 9, 1984, p. 3.

now starting to be presented in Japan, in response to International Accounting Standard No. 3, "Consolidated Financial Statements," issued by the International Accounting Standards Committee. And, before the "Seventh Council Directive Concerning Consolidated Accounts" of the European Economic Community, "Consolidation was only legally required in a minority of Community member states.[2]"

Also, an explicit argument against ever presenting consolidated financial statements can be found in the writings of a widely cited critic of present generally accepted accounting principles. He suggested an alternative to consolidation: "annexures to the financial statements of the holding company, simple aggregative statements of the assets and liabilities and profit and loss account items of all the subsidiaries."[3] He confessed that he "has been guilty as anyone else in perpetuating the acceptance of the consolidation solution."[4] But he has repented: ". . . it now seems that the alternative is much more easy to defend on logical and practical grounds, and that the result is far more comprehensible and realistic than the product of the consolidation process."[5]

The main objections to presenting consolidated financial statements stem from concerns about undisclosed restrictions on transfers of resources among members of consolidated groups, discussed in Chapter 1, presenting the consolidated group as if it were a single legal entity by ignoring legal boundaries, and the possibility that financial difficulties of members of the group will be obscured. Most observers who support consolidation agree that those concerns are real. But they believe the concerns can be overcome by disclosures and should not be allowed to prevent users from receiving what they believe to be the benefit of consolidation, which is the presentation of what is believed to be the substance of the relationships and events and not merely their legal forms.

DEFINITION OF CONSOLIDATED REPORTING ENTITY

Because reporting entities in consolidated financial statements transcend the legal boundaries of single-member companies, the nature of the consolidated reporting

---

[2]Price Waterhouse EEC Bulletin, "Special Supplement on the EEC Seventh Directive, Consolidated Financial Statements," 1983, p. 2.

[3]R. J. Chambers, "Consolidated Statements Are Not Really Necessary," *Australian Accountant*, February 1968, p. 90.

[4]Chambers, "Consolidated Statements," p. 92.

[5]Chambers, "Consolidated Statements," p. 92.

entity is a primary issue. Authoritative accounting bodies have defined that entity in "as if" terms. For example, ARB No. 51 says (paragraph 1) that consolidated financial statements "present . . . the results of operations and the financial position of a parent company and its subsidiaries essentially as if the group were a single company with one or more branches or divisions." And International Accounting Standard No. 3 defines (paragraph 4) *consolidated financial statements* as "statements which present the assets, liabilities, stockholders' accounts, revenue, and expenses of a parent company and its subsidiaries as those of a single enterprise."

A consolidated reporting entity is not a single company or any other type of single enterprise. It is, as discussed in Chapter 1, a group of companies united for economic activity by common control.

Defining the reporting entity in consolidated financial statements in "as if" terms turns the statements into pro forma information. It provides precedent for injecting other pro forma aspects into purportedly factual parts of financial reports. Such a tendency should be resisted wherever it is accepted or proposed in financial reporting. Pro forma information included in financial reports should be labeled as such.

CONSOLIDATION POLICY

When ARB No. 51 was issued in 1959, most companies were in single lines of business. The 1960s conglomeration wave had not yet started, an era in which groups of companies under common control operating in a number of unrelated kinds of business became increasingly more common. That a reporting entity should present a simple whole was then still taken for granted. Presenting dissimilar operations in a single set of financial statements was considered less meaningful.

ARB No. 51 reflects that attitude. It condones and even encourages exclusion from consolidation of subsidiaries because of the dissimilarity of their operations from those of the parent company.

That justification for such exclusion is long gone. Many sets of consolidated statements of companies whose stock is publicly traded now present the financial affairs of companies that have disparate kinds of operations. Such conglomerations are no longer disaggregated by excluding subsidiaries from consolidation; that is now done by segment reporting in addition to rather than as a substitute for full consolidation.

New, valid reasons for not consolidating selected types of subsidiaries, new benefits to the users of financial reports, should be found, to continue excluding subsidiaries from consolidation.

PROPORTIONAL CONSOLIDATION

Under proportional consolidation, as its name implies, an investor records its proportionate share in each of the investee's assets, liabilities, revenues, and expenses by combining, line by line, those amounts directly with its own assets, liabilities, revenues, and expenses.

That is one of about five methods commonly used in accounting for investments in real estate partnerships and in construction joint ventures. It has not generally been used in accounting for other types of investments, but it has some appealing characteristics. For one, an investor does not present minority interest, because there is none to present. Proportional consolidation reports only attributes of the consolidated group.

To present, say, 80% of each of an investee's assets and 80% of each of the investee's liabilities in the financial statements of an investor that owns 80% of the voting stock of the investee seems anomalous to some. But that seems to others to be no more anomalous than including 100% of each of the investee's assets and 100% of the investee's liabilities in the financial statements of that investor, and then reporting on the right side of the investor's balance sheet a nondescript amount (discussed in the next section) equal to 20% of the carrying amount of the equity of the investee, attributable to stockholders outside the consolidated group.

TREATMENT OF MINORITY STOCKHOLDING

Minority interest is reported only in consolidated financial statements. It has no counterpart elsewhere in financial reporting. It fits neatly into no category. For many years three interpretations of minority interest have coexisted uneasily. Some have held it is debt. Some have held it is equity. And some have held it is neither debt nor equity.

These statements support the interpretation that minority interest is debt:

1917: The proper practice is to take up as a *liability* the par value of the outstanding stock [held by the minority stockholders], together with its relative share of surplus. . . .[6]

1932: . . . report the minority interest under the head of "deferred *liabilities.*"[7]

1975: In substance, minority stockholders are a special class of *creditors* of the consolidated entity. . . .[8]

1981: Any minority interest in subsidiaries is shown as the last item of *liabilities.*[9]

These support the interpretation that it is equity:

1908: Under *capital stocks* will be included . . . such part of the stocks of the subsidiary companies as are not owned by the holding company. . . .[10]

1924: The *capital stock* . . . should . . . consist of the capital stock of the parent company together with . . . the minority interests (if any) in the subsidiaries.[11]

1946: Both groups of owners, majority and minority, must therefore be shown in the *proprietorship* section.[12]

1966: In theory, the minority interest is clearly part of the *ownership equity* on the consolidated balance sheet. The minority interest is certainly *not an unliquidated obligation* in any sense, and *classifying it in the no-man's land between liability and capital simply avoids the issue.*[13]

---

[6]Arthur Lowes Dickinson, *Accounting Practice and Procedure* (New York: Ronald Press Company, 1917), p. 183 (emphasis added).

[7]W. A. Paton, ed., *Accountants' Handbook,* 2nd ed. (New York: Ronald Press Company, 1932), p. 1041 (emphasis added).

[8]Walter B. Meigs, A. N. Mosich, and E. John Larsen, *Modern Advanced Accounting* (New York: McGraw-Hill Book Company, 1975), p. 187 (emphasis added).

[9]Roderick K. Macleod, "Financial Statements: Form and Content," in Lee J. Seidler and D. R. Carmichael, eds., *Accountants' Handbook,* 6th ed. (New York: John Wiley & Sons, 1981), p. 4.15 (emphasis added).

[10]William M. Lybrand, "The Accounting of Industrial Enterprises," *Journal of Accountancy,* December 1908, p. 120 (emphasis added).

[11]W. A. Paton, *Accounting,* (New York: MacMillan Company, 1924), p. 507 (emphasis added).

[12]Roy B. Kester, *Advanced Accounting* (New York: Ronald Press Company, 1946), p. 585 (emphasis added).

[13]Walter B. Meigs, Charles E. Johnson, and Thomas Keller, *Advanced Accounting* (New York: McGraw-Hill Book Company, 1966), pp. 263–264 (emphasis added).

1980: Minority interests . . . are part of *equity*.[14]

And these support the intepretation that it is neither debt nor equity:

1941: The minority interest should be shown as *a distinct element between the liabilities proper and the capital and surplus* attaching to the dominant interest.[15]

1949: The minority interest . . . is normally shown on the consolidated balance sheet under a *separate caption just preceding the net worth section*.[16]

1976: The minority interest in the equity of consolidated companies should be classified in the consolidated balance sheet as a *separate item* and should *not* be shown as *part of stockholders' equity*.[17]

Settling the issue will require rethinking of basic ideas concerning the elements of financial statements.

PURCHASE METHOD VERSUS POOLING OF INTERESTS METHOD

Some of the 12 criteria that must all be met for a business combination to qualify for the pooling of interests method, discussed in Chapter 2, can easily be violated virtually at will. A free choice alternative is, therefore, in effect, available under present principles to use the pooling of interests method or the purchase method to account for a combination that can qualify for the pooling of interests method.

The theory supporting each method is plausible.

The theory supporting the pooling of interests method holds that the method reflects an amalgamation of two streams, previously running separately and presently running together, neither one augmented or diminished by their joining. The history of the amalgamated stream becomes, therefore, the sum of the histories of its tributaries.

The theory supporting the purchase method holds that in each business com-

---

[14]Financial Accounting Standards Board, Statement of Financial Accounting Concepts No. 3, "Elements of Financial Statements of Business Enterprises," 1980, paragraph 179 (emphasis added).

[15]W. A. Paton, *Advanced Accounting* (New York: MacMillan Company, 1941), p. 803 (emphasis added).

[16]Wilbert E. Karrenbrock and Harry Simons, *Advanced Accounting* (Cincinnati: Southwestern Publishing Company, 1949), p. 189 (emphasis added).

[17]International Accounting Standards Committee, International Accounting Standard 3, "Consolidated Financial Statements," 1976, paragraph 43 (emphasis added).

bination, one company acquires one or more other companies. The acquirer continues; the acquired disappear. The history of the combined enterprise is the history of the acquirer. Its acquisition of the acquired is accounted for as is the acquisition by a company of any other assets.

The pooling of interests method generally produces higher reported net income and more conservative balance sheets than the purchase method.

The existence of the de facto free choice alternative of the two methods harms comparability.

ACCOUNTING FOR ISSUANCES OF STOCK BY A SUBSIDIARY

Chapter 7 indicates the alternative treatments now generally accepted for reporting in consolidated financial statements or by the equity method of issuances by an investee of its own stock. The difference between (1) the proceeds received by the investee and (2) the book value per share of its shares outstanding when the new shares were issued, times the number of shares issued, is treated as either (1) a gain or loss in the consolidated income statement or in the investor's income statement or (2) an adjustment to consolidated paid-in capital or to the investor's paid-in capital.

Paragraph 19e of APB Opinion 18, "The Equity Method of Accounting for Investments in Common Stock," states: "A transaction of an investee of a capital nature that affects the investor's share of stockholders' equity of the investee should be accounted for as if the investee were a consolidated subsidiary." At issue, then, is the treatment in consolidation of issuances by a consolidated subsidiary of its stock to other than members of the consolidated group.

As indicated in Chapter 7, APB Opinion 18 requires recognition of a gain or loss on the sale by an investor of stock of an investee accounted for by the equity method. Also as indicated there, that treatment is consistently applied in consolidation to the sale by the parent company of the stock of a consolidated subsidiary. Some hold that the effects of the issuance by a subsidiary of its own stock are sufficiently similar to the effects of a sale of stock of a subsidiary by its parent company that they should also result in reporting a gain or loss on the transaction.

Others hold that the effects differ sufficiently to require different accounting for issuances of stock by a subsidiary, specifically, that consolidated paid-in capital should be charged or credited with the effects of the transaction. The differences they see include these:

The earnings process for the parent company is culminated by the parent company's sale of subsidiary stock but not by an issuance by a subsidiary of its stock.

The parent company has disposed of part of its investment by its sale of stock of a subsidiary, but it has not disposed of part of its investment by issuance by a subsidiary of its stock.

The two types of transactions result in different percentages of ownership of the subsidiary's stock by the parent company after the transactions are finished.[18]

As indicated in Chapter 7, the AICPA's Accounting Standards Executive Committee stated an advisory conclusion that differences determined on issuances by an investee of its own stock should be recognized as gains or losses.[19]

MERITS OF EQUITY METHOD

Justification for the equity method stems from the presumption that an investor required to use that method has more than a passive investment. For the equity method to be used, the investor has to have the ability to exercise significant influence over the financial and operating activities of the investee, including its dividend policies. Those who support use of the equity method believe it best meets the objective of accrual accounting, because under that method, the investor recognizes changes in the economic resources (including the earnings and losses) of the investee in the periods in which they are recorded in the accounts of the investee.

Others criticize the equity method because they believe an entity should not reflect in its financial statements changes in the recorded amounts of assets and liabilities of another entity. Further, they question recognition of changes in the carrying amount of the investment based on the earnings or losses of the investee while ignoring other factors that also affect the investment, such as changes in the market value of the investment securities.

---

[18]These arguments were taken from AICPA Issues Paper, "Accounting in Consolidation for Issuances of a Subsidiary's Stock," June 3, 1980.

[19]Also taken from AICPA, Issues Paper, "Accounting in Consolidation for Issuances of a Subsidiary's Stock," June 3, 1980.

GAAP FOR FOREIGN OPERATIONS

The current standard on accounting for foreign operations by translation, FASB Statement No. 52, "Foreign Currency Translation," requires a translation method, the current rate method, that is one in a line of methods that have been used to translate amounts originally stated in terms of a currency other than the reporting currency. At least three translation methods preceded the current rate method: the current–noncurrent method, the monetary–nonmonetary method, and the temporal method. Each of the two most recent translation methods, the temporal and current rate methods, has been vigorously defended and opposed over the last nine years.

Each has a fatal flaw.

Fatal Flaw of the Temporal Method

The fatal flaw of the temporal method of translation is practical: It gives results contrary to the economic effects of key events it recognizes, changes in foreign exchange rates. A change in a foreign exchange rate may be clearly beneficial to a consolidated group of companies in terms of the reporting currency, but the temporal method could cause the group to report in the period of the change that it caused detrimental effects.

To illustrate: While a foreign operation has inventory carried at cost of £(U.K.) 1,000 and has a debt of £500, the foreign exchange rate between U.S. dollars and U.K. pounds changes from $2.00/£1 to $2.50/£1. That event has two effects on the company from the perspective of U.S. investors.

The first effect is that it increases the company's debt from the equivalent of $500 × 2 = $1,000 to the equivalent of $500 × 2.50 = $1,250. Because cash, regardless of its country of origin, is considered to be a liquid asset and therefore never unrealized, gains or losses pertaining to holdings of cash or receivables or payables in cash are recognized when any change in them takes place. And the temporal principle reflects that aspect of present accounting rules; it recognizes the increase in the dollar equivalent of the debt of $250 as a loss in the period in which the rate changes.

But present-day accounting does not immediately recognize all changes related to nonmonetary assets or liabilities when they occur. It ordinarily recognizes changes in those items only when their quantities change, not when their costs or prices change. Changes in foreign exchange rates do not change the quantities of nonmonetary assets or liabilities. They do, however, change the prospects in terms of the domestic currency of receiving or giving up wealth when those items are realized by selling or redeeming them for money.

The second effect is such a change in prospects. The change in the foreign exchange rate in the illustration changes the prospects in terms of dollars of realizing benefit from the inventory the company holds. With the inventory carried in the foreign currency financial statements of the foreign operation at the lower of cost and market, the inventory presumably can be sold for the £1,000 at which it is shown or more. Before the change in rate, the inventory presumably could be sold for the equivalent of $2,000 or more. After the change it presumably could be sold for the equivalent of $2,500 or more. In any event, the increase in dollar prospects is no less than the equivalent of $500.

Overall, therefore, the company has benefited in U.S. dollar terms from the change in the foreign exchange rate. Its inventory became at least $500 more valuable while its debt became only $250 more burdensome. Overall, the company benefited by at least $250. But the temporal method requires recognition in the period the rate changes not of that blessing but of a loss of $250! The benefit of the foreign exchange rate change is recognized not in the period in which the detriment is recognized but later, when the inventory is sold.

Solely to avoid such misleading reports, companies that had been required to apply the temporal method entered into transactions that rectified the reports though they had no good business purpose and often caused actual expenses or losses.

Fatal Flaw of the Current Rate Method

The current rate method's fatal flaw is structural; it introduces multiple units of measure into a single calculation, such as adding a single column of amounts: The objective "to use a 'single unit of measure' for financial statements that include translated foreign amounts . . . was not adopted."[20] But such a calculation requires a single unit of measure: ". . . a single perspective is essential for a valid addition and subtraction . . ."[21]

To illustrate: A U.S. parent company and its U.K. subsidiary each buy the same kind of machine with a five-year life at the same time. The parent company buys one for $1,000 and the subsidiary buys one for £400, when $2.50 buys

[20]FASB Statement No. 52, "Foreign Currency Translation," paragraphs 70 and 75.
[21]Statement by dissenters, FASB Statement No. 52, "Foreign Currency Translation."

£1. Using the current rate method of translation, the machines would be presented in a consolidated balance sheet stated in dollars at the date of acquisition at a total acquisition cost of $1,000 plus (£400 × $2.5/£1) = $2,000, a satisfactory presentation in dollars of their total acquisition cost.

During the following reporting period, $2 buys £1. Straight line depreciation on the two machines in the consolidated income statement under the current rate method consists of $200 on the machine bought by the parent company plus £80 × $2/£1 = $160 on the machine bought by the subsidiary. Though each machine cost the same in terms of dollars, the equivalent of $1,000, depreciation on them based on their acquisition costs using the same depreciation method is presented at different amounts. The first amount is measured and presented in dollars. The second is measured in pounds and the measurement is multiplied by two, a number that is not a measurement conversion factor and that therefore does not convert the pound measurement into a measurement in another scale, in dollars. Total reported depreciation of $360 is therefore the result of adding an amount measured in dollars to an amount measured in pounds.

Net income is calculated on the face of the income statement—net income is only calculated; it is not measured—using the total amount of depreciation, which is determined by the invalid process of adding two amounts with different units of measure. Neither total depreciation nor net income calculated that way has any significance beyond that of a pure number, and such a number cannot help anyone who is informed of it unless it approximates a number that would be derived by valid calculation.

A Way Out?

The developer of the temporal principle acknowledged that it has the fatal flaw described above but he contended that translation involves a dilemma in that any other translation method would also have a fatal flaw: "The dilemma is . . . unresolvable as long as the historical-cost basis of accounting continues to be used."[22]

However, that developer might have given us a way out of the dilemma. Though he called his system a system of translation, he did not refer to translation in the title of his study. He merely referred to "reporting foreign operations."

[22]Leonard Lorensen, Accounting Research Study No. 12, *Reporting Foreign Operations of U. S. Companies in U. S. Dollars* (New York: American Institute of Certified Public Accountants, 1972), p. xii.

Maybe our mistake has been to try to translate foreign currency financial statements rather than to search for principles with which to report foreign operations. Such principles would reflect the unique aspect of such operations, which is that they deal in markets in which the mediums of exchange are currencies other than the reporting currency of the financial statements in which the operations are reported.

Searching for GAAP for foreign operations would be better than acquiescing in the dilemma of translation.

Index